FAITH AND

FAITH AND SWORD

A Short History of Christian–Muslim Conflict

SECOND EXPANDED EDITION

Alan G. Jamieson

REAKTION BOOKS

Published by Reaktion Books Ltd
Unit 32, Waterside
44–48 Wharf Road
London N1 7UX, UK
www.reaktionbooks.co.uk

First published 2006
Second expanded edition published 2016

Printed and bound in Great Britain by Bell & Bain, Glasgow

A catalogue record for this book is available
from the British Library

ISBN 978 1 78023 672 8

CONTENTS

LIST OF MAPS

Arabic and Turkish spellings have been simplified throughout, and where an English version of an Arabic or Turkish name is common, e.g., Saladin, it has been used.

1

INTRODUCING THE LONGEST WAR

It had been a long day for the Arab mayor of Jerusalem, Hussein Selim al-Husaini. Once the Ottoman Turkish forces had left Jerusalem, the mayor had borrowed a white sheet from an American missionary and set out on the morning of 9 December 1917 to surrender the holy city of three world religions, Judaism, Christianity and Islam, to the approaching British army. First he met two army cooks who had blundered into Jerusalem in search of water, but they felt unable to accept the responsibility of taking the surrender. Then the mayor encountered two infantry sergeants patrolling on the Lifta–Jerusalem road. They declined the honour as well, but had their photograph taken with the mayor and his party. Eventually, before the end of the day, the mayor worked his way up the British chain of command until he reached Major-General J.S.M. Shea of the 60th (London) Division, who was ready to accept his surrender of the city on behalf of General Sir Edmund Allenby, the British commander-in-chief.

Allenby made his formal entry into Jerusalem via the Jaffa Gate at noon on 11 December 1917. To show his respect for the holy city, the general entered on foot. In his proclamation to the inhabitants of 'Jerusalem the Blessed', Allenby made it clear that he would respect and protect the holy places of all the three religions that held the city to be sacred. The British prime minister, David Lloyd George, had asked Allenby to capture Jerusalem as a Christmas present for the British nation. He had carried out that task with two weeks to spare, and not a single sacred building had been damaged.

General Allenby was the first Christian conqueror of Jerusalem since 1099, when the city had been stormed by the soldiers of the First Crusade, who had massacred the Muslim and Jewish inhabitants. Allenby had tactfully avoided any mention of crusades in his proclamation to the people of Jerusalem, but press accounts of his success were less reticent. British propaganda sought to make much of the capture of Jerusalem from the Turks at the end of 1917, but the war-weary allied populations were largely unimpressed. Crusader imagery could not offset the grim realities of a bad year for the allied cause, with events such as the French army mutinies, the slaughter of British troops in the mud of Passchendaele, Russian withdrawal from the war and Italian defeat at Caporetto. The year 1918 brought further crises, but in the end the allied cause was victorious. In the autumn of 1918 Turkish resistance in the Middle East finally collapsed and an armistice was agreed. Allied forces took possession of Constantinople, which had been lost by the Christians in 1453, and the Ottoman empire, for centuries the most powerful Muslim opponent of Christian Europe, lay prostrate. When Turkey rose again after 1919 under the leadership of Mustafa Kemal (Ataturk), it would be a very different state, committed to secularism, modernization and other aspects of Westernization.

The Turks lost the Arab parts of their empire. Despite British promises of independence for the Arabs, these territories were divided between the French and the British. France was to receive Syria, but local Arabs declared Prince Feisal king of Syria in March 1920. Four months later, French troops under General Henri Gouraud swept aside Arab resistance and expelled Feisal from the Syrian capital Damascus. The British would later make him king of Iraq. General Gouraud, who had lost an arm fighting the Turks at Gallipoli in 1915, was to prove less tactful than General Allenby. Once he was in control of Damascus, Gouraud went to the tomb of Saladin, perhaps the greatest Muslim hero in the centuries-long struggle between Christianity and Islam, and boldly declared: 'Saladin, we have returned. My presence here consecrates the cross over the crescent.'

In France the memory of that country's major role in the Crusades had never been forgotten, but Gouraud's triumphalism also reflected the view of Christians in many countries. For them the victory of the allied powers over the Ottoman empire represented a victory of Christianity over Islam, marking the end of what had been perhaps the longest conflict in human history. For almost 1,300 years Christians and Muslims had fought frequent and bitter wars, and for most of that period the Muslims had generally had the better of the struggle. However, from the seventeenth century onwards the power of Christian Europe grew dramatically. With the division of the Ottoman empire after the allied victory in 1918, only a handful of Muslim states were not part of one of the European colonial empires. The triumph of the Christians seemed complete. Yet the sources of the power that gave the Christians victory also undermined any idea that this success was principally based on a religious commitment. The superior economic and military power of the Christian West sprang from the scientific revolution in the seventeenth century, the secular spirit of enquiry of the eighteenth-century Enlightenment, and, above all, from the nineteenth-century Industrial Revolution. Christianity may have helped to shape the conditions that gave birth to these revolutionary changes, but the wider implications of those changes challenged all forms of religious belief, including both Islam and Christianity.

The destruction of the Ottoman empire at the end of the First World War ended the Christian–Muslim contest that had its basis in religious rivalry, but a new type of struggle could still break out and continue the conflict between the two sides. Muslims were the principal victims of European imperialism, and between 1920 and 1970 they were to fight successfully to free themselves from this foreign domination. The nature of the conflict had changed, however, with religious elements being less important to both sides. The Christian West became increasingly secular in its outlook, while Muslim resistance movements saw imported doctrines such as nationalism and socialism as being more important than their religious identity.

The Second World War made it clear that European states like Britain and France were no longer world powers and leadership of the West passed to the United States of America. Apart from short wars with the Barbary pirates and clashes with Muslim rebels in the Philippines, the USA had little past history of serious conflict with the Islamic world, so its dominance might well have been acceptable to Muslim countries. However, changes in the Middle East made the United States determined to play an active role in the Islamic world. The need to safeguard the vast oil supplies found in the region from enemies such as the Soviet Union made American intervention in some form inevitable.

In addition, changes in the relations between Muslims and Jews added another unstable element to the region. For centuries Jews had found refuge from Christian oppression by moving to Muslim lands, and in the Christian–Muslim conflict had almost always supported the latter. After the establishment of Israel in 1948 a bitter hatred steadily grew up between Jews and Muslims, with many Arabs seeing the new state as a Western colony thrust into their midst, a modern version of the Christian states established for a time by the medieval crusaders. The United States supported Israel, leading some Arab countries to turn to the Soviet Union for support.

Despite Soviet assistance, the Arab states failed to crush Israel and their repeated failures began to discredit secular nationalism in the eyes of many Muslims. Some took the view that Arab failure was not due to insufficient mastery of Western modernization, but was caused by turning away from traditional Islamic beliefs. Only by a return to such beliefs, claimed the Islamic fundamentalists, could Muslim countries stand up to the West and its proxies. It was not so much the Christianity of the West that the fundamentalists hated, since that religion had been in serious decline in most Western countries for decades, as its secularism. To them the capitalist West was just as godless as the communist Soviet bloc. After the Iranian revolution of 1979, when the pro-Western shah was overthrown and replaced by an Islamic religious government, Islamic fundamentalism became a major force in the Muslim world.

The United States was happy to support such Muslim fervour when it was directed against its Cold War enemy the Soviet Union after the Soviet invasion of Afghanistan at the end of 1979. However, the ten-year guerrilla struggle in that country not only defeated the Soviets but also built up a formidable Islamic military organization with international links. After the collapse of the Soviet Union in the years 1989–91, some Islamic fundamentalists saw its demise as largely due to their own efforts in Afghanistan. Having disposed of one godless superpower, they believed they might be able to humble the remaining one, the United States. Furthermore, hostility to the Americans increased after the First Gulf War brought large American garrisons into the Middle East for the first time. Terrorist attacks on Americans increased and some observers in the United States claimed Islamic fundamentalism had now replaced Soviet communism as the principal threat to the West. Nevertheless it seemed during the 1990s that Islamic terrorism was no greater threat to international peace than other forms of terrorism that had plagued the world since the 1960s. Then came the events of 11 September 2001.

On that morning Islamic terrorists crashed hijacked airliners into the World Trade Center in New York and the Pentagon in Washington, DC, and it appeared that the Christian–Muslim conflict might be re-ignited on a new and vaster scale. Western commentators seemed baffled when the alleged mastermind behind the atrocities, Osama bin Laden, put forward Muslim grievances reaching back to the expulsion of the Islamic population of al-Andalus (modern Spain and Portugal) centuries ago. Yet it seemed natural for American leaders to talk of crusades and call on the Christian God to support their war against terrorism. Both sides were looking to that earlier struggle to vindicate their position.

America hit back after 9/11 by invading Afghanistan in late 2001, driving Osama bin Laden into hiding in Pakistan. Then, instead of concentrating on bin Laden, the USA chose to invade Iraq in 2003, claiming its ruler, Saddam Hussein, had weapons of mass destruction that might fall into terrorist hands. Iraq was soon conquered and its ruler overthrown. The US conventional military attacks on Afghanistan and Iraq appeared to be swift victories, but by bringing Western armies into the heartlands of the Muslim world, they only inflamed conflict between Islamic militants and the West.

Muslim guerrilla resistance in both Afghanistan and Iraq steadily wore down the resolve of the USA and its allies. In Iraq the Americans managed to reduce violence to an acceptable level by 2009 and at the end of 2011 their military forces withdrew from that country. After an intensified struggle in Afghanistan, it seemed the conflict there might be winding down after 2011 and the foreign military presence was considerably reduced by 2014. However, the so-called 'Arab Spring' of 2011, when Muslim populations rose against their oppressive Muslim rulers in various countries, created widespread turmoil which allowed the revival of Islamic terrorist groups who turned the insurgents not just against their national governments but against the West. The most successful of these groups currently calls itself Islamic State, but it is also known as ISIS or ISIL, or as Da'esh by others. The acronym ISIS – Islamic State in Iraq and Syria – sums up its achievement. It has created its own state straddling eastern Syria and western Iraq and has affiliated groups in other countries, notably Afghanistan, Libya and Egypt. The ISIS challenge has brought American and other Western troops back to Iraq and has prevented their complete withdrawal from Afghanistan. At present the West seeks to curb ISIS by a bombing campaign from the air, but some form of military action on the ground seems increasingly likely if that terror group is to be eliminated.

The renewed conflict between the West and parts of the Muslim world seems to have some continuity with the great Christian–Muslim religious struggle before 1918, but there are also factors that make it significantly different from its predecessor. One such factor is the growing presence of Muslim populations within Western countries.

For most of the long Christian–Muslim religious conflict, there were large Christian and Jewish populations within the Islamic world, but almost no Muslims in Christian countries. Today the situation is very different. Jews are now few in Muslim states, most having left for Israel, while small Christian minorities in Muslim countries such as Iraq have been killed or driven out in the ongoing conflict. Only their comparatively large size has allowed Christian communities in Lebanon (the Maronites) and Egypt (the Copts) to survive Muslim hostility and even they are under increasing pressure.

While Jews and Christians have disappeared from Muslim lands, Muslim populations have grown in the West. This is largely a European phenomenon, as Muslims constitute only a small percentage of the population of North America (usa and Canada). The large Muslim population that lived in the Iberian peninsula for centuries is long gone (Muslims comprise barely 2 per cent of Spain's population), but the Muslim populations that remained in the Balkans as the Ottoman empire retreated are still substantial. Albania and Kosovo are Europe's only Muslim majority countries, but in both Bosnia and Macedonia Muslims will soon make up half the population. Yet it is not the survival of Muslim populations in the Balkans that is the most significant change in Europe. The real novelty is the steady growth of Muslim populations in Western European countries. Muslims now form almost 10 per cent of the population of France, while in countries such as Germany, the Netherlands and Great Britain they comprise around 5 per cent of the population. The influx of Muslim refugees into Europe in 2015 can only increase these Muslim populations, especially in Germany, Austria and Sweden, which have granted asylum to the largest volume of Syrian refugees. The impact that the growing Muslim populations will have on the policies of European governments towards the Islamic world is yet to be seen.

It is the aim of this book to give an outline of the course of Christian–Muslim conflict across the centuries, showing how this longest of wars changed over time. Of course, conflict was not the only theme in Christian–Muslim relations and there were periods of comparative peace when trading activities and cultural exchanges could bring the two sides together. Nevertheless, on both sides an ideology of holy war had grown up and persisted over the years. The religious war period from the death of the Prophet Muhammad in 632 to the end of the Ottoman empire in 1918 will be covered, as well as the Muslim struggle against Western imperialism from 1920 to 1970 and the growing hostilities between the United States and Islamic fundamentalists from the 1970s onwards. After the atrocities of 9/11, the successful invasions of Afghanistan in 2001 and Iraq in 2003 seemed to promise an early victory for the USA and its allies, but the persistence of Islamic militancy in those countries and elsewhere – above all the rise of ISIS – seems to promise that this conflict, in its new form, will continue for years to come.

2

THE ARAB CONQUESTS,
632–750

AN INEVITABLE CONFLICT?

The three great monotheistic religions of the world, Judaism, Christianity and Islam, make exclusive claims yet have much in common. All look back to Abraham as the origin of their religious beliefs, but each claims a special relationship with God. Historically, the Christians believed their religion had superseded that of the Jews, while Muslims were convinced that God's words to the Prophet Muhammad represented His final revelation, thus making Islam superior to both Christianity and Judaism. Since each religion made claims to universal validity, conflict between them seemed inevitable, with armed conflict always a possibility, especially between Christians and Muslims.

Bar Kochba's failed revolt against the Romans in AD 131–5 was the last serious outbreak of Jewish militancy until the mid-twentieth century. In the intervening period the Jews struggled to preserve their community and usually found more tolerance under Muslim rule than under Christian government. The religion of Jesus Christ was in origin anything but martial, being more concerned with love and peace than with power and aggression. However, after the Emperor Constantine converted to Christianity in 312 and set up a new, Christian capital at Constantinople in 330, Christianity became wedded to secular power as much as to religious belief. In 391 the Emperor Theodosius made it the official religion of the Roman empire. The empire was divided in 395 into western and eastern parts, each with its own ruler. The last emperor in the west fell in 476 as a consequence of the barbarian invasions. The empire lived on in the east, but its culture became increasingly Greek, so that later historians have labelled it the Byzantine empire (from Byzantium, the former Greek name of Constantinople) to mark its distinctive civilization. Nevertheless, its citizens always called themselves 'Romans', and when the Ottoman sultan finally took Constantinople in 1453 he added 'Rum Kayseri' ('Roman Caesar') to his titles.

The Emperor Justinian regained a section of the west (Italy, Sicily, North Africa and part of Spain) in the mid-sixth century, but the most prolonged Byzantine struggle at this time was with the Sassanid empire of Persia, whose religion was Zoroastrianism. Although Christians were always struggling to agree on what constituted a 'just war', there could be few doubts about the justice of a war against non-Christians. The Emperor Heraclius was to embrace a concept of 'holy war' in his campaigns against the Persians during the 620s, more than a decade before the Arabs brought Islamic holy war to his territories.

For Muslims, the *jihād* (literally 'striving') or holy war was a major feature of their faith from the very start. Christianity had achieved secular and military power by taking over an existing empire from within. From the outset Islam was created by an Arab warrior society and it was identified with military success. Although Muslim commitment to the jihad would wax and wane over the centuries, it could never totally disappear. Between Muslim lands and infidel lands there could never be lasting peace, only occasional truces. Muslims did not seek to convert people to their faith by force, but they did seek to remove all obstacles, especially infidel governments, from the path to conversion.

This fervour has led some Christian commentators to see Islam as being uniquely committed to war. One of the proofs put forward by Thomas Aquinas, the great Christian medieval philosopher, that Islam was not a true faith was that it was a religion of violence and war. Such a view has been reiterated by secular commentators in more recent times. Yet since most societies up to modern times were organized around military capability for war, it seems perverse to single out Muslim societies as being especially militant. Both the Christian Byzantines and the Muslims viewed medieval crusaders from western Europe as uncivilized and obsessed with violence. Once victorious, the Muslims were far more generous and tolerant to conquered peoples than were victorious Christians. Nevertheless, Islam first burst onto the stage of world history in a wave of Arab military conquest that was to create an empire stretching from the shores of the Atlantic Ocean to the borders of China.

OUT OF ARABIA

After the death of the Prophet Muhammad in 632, Abu Bakr became the first caliph (successor) and many of the tribes in the Arabian peninsula renounced their earlier conversion to Islam. Military action was necessary to return them to the true path, and one way of deflecting the violent impulses within Arabia was to step up the raiding of the territories of the Byzantine and Persian empires to the north. While it is unlikely that the Arabs had any master plan for world conquest, their onslaught on the Byzantine and Persian empires should not be seen as an uncontrolled nomadic wave driven solely by religious fervour. Rather it was the expansion of a new state based on Medina. The caliphs and their advisers provided an element of central direction for the armies of pastoral nomads drawn from north and central Arabia and mountain people from Yemen. If the pace of advance was rapid this had less to do with the religious fervour of the attackers than the weakness of the societies under attack, where the Arabs found populations ready to forsake their imperial masters. Raids turned into conquests and the Arabs were ready to expand just as far and as fast as Byzantine and Persian weakness would allow them.

Between 602 and 628 the two great empires had engaged in a bitter and exhausting war. Initially the Sassanid Persians had been very successful. In 614 they stormed Jerusalem and took away the relic of the True Cross. By 620 the Persians had occupied Syria, Palestine and Egypt, and raided almost to the walls of Constantinople. Then the Byzantine emperor Heraclius struck back. In 622 he declared what amounted to a holy war against the infidel Persians, aimed at saving Christendom, recapturing the Holy Land and restoring the True Cross to Jerusalem. Carrying the war into Persian territory, Heraclius eventually forced a Persian surrender in 628. They returned the captured Byzantine lands and gave back the True Cross, which Heraclius personally returned to Jerusalem in 630. By the time the Persians were defeated both empires were exhausted and much of the Middle East had been ravaged by war. To pay for the conflict, the Byzantines imposed heavy taxes on their provinces, which further alienated many of their subjects; they also cut back their army and reduced subsidies to allies such as the Christian Arab tribes who protected their frontier with Arabia.

The first caliph, Abu Bakr, sent Arab forces into both Iraq against the Persians and into Palestine against the Byzantines. In 633 the Arabs defeated and killed the Byzantine military commander in Palestine. The Emperor Heraclius then sent an army under his brother Theodore against the Arab invaders (called 'Saracens' by the Byzantines). Forewarned of its approach, the caliph ordered Khalid ibn al-Walid to bring forces from Iraq to reinforce the Arab army in Palestine. In July 634 Khalid defeated Theodore's army at Ajnadain and took possession of all of Palestine except Jerusalem and a few other towns. In 635 the Arab armies swept into Syria, capturing Damascus, Homs and Aleppo.

Why had the Byzantine army, so recently victorious over Persia, failed to defeat the Arab attacks? In large part this failure was due to the Byzantines underestimating their enemy. Arab raids had been going on for centuries, but they were usually no more than a minor nuisance. The Byzantines were slow to appreciate that the new Arab incursions were something different. Although soon forced to recognize that the Arabs were better armed and organized than in the past, the Byzantines failed to appreciate the new power that Muslim religious fervour gave to the Arab armies. Ill-informed about the nature of Islam, Emperor Heraclius simply did not see it as a serious threat to Christendom in the way the Persian onslaught had been. By the time he changed his views, it was too late.

The Arabs had many of the advantages that over the centuries enabled nomadic warriors to triumph over rich, settled, more technologically advanced societies. They had highly mobile forces; their warriors were used to hardship and war; and past conflicts had ensured that only the best military commanders had risen to the top in their forces. In the case of the Arabs, commitment to their new religion further strengthened the solidarity and aggression of all nomad warriors. One military skill the Arabs initially lacked was any experience in siege warfare, yet they proved able to force great cities to surrender. This was partly because Arab campaigns against the Byzantines were usually decided on the field of battle. Once besieged cities knew the Byzantine forces had been defeated and that no relief force would reach them, surrender became the only option. In addition, many elements within city populations, such as Jews and non-Orthodox Christians, did not support the Byzantines. They were ready to surrender to the Arabs, especially as the invaders soon became known for their generous treatment of conquered peoples.

City dwellers might also believe that nomad conquest would not be long-lasting. Historically this has usually been true. For example, even the greatest of nomad conquerors, the Mongols, were soon submerged by the superior Chinese civilization that was one of their greatest conquests. The Arabs, however, were to be the exception to this rule. They were to leave one of the world's great religions, Islam, and one of the world's great languages, Arabic, spread across their wide conquests.

In 636 Heraclius assembled a large army at Antioch and then forced the Arabs out of Syria. The Byzantines pursued their enemy, but at the River Yarmuk in August 636 an Arab army under Khalid ibn al-Walid chose to confront them. The Byzantine army, commanded by Theodore Trithyrius, the imperial treasurer, and the Armenian prince Vahan, outnumbered the Arabs, but was composed of a mixture of forces, including Armenians, Christian Arabs, Syrians and Greeks. Thanks to a sandstorm that temporarily blinded their enemies, and the alleged defection of Christian Arabs from the Byzantine side, Khalid's attacking army won a major victory, in which both the enemy commanders were killed. Heraclius now withdrew to Constantinople, taking care that the relic of the True Cross was smuggled out of Jerusalem and taken to the Byzantine capital as well. The Arabs began the siege of Jerusalem in July 637 and the holy city was surrendered by the Christian patriarch Sophronius in February 638. Syria and Palestine were now completely under Arab control. In Iraq the Arabs gained victories over the Persians, and the Persian empire began to fall apart as the Arabs made further advances.

The conquest of Egypt was undertaken by Amr ibn al-As, largely on his own initiative, and he advanced across Sinai from Palestine towards the end of 639. Defeating a Byzantine force at Heliopolis, Amr went on to besiege Babylon, a fortress near the site of modern Cairo. It surrendered in 641, the year of Heraclius's death, and the garrison was allowed to withdraw to Alexandria, the capital of Egypt and the base for the Byzantine fleet in the Levant. Amr then besieged Alexandria, and by late 641 Cyrus, the Byzantine viceroy, was ready to surrender. He was given generous terms and the garrison was allowed to leave the country. By 643 the conquest of Egypt had been completed, but in 644, after hearing news of Amr's recall to Medina, the Byzantines sent a fleet and army to regain their lost province. Alexandria was retaken in early 645, but when the Byzantines advanced on the new Arab capital at Fustat they were defeated by Amr, who had returned to his post. The Byzantine commander was so disgusted at the lack of support he received from local Christians that he did not defend Alexandria, sailing away to Constantinople instead. The Arabs had less success when they advanced up the River Nile in 652, being repulsed by the Christians of Nubia. Nevertheless, within less than a decade the Byzantine empire had lost three of its most wealthy provinces, Syria, Palestine and Egypt.

The Byzantine naval intervention at Alexandria in 645 was a warning to the Arabs that if they wished to preserve their conquests they would need to obtain superiority at sea as well as on land. The Arabs were not without maritime traditions, with Arab ships active on the Red Sea, Persian Gulf and Indian Ocean, but most of the desert tribesmen who spearheaded the conquest were strangers to salt water. Nevertheless, the local maritime experts of Syria and Egypt, especially the Christian Copts in the latter country, were more than ready to assist their new masters in acquiring maritime skills. Abdullah ibn Saad, governor of Egypt, and Muawiya ibn abi Safian, governor of Syria, were active promoters of the new Arab navy. In 649 the Arab fleet took Cyprus from the Byzantines and in 655, in the so-called Battle of the Masts off the south coast of Anatolia, it inflicted a major defeat on the fleet of Emperor Constans ii, with the emperor himself narrowly escaping death in the battle. Having been soundly beaten on both land and sea, the future of the Byzantines looked grim, but they received a temporary reprieve when civil war erupted among the Arabs.

The murder of the caliph Uthman by fellow Muslims in 656 at Medina threw the Arab world into confusion. The new caliph Ali had to fight various opponents, but was eventually overcome by Muawiya, the governor of Syria, and killed in 661. Muawiya founded the Umayyad dynasty that was to reign over the Arabs for almost one hundred years. The new ruler moved the Arab capital from Medina to Damascus in Syria and he took a close interest in further Muslim attacks on the Christians in the Mediterranean world.

TO CONSTANTINOPLE AND CARTHAGE

After 670 Caliph Muawiya began to prepare a major assault on the Byzantine capital, Constantinople. After securing Cyprus and Rhodes as bases, the Arab fleets moved steadily northwards through the Aegean Sea. Eventually Arab warships passed through the Dardanelles and into the Sea of Marmara (Constantinople lay on the northern shore of that sea, on the Bosphorus, the channel leading into the Black Sea). The Arabs set up a base at Cyzicus on the southern shore of the Marmara. Only in 674 did the caliph's son, Yazid, begin a land and sea blockade of Constantinople, a siege that would last for five years. It was not a continuous effort, since Arab forces retired to Cyzicus and even back into the Aegean during the winter months, but the Byzantine capital faced a major threat.

The great walls of Constantinople remained unbreached, however, and the Byzantine fleet was undefeated. The real salvation for the

Europe and the Middle East at the time of the Arab conquests.

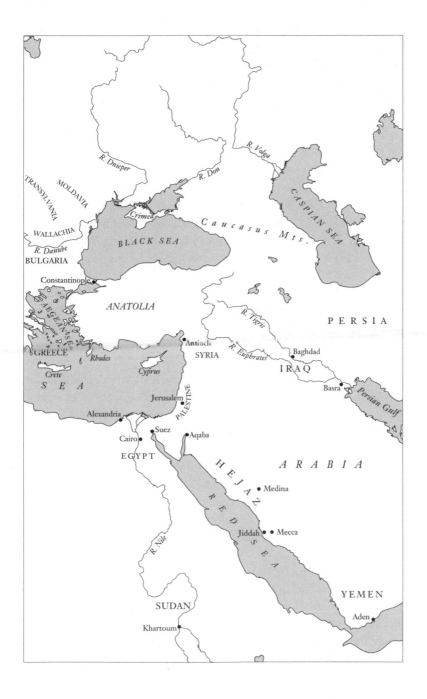

Byzantines was their use of a new secret weapon, 'Greek Fire'. Said to have been invented by Callinicus, an architect and chemist from Syria, the exact formula for this incendiary mixture remains unknown, although it was probably composed of a mixture of flammable materials such as sulphur and pitch in a petroleum base. This compound was sprayed on the enemy from tubes through which it was forced under pressure by pumps. Apparently 'Greek Fire' ignited spontaneously and could not be extinguished by water. Equipped with this new weapon, Byzantine warships inflicted heavy losses on the ships of the blockading Arab fleet.

By the summer of 678 it was clear that the Arabs could not take Constantinople, and the remains of their army and fleet withdrew. The failed siege was the first major defeat for the Arabs. When Caliph Muawiya came to make peace with the Byzantine emperor, Constantine IV, in 679, he was the one who had to make concessions. The Arabs agreed to a long truce, withdrew from Rhodes and Cyprus, and even promised to pay an annual tribute to the Byzantine emperor. Muawiya died in the following year, having seen the Arab fleet he had helped to create almost destroyed. Nevertheless, this was only a temporary setback for the Islamic conquerors.

A bigger problem for the Arabs was the civil war that broke out among them after Muawiya's death and further delayed advances against the infidel. Husayn, the son of Ali, tried to overthrow the Umayyads, but was swiftly crushed. Other opponents then took up the struggle against the ruling house, but by 685 they too had been defeated. Husayn and his father Ali were treated as sacred martyrs by the Shiite version of Islam that grew up soon afterwards. The Shia ('party of Ali') refused to recognize the caliphs that came after them. Shiism became the expression in religious terms of opposition to the established order, acceptance of which meant conformity to Sunni, or mainstream, Islamic doctrine.

War between the Byzantines and the Arabs resumed in the 690s, with the Arabs taking Cyprus once again and making progress in Armenia. The main area of conflict between the two sides, however, was now to be in the old Roman province of Africa (modern Tunisia), where the Byzantines had a major base at Carthage. Arabs from Egypt had been pushing westwards across North Africa since the late 660s, and faced opposition from both the Byzantines and the local Berber tribes, most of whom were pagans, although some had converted to Judaism. In 670 the Arabs established a base at Kairouan in Tunisia, and in the early 680s they launched a bold westward advance that was said to have reached the shores of the Atlantic Ocean in Morocco. However, the Arab commander had over-reached himself. He was defeated and killed near Tahuda in Algeria by a coalition of Berber tribes and Byzantines. The victors then pushed the Arabs right back to the borders of Egypt.

In 693 the Arabs launched a new offensive across North Africa and in 695 they took Carthage from the Byzantines. Then a Berber uprising led by a mysterious female ruler known as al-Kahina, possibly a Jewish Berber, threatened Arab control. To exploit this development, Emperor Leontius sent a Byzantine army and fleet to recapture Carthage, an objective they quickly achieved. Once again the Arabs had to rally their forces and counter-attack. They defeated al-Kahina and in 698 drove the Byzantines out of Carthage. The surviving Byzantine forces sailed back to Constantinople and overthrew Emperor Leontius. He was replaced by Tiberius III, who was to enjoy some military success against the Arabs in Armenia and Cilicia in the years 700–04. The Byzantines, however, never attempted to regain their lost territories in North Africa, and many Christians from that area fled abroad.

Since Carthage harbour seemed too vulnerable to attack from the sea, a new Arab naval base was built at Tunis by connecting an inland lake to the sea by a canal through the coastal strip. The governor of Egypt sent 1,000 Christian Coptic shipwrights to populate the new city and to construct a fleet of 100 warships. The new governor of North Africa, Musa ibn Nusayr, used this new fleet to raid widely in the western Mediterranean, the first time this area had been attacked by Arab sea power. He also used military and diplomatic means to bring the Berbers under control and encourage them to convert to Islam. By the early years of the eighth century the Arabs had extended their control to the shores of the Atlantic. The next target for conquest was the Visigothic kingdom of Spain.

INTO SPAIN

The Visigoths had settled in the Iberian peninsula during the barbarian invasions and converted to Christianity. At the start of the eighth century their kingdom was torn by internal divisions, and some groups in the population, such as the much-persecuted Jews, would not have been averse to Muslim conquest. After the death of King Wittiza in 710, a civil war between noble factions ensued. King Roderic (Rodrigo) gained control of the Visigothic capital, Toledo, and much of southern Iberia. A rival monarch, Achila II, took over Barcelona, the Ebro valley and Septimania, the Visigothic enclave in south-western France that had its capital at Narbonne.

In 711 Tariq ibn Ziyad, governor of Tangier, led an Arab and Berber force into Spain. Tariq crossed to Gibraltar (which was named after him: Jebel Tariq, 'Tariq's mountain') and later encountered a Visigothic army, under King Roderic. In a battle probably fought somewhere between Algeciras and Jerez, Tariq defeated and killed Roderic. The Muslims then pushed northwards and captured Toledo. Musa ibn Nusayr, the governor of North Africa, subsequently brought over another army of Arabs and Berbers (Iberian Christians called all their Muslim foes 'Moors') and moved further into Iberia. By 714 Muslim forces had reached the Ebro valley and taken Saragossa. The last Visigothic ruler, Achila II's successor Ardo, tried to hold out in Septimania, but the Muslims took Narbonne in 720. The Arabs called their new Iberian conquest al-Andalus and its capital was moved from Toledo to Seville, and later to Córdoba.

Possession of Narbonne gave the Muslims a forward base from which to raid widely into France, although an attempt to capture Toulouse in 721 was defeated. In 732 a Muslim force occupied Bordeaux and then moved north towards the River Loire. While advancing along the road from Poitiers to Tours the Muslims, led by Abdar-Rahman al-Ghafiqi, met a Frankish army under Charles Martel, which inflicted a heavy defeat upon them, killing the Muslim commander. Later chroniclers and historians have made much of the battle of Tours (or Poitiers), claiming that it was a turning point in world history, a victory that halted the Muslim advance into western Europe. The decisive nature of the battle was probably not so obvious at the time. A Berber revolt in North Africa and Iberia in 740–41 probably did more to curtail Muslim raiding north of the Pyrenees. Nevertheless, such raiding soon began again, Lyon, for example, being attacked in 743. Only the prolonged campaigning of Pepin, son of Charles Martel, finally led to the capture of Narbonne by the Franks in 759 and the expulsion of the Muslims from France.

By the 750s the Arab conquests were finally running out of steam. Even in Spain the Christians had been regaining ground in the north-west of the country. The traditional start of the Iberian *Reconquista* (Reconquest) is said to be the victory of Pelayo over the Arab governor of Gijon at Covadonga around 720, but Muslim withdrawal from north-west Spain was caused less by Christian resistance than by Arab–Berber conflict during the 740s and widespread famine in the 750s. The Asturian kings Alfonso i and his son Fruela i followed up the Muslim retreat by expanding their authority into Galicia and the Basque country between 740 and 770. This expansion laid the basis for sustainable Christian resistance. More important than the Christian efforts in France and Spain, however, was the Byzantine resistance to a second great Muslim siege of Constantinople in 717–18 and the Byzantine military revival that followed this success. Yet perhaps the principal reason for the end of Arab expansionism was political change at the heart of the empire, when in 750 the Umayyad dynasty was overthrown by the Abbasids.

CONQUERORS AND CONQUERED

Before 632 the great centres of Christianity had been around the shores of the Mediterranean. Then the Arab conquests had brought Christian lands such as Syria, Palestine, Egypt, North Africa and Iberia under Muslim rule. Islam's victories had turned Europe into Christianity's last remaining base, while blocking direct European access to other world civilizations. Christendom would now be based on the remnants of the Byzantine empire and on the emerging states of western and northern Europe. How the remaining Christian lands reacted to the continuing challenge of Islam would be a major factor in shaping their future – but what was to become of the populations of those formerly Christian territories now under Arab rule?

One of the ironies of the Arab conquests was that the Arabs were initially reluctant to encourage conversions to Islam among the conquered peoples. Arab garrisons held strategic points in the conquered lands, but day-to-day administration was largely left to officials inherited from the defeated Byzantine and Persian empires. Non-Muslims were given the status of *dhimmis,* followers of the religions tolerated by law, chiefly Christians and Jews. Their tax burden was lighter than under their former rulers, but it was still heavier than taxes on Muslims. As the years passed, non-Arab converts to Islam (called *mawalis*) increased in number, but the Arabs refused to grant them full equality with Arab Muslims, especially with regard to taxes. Mawali resentment at their position found religious expression in the rise of the Shiite version of Islamic doctrine, which stressed the rights of the oppressed. The Hashemite branch of Shiism stirred up mawalis and others in the Khurasan area of Persia and a revolt, led by the Abbasid family, broke out in 747. The rebels defeated the

Umayyads in 750 and Abul-Abbas became caliph. A determined effort was then made to kill all the remaining members of the Umayyad royal house.

The new Abbasid rulers, who dropped their Shiite supporters and became orthodox Sunnis once they had achieved power, were to produce changes that had considerable impact on the Christian–Muslim conflict. To satisfy the mawalis, Islam became the badge of identity within the empire, not Arab ethnic status. The Abbasids shifted the focus of the empire eastwards, away from the Mediterranean, and the capital was moved from Damascus to the new city of Baghdad in Iraq. Partly because of the origins of their rebellion, the Abbasids favoured a version of Islamic empire that looked to the example of Persian empires of the past, especially in giving great power to the ruler, in this case the caliph. Although ready to continue the jihad against the Byzantine Christians if required, the Abbasids took less and less interest in the Mediterranean world. They did little to prevent Muslim states in that area from breaking away from the empire, and this fragmentation was eventually to provide opportunities for Christian reconquest.

3

BYZANTINE DEFIANCE,
750–1000

THE BYZANTINE ROCK

Between the 630s and the 750s the Muslim conquerors had been victorious from the shores of the Atlantic Ocean to the borders of China. Within that great area only one important state had successfully defied them: the Byzantine empire. Battered and shorn of some of its richest provinces, the empire continued to hold out against the Muslims, even when they reached the very walls of Constantinople. Behind the Byzantine breakwater sheltered not only the empire's own Christians, but also those of western Europe. Whatever the success of Charles Martel at the battle of Tours, it was primarily the Byzantines who held back the Muslim tide, and were to continue to do so for centuries.

Despite the creation of a western Holy Roman Empire by Charlemagne in 800, the western Christians were not strong enough to make a major military impact on the Muslim world until the eleventh century. And when they did so, they soon showed themselves ready to use that power against the Byzantines as well as the Muslims. Although the formal separation of eastern (Orthodox) Christianity from western (Catholic) Christianity did not take place until 1054, the two churches had been drawing apart for centuries before that, with doctrinal differences turning into mutual hostility. The western Christians (known as 'Franks' to both Byzantines and Muslims) repaid Byzantine constancy in the Christian cause by sacking Constantinople in 1204 and doing more damage to the city than the final Muslim conquest in 1453.

All this lay in the distant future, however, when the second great Muslim siege of Constantinople took place in 717–18. Muslim preparations for the assault had been detected as early as 715, and Emperor Anastasius II had sought to put his capital in a state of defence. He also assembled forces in Rhodes to launch a pre-emptive attack on the Muslim fleet. However, those forces mutinied, returned to Constantinople and overthrew the emperor. His replacement, Theodosius III, had a short career, being overthrown in his turn in March 717 by the soldier who became Emperor Leo III, one of the greatest of Byzantine rulers.

Leo was also aware of Muslim intentions and renewed the defensive preparations begun by Anastasius. Thus when the Muslim army, commanded by the caliph's brother Maslama, crossed the Dardanelles into Thrace and besieged the land walls of Constantinople in August 717 the city was ready to resist the enemy. Shortly afterwards the Muslim fleet appeared in the Sea of Marmara, only to find the Byzantine naval forces secure in the Golden Horn, which was closed with an iron chain across the entrance. Leo led sorties by his fleet, and 'Greek Fire' inflicted as much damage on the Muslim fleet as it had during the first great siege during the 670s. Unlike the first siege, the Muslims did not retire when winter came, but continued their blockade on land and sea during the winter of 717–18. This proved one of the coldest winters in living memory and inflicted severe losses on the Muslim forces. In the spring of 718 a supply fleet from Egypt reinforced the Muslim besiegers. Christian sailors on the newly arrived vessels defected to the Byzantines and supplied Leo with valuable intelligence that enabled him to mount further damaging attacks on the Muslim fleet. The final blow for the Muslims came when the Bulgars agreed to support the Byzantine emperor and attacked the Muslim army from the rear. In August 718 Maslama lifted the siege and withdrew what was left of the Muslim army and fleet, having suffered a major defeat. More than 700 years would pass before another Muslim army mounted a serious attack on Constantinople.

The Emperor Leo III had further successes against the Muslims in Anatolia, including a major victory over them at Akroinen in 740. However, he also inflicted serious damage on the Christian world by unleashing the iconoclast religious controversy. By the time of his death in 741, Leo had created deep divisions within the Byzantine empire. In 746 his son, Constantine V, took the war into enemy territory by initiating operations in Muslim Syria. Success on land was matched by success at sea: the Byzantine navy defeated the Egyptian and Syrian fleets at the battle of Ceramea in 747 and recaptured Cyprus. For the next fifty years the Byzantines were to have the advantage over the Muslims at sea.

By the mid-eighth century a new military system was well established within the Byzantine empire. The armies of the Byzantine empire were transformed into an elite expeditionary guard named *tagmata* and into military districts called themes (*themata*). Each theme was commanded by a *strategos*, or general, with civil and military authority over his district. Leo III, for example, had been *strategos* of the important theme of Anatolikon before he seized the throne. The soldiers of the thematic armies acquired tax-exempt lands and preserved the core of the empire, thus avoiding the high costs that had been imposed by the armies of mercenaries usually assembled by the Byzantines in the period before the Arab invasions. If a Byzantine emperor wished to launch an expedition against the Muslims or the Bulgars, he would send *tagmata* from the capital to join up with troops from the themes nearest to the relevant enemy frontier.

Emperor Leo IV resumed the war against the Muslims in the second half of the eighth century with some success, but after his death in 780 the Muslims began to regain the upper hand. An invasion of Anatolia in 782 by the caliph's son Harun al-Rashid forced a humiliating peace on Empress Irene. Harun's reign (786–809) is usually regarded as the high point of the Abbasid dynasty. He carried out many raids on Byzantine territory, but never made any attempt at permanent conquest. By the year 800 the border between the Byzantine and Muslim empires had settled on the line of the Taurus mountains in eastern Anatolia.

It was to remain on that line for most of the next two hundred years. Depending on who had control of the Taurus passes, Muslim raiders would sweep into Anatolia or Byzantine armies would move into Syria, but neither side made permanent gains until the Byzantine advance in the second half of the tenth century. Harun al-Rashid and later rulers still invoked the jihad in their wars with the Byzantines, but they were now ready to accept a stalemate with their Christian enemies. Harun took little interest in Christian–Muslim conflict elsewhere in the Mediterranean area, chiefly because by 800 Spain, Morocco and Tunisia had all separated from the original Arab empire and become new Muslim states.

SPAIN BREAKS AWAY

When the Abbasids had come to power in 750 they tried to kill all members of the defeated Umayyad dynasty. To a large extent they succeeded, but one Umayyad prince, Abd al-Rahman, escaped the slaughter and fled westwards. He eventually reached al-Andalus in 755 and cultivated local support. Then Abd al-Rahman seized Córdoba, refused allegiance to the Abbasids, and in 756 proclaimed himself emir (prince) of an independent al-Andalus. Córdoba was to be the capital of the Umayyad state in Spain for the next three centuries. The new emir found the subjugation of al-Andalus a hard task, with Abbasid agents stirring up local resistance. Toledo and its region submitted only in the mid-760s; Seville was subdued during the 770s, and the Ebro valley was secured only around 780.

The Christian states in Spain made few significant advances against the Muslims in the late eighth century, but the growing power of the Frankish kingdom north of the Pyrenees seemed to pose a threat to al-Andalus. In 778, with Abd al-Rahman's armies approaching from the south, the Muslim ruler of Saragossa turned to the Frankish ruler, Charlemagne, for support. Charlemagne crossed the Pyrenees, but when his army reached Saragossa its ruler changed his mind about enlisting Christian support and refused to admit the Franks. A siege was begun, but then news of rebellions back home forced Charlemagne to withdraw across the Pyrenees, leaving Saragossa to fall to Abd al-Rahman the following year. During Charlemagne's retreat, his rearguard, commanded by Roland, was cut off in the Pass of Roncesvalles and destroyed. Those responsible for this attack were probably Basques, but in the great medieval epic written about the event, the *Song of Roland*, they were portrayed as Muslims so as to encourage later Christian warriors to take up the struggle against the infidel. In 801 the Franks seized Barcelona from the Muslims and laid the basis of a Christian state in the north-east of the Iberian peninsula to match those already established in the north and north-west.

Charlemagne's rebuff in Spain in 778 was a minor episode in his great career. In 800 the pope crowned him Holy Roman Emperor in Rome, the first emperor in the West since 476. The Byzantines refused to recognize Charlemagne's imperial status, but his elevation did mark the growing power of western Christians. Nevertheless, it was to be many years before such power had a major impact on the Christian–Muslim balance of forces. The ninth century was to witness a revival of Muslim sea power in the Mediterranean, which led to new conquests.

ISLAND BASES AND PIRATE NESTS

The breakaway Muslim states in the Mediterranean took a strong interest in sea power, and during the ninth and tenth centuries much of the Mediterranean was turned into a Muslim lake. This permitted the capture or recapture from the Christians of Cyprus, Crete, Sicily, Corsica, Sardinia and the Balearic Islands. From these islands, and with forward bases – or rather pirate nests – on the French and Italian coast-lines, Muslim fleets and sea raiders pushed the Christians back into the northern waters of the Aegean, Adriatic and Mediterranean seas. The main west-to-east trade route through the Mediterranean was now under Muslim control, aiding trade and the passage of Muslim pilgrims on their way to Mecca. Christian efforts to combat Muslim sea power in these centuries had only limited success, and the situation would not change until the eleventh century.

The first important Muslim success was to take the island of Crete from the Byzantines. Rebellious Muslim corsairs who had been driven out of al-Andalus came to the island around 824 and by 827 they had secured complete control of it. This Muslim conquest altered the strategic picture in the eastern Mediterranean, enabling corsairs from Crete to raid widely in the Aegean Sea and even venture into the Sea of Marmara. The Byzantines failed to recapture Crete, but they did raid Egyptian ports from which the Cretan corsairs were receiving supplies.

From 860 the Abbasid caliphate sought to revive its sea power in the Mediterranean, creating naval bases at Tripoli in Syria and Tarsus in Cilicia. A victory by a Tarsiote squadron over a Byzantine fleet in 898 permitted Abbasid ships to begin raiding in the Aegean Sea. In 904 a fleet under Leo of Tripoli, a former Byzantine seaman who had converted to Islam, made a devastating attack on Thessalonica, one of the great cities of the Byzantine empire. Leo's corsairs were said to have killed 5,000 people, freed 4,000 Muslim prisoners, captured 60 ships and carried away thousands of men, women and children to be sold into slavery. A Byzantine naval campaign in 910–12 sought to destroy Leo and his equally formidable ally Damianos of Tarsus, another convert to Islam, but it ended in failure. Only after 950 did the Byzantine military revival on land and sea start to do serious damage to the Muslims. By the end of the tenth century, both Tarsus and the island of Crete were back in Byzantine hands.

If the loss of Crete in the 820s was a major blow to the Christians of the eastern Mediterranean, then the Muslim attack on Sicily during the same decade was to have even more far-reaching consequences for Christians in the central Mediterranean. The Byzantine-held island of Sicily, commanding the narrowest point of the Mediterranean Sea, had been raided sporadically by the Muslims since the seventh century, but it was only in the ninth century that its actual conquest began. In 825 Euphemius, a rebellious Byzantine admiral, took control of Sicily, but he was defeated by imperial forces and fled to Tunisia, which was then an independent Muslim state under the Aghlabid dynasty. Euphemius urged the Aghlabid ruler, Ziyadat-Allah I, to invade Sicily, which he did in 827, landing his forces at Mazara. Progress proved slow for the invaders, however, and it was not until 831 that they captured Palermo, which was to become the capital of Muslim Sicily. Messina fell in 843, giving the Muslims control of the strait between Sicily and Italy, and all the offshore islands were secured – Malta, for example, being taken by the Muslims in 870. Syracuse, the principal Byzantine base on Sicily, finally surrendered to the Muslims in 878. The last major Christian outpost on the island, Taormina, fell in 902, but the fall of Syracuse signalled the success of the Muslim conquest.

Long before Syracuse fell, however, Sicily was being used as a base for Muslim attacks along the eastern and western coasts of Italy. This was followed by a Muslim invasion of Calabria and Apulia, with the invaders capturing Brindisi in 838, Taranto in 839 and Bari in 841. On the western coast of Italy Muslim raiders reached Ostia in 846 and sailed up the River Tiber to Rome. The walled city was too strong to attack, but the basilica of St Peter's lay defenceless outside the walls. To the horror of the pope and all western Christians, the basilica was sacked by the Muslims, who sailed away unmolested. This provocation led the pope to call on the secular powers to defend the Church and to offer spiritual benefits to Christians who would fight the Muslims. More practically, Pope Leo IV built walls around St Peter's and assisted in the formation of a Christian fleet, which defeated later Muslim raiders off Ostia.

The Holy Roman Emperor came to assist the pope and even entered into an uneasy alliance with the Byzantines in the common Christian struggle against the Muslims. The Byzantines, however, declined to recognize the imperial status of the western emperor, calling him 'King of the Germans', and pushed their own claims to southern Italy as former Byzantine territory. A joint Frankish-Byzantine siege of Bari was defeated in 869, but Emperor Louis II captured the city without significant Byzantine aid in 871. Muslim-held Capua was taken by the western emperor in 873 and the Byzantines recaptured Taranto in 880. When Louis II died in 875, the Byzantines took control of Bari, and it was to be the capital of their Italian territories for next two hundred years. During the tenth century the western emperors of the Ottonian dynasty took some interest in southern Italy, fighting both Byzantines and Muslims. After the crushing defeat of Emperor Otto II near Cape Colonne in Calabria in 982 by a Muslim army from Sicily, however, the western emperors increasingly left southern Italy to the pope and the Byzantines.

By 880 the Muslim occupation of large areas of southern Italy was at an end, but Muslim corsairs continued to ravage the Italian coast. Muslim control of the sea meant that they could establish surprisingly long-lived pirate bases deep in enemy territory. From such bases raids could be made on the surrounding countryside to take slaves and seize booty. Between 881 and 883 Christian forces drove Muslim pirates from bases below the volcano of Vesuvius and in the Gulf of Salerno, but they merely moved to reinforce another pirate nest that had been established on the River Garigiliano to the north of Naples. From this base Muslim raiders could sweep across Campania and Latium, almost to the gates of Rome, and in 884 the abbey at Monte Cassino was sacked. Christian efforts to remove this Muslim base were repeatedly unsuccessful. Only in 915 did a Byzantine fleet blockade the mouth of the River Garigliano while troops of a papal alliance attacked the Muslims. Ignoring prohibitions on the clergy being involved in bloodshed, Pope John x was said to have led his soldiers personally when they destroyed the Muslim base.

A similar Muslim enclave was set up at Fraxinetum (La Garde-Freinet) near Saint-Tropez on the south coast of France around 890 by Muslim corsairs from al-Andalus. From this base they raided west to Marseille, north to Vienne, east to Asti, and north-east to the abbey of St Gall in Switzerland. Christian attempts to expel the Muslims in 931 and 942 were unsuccessful. Not until 972 did the counts of Provence and Turin lead a joint Christian army that finally destroyed their base.

The long survival of these Muslim raider bases showed the benefits of control of the sea. As well as living off the local countryside, they could easily be supplied from Muslim ports. This capacity of sea power to sustain distant bases deep in enemy territory was to be demonstrated again during the Crusades, but then it would be Christian sea power sustaining Christian enclaves deep inside Muslim territory.

SPAIN: MUSLIM SUCCESS OR STALEMATE?

During the first half of the ninth century the Umayyad dynasty in al-Andalus remained strong, but in the second half of the century civil wars among the Muslims became more common. The Christians exploited this development and were able to continue their slow advance southwards in Iberia. They had been heartened by the discovery around 820 of the supposed relics of St James the Apostle (later patron saint of Spain), which were to be housed in the cathedral at Santiago de Compostela in north-west Spain. Santiago was to become a place of Christian pilgrimage in western Europe second only to Rome itself. As early as 822 at the battle of Clavijo, St James was said to have appeared to inspire the Christian army of King Ramiro of Asturias to defeat the Moors. Visions of 'Santiago Matamoros' (St James the Moorslayer) were to inspire Christian armies to victory in later battles.

In the tenth century, however, Muslim power in Iberia was to reach its zenith. Muslim fortunes revived rapidly after Abd al-Rahman III came to the throne in 912. He crushed Muslim rebels and led repeated campaigns against the Christian states in northern Iberia. After defeating the combined armies of León and Castile at Tudela in 918, he inflicted another defeat on the Christians in 920 at Val de Junqueras, only 40 miles from the Bay of Biscay. In 924 he sacked Pamplona, the capital of Navarre.

In 929 Abd al-Rahman III crowned his success by declaring himself caliph, which now meant the Muslim world had three caliphs. The original one was the Abbasid caliph in Baghdad, but early in the tenth century the Fatimids, break-away rulers of part of North Africa (and later Egypt) and zealous Shiites, declared their leader to be caliph. This proliferation of leaders of the faithful could do little to enhance the unity of Islam. The Fatimid fleet posed a major threat to al-Andalus, so Abd al-Rahman strengthened his own naval forces, a development further encouraged by the raids of pagan Vikings coming down to the Mediterranean from northern seas. Fortunately for Abd al-Rahman and his successors, the Fatimids chose to expand eastwards into Egypt and beyond, not northwards into al-Andalus. Thus the Umayyad caliph could concentrate on his wars with the Iberian Christians.

Abd al-Rahman sacked Burgos in 934, but in 939 he was defeated by a Christian army under King Ramiro II of León at the battle of Simancas, near Valladolid. The caliph was lucky to escape with his life and never again would he take the field in person against the Christians. Ramiro was the most determined Christian opponent of the Muslims, but after his death in 951 Christian fortunes declined. Before Abd al-Rahman died in 961 most of the Christian rulers in Iberia had recognized him as their overlord. The Umayyad dynasty had reached its peak and the city of Córdoba was for a time a worthy rival to Baghdad or Constantinople.

Abd al-Rahman's son and successor died in 976, leaving a child as heir, and real power passed to the vizier (*wazir*), the caliph's chief minister. This was Muhammad ibn Abi Amir, and after defeating the Christians at Rueda in 981 he took the title al-Mansur ('the Victorious'), which led to his being known to the Christians as Almanzor. He led campaigns against the Christians almost every year and enjoyed considerable success. In 985 Almanzor sacked Barcelona and in 988 it was the turn of León. In 997 he campaigned in the mountains of Galicia and attacked Santiago de Compostela. The town and the cathedral were destroyed, but Almanzor left the reputed tomb of St James undamaged. He took away the church bells, which were not recovered from Córdoba until it fell to the Christians in 1236. This attack on perhaps the second holiest Christian site in western Europe was a great blow to the Christians, humiliated by their inability to defend it. The attack on St Peter's at Rome in 846 had brought some Christian military reaction, but the sacking of Santiago brought little or none. Almanzor seemed invincible, but in 1002 he died while returning from a campaign in Castile.

Even more than Abd al-Rahman III, Almanzor had reduced the Christian kingdoms of Iberia to subservience. Yet, like his predecessor, he did not think in terms of conquering those Christian lands. For all the success of the Muslim rulers, they seemed ready to accept a territorial stalemate along a recognized border. This cut a diagonal line across Iberia, leaving perhaps a third of the peninsula to the Christians in the north. Behind the border states of Badajoz, Toledo and Saragossa, the centre and south of Iberia remained the heartland of al-Andalus. Thus in Spain, as along the Taurus mountains of Anatolia, the Muslims seemed ready to accept a balance of forces, but soon that balance would begin to shift in favour of the Christians.

BYZANTINE REVIVAL

After the death of Harun al-Rashid in 809, his sons fought each other for the throne and al-Mamun did not emerge as victor until 813. During the 830s he and his successor, al-Mutasim, waged a largely successful series of campaigns against the Byzantine emperor Theophilus, often crossing the Taurus passes and ravaging Anatolia. However, the Muslim armies that undertook these campaigns were changing in composition and this was to have long-lasting effects. Since taking power in 750 the Abbasids had favoured non-Arab, chiefly Persian, troops. Now a new element began to take over: the Turks. Some were mercenaries; others were captives or slaves brought from Central Asia and later converted to Islam. The slave (Mamluk) army now began to emerge as a feature of Muslim military organization and was to remain so for centuries. Its advantage for the ruler was that Mamluks were his personal soldiers, not troops provided by potentially rebellious nobles. The disadvantage was that if the ruler was weak, the Mamluks could all too easily become the dominant force in government. From 860 onwards military commanders were usually more powerful than the Abbasid caliph, and after 945 the caliph was little more than a religious figurehead.

Unfortunately for the Muslims, the breakdown of Abbasid government coincided with a Byzantine military revival. Emperor Basil I seized power in 867 and took control of the Taurus passes, where he built fortifications. He then launched a series of campaigns into Muslim territory between 871 and 879. Samosata, on the upper Euphrates river, was occupied in 873, and during the campaign of 878–79 both Cappadocia and Cilicia were freed from Muslim rule. In southern Italy, Bari, Taranto and Calabria were cleared of Muslims and returned to Byzantine rule. By the time of Basil's death in 886, he had clearly re-established the Byzantine empire as a major military power.

Towards the end of the ninth century and in the first half of the tenth, however, that power was more likely to be used in the Balkan peninsula against pagan or Christianized tribes moving in from the steppes than against the Muslims. One of the principal military weaknesses of the Byzantine empire was the possibility of having to fight on two fronts at the same time. In the east were the Muslims and in the west various hostile Balkan tribes, with the Bulgars as the principal threat at the end of the ninth century.

During the reign of Emperor Romanus I Lecapanus (920–44), the Byzantine empire began to enjoy increasing success in its conflict with the Muslims, with John Kourkouas as the most successful Byzantine commander. The Abbasid caliph in Baghdad was largely incapable of organizing Muslim resistance, so border defence was left to local rulers. The most important of these was Ali ibn Hamdan, known as Sayf al-Dawlah, who seized power in Aleppo in 944. For some years he enjoyed successes against the Byzantines, but after 955 the Muslims found it hard to resist the attacks of a group of brilliant Byzantine generals, most notably Nicephorus and Leo Phocas, and John Tzimisces.

In 960 Leo Phocas defeated Sayf al-Dawlah at the Kylindros pass in the Taurus mountains, and in 961, taking advantage of growing Byzantine naval power, Nicephorus Phocas took Crete from the Muslims. In 963 Nicephorus captured Aleppo, and at the end of the year seized the imperial throne, becoming Emperor Nicephorus II Phocas.

Nicephorus attacked the Muslims in south-east Anatolia in 964, occupying Adana. Tarsus fell in 965, and Cyprus was retaken by the Byzantines in the same year. Sayf al-Dawlah died in 967 and Aleppo was soon just a vassal state of the Byzantines. In 968 the emperor invaded Syria, sacking Homs and Hama and ravaging the coast from Tripoli back to Tarsus. In 969 the great city of Antioch, capital of Syria in Roman times, was recaptured by the Byzantine general Michael Bourtzes after more than 300 years in Muslim hands. At the end of 969 Nicephorus was murdered and replaced by John Tzimisces, who became Emperor John I. Wars in the Balkans detained John for some years, but by 974 his presence was urgently required on the empire's eastern frontiers.

The Fatimid caliph had taken over Egypt in 969 and then sent his forces into Palestine and Syria. From 970 onwards the Fatimids were the principal defenders of the Muslim frontier against the Byzantines. A Fatimid attack on Antioch had been repulsed in 971, but Fatimid forces had then defeated a Byzantine force at Amida in 973. In 974 John invaded Muslim territory and at first thought of launching an attack on the Abbasid caliph in Baghdad. While Abbasid weakness seemed to invite such an attack, however, the reality of the Fatimid threat had to have priority. In 975 the emperor led a major invasion of Fatimid-held Syria. Homs and Damascus surrendered with little resistance, but Tripoli repulsed the Byzantines. Nevertheless, Syria had largely been taken under Byzantine control for the first time since the days of Heraclius.

The campaigns of Nicephorus Phocas and John Tzimisces once again made the Byzantine empire a great power in the east. Significantly, they were also consciously holy wars, the first since Heraclius's war with the Persians. In previous wars with the Muslims the Byzantines had all too often been on the defensive, with the retaining of Christian territory their aim, not its expansion. However, both Nicephorus and John declared their wars to be for the glory of Christendom, aimed at rescuing the holy places and destroying Islam. The Arabs had always been readier to see war as a religious matter, but over the years their raids on Christian territory had lost much of their religious significance and had become merely plundering expeditions. The new Christian holy war forced the Muslims to try to rekindle some of their own fervour. In 974 riots in Baghdad forced the Abbasid caliph, who personally was not sorry to see his rival the Fatimid caliph beaten by the Christians, to proclaim a holy war, a jihad, against the Byzantines.

Emperor John I had no more great victories. He died early in 976, possibly poisoned, and his successor Basil II became known as the 'Bulgar Slayer' because so much of his reign was spent in fighting in the Balkans. Nevertheless, Basil did campaign in Syria in 995 to restore Byzantine suzerainty over Aleppo, and in 999 he led an army down the coast as far as Tripoli. The dispirited Muslims made no attempt to recapture the land and cities reoccupied by the Byzantines since 960. By the year 1000 it was clear that the balance of forces had shifted in favour of the Christians on the Byzantine-Muslim frontier. The century that was about to dawn was to see major Christian victories throughout the Mediterranean world.

4

RISE OF THE WEST: CHRISTIAN ADVANCES IN THE ELEVENTH CENTURY

NEW FORCES

The eleventh century was an important turning point in the struggle between Christians and Muslims. For the first time in nearly four centuries the Christians made major advances, recapturing territory long held by the Muslims. This progress was due to major changes on both sides. On the Christian side, the greatest change was the rise to military and naval power of the states of western Europe. The Iberian kingdoms made significant advances against the Moors; Norman adventurers conquered Muslim Sicily; the Italian maritime states of Venice, Genoa and Pisa asserted Christian naval superiority in the Mediterranean; and finally, and most famously, the First Crusade made its difficult way from western Europe to Palestine and took Jerusalem from the Muslims in 1099.

For at least the first half of the eleventh century it seemed that the Byzantine Christians would share in these advances, but their power was steadily undermined by new forces in both west and east. In the west some of the rising Christian powers – especially the Normans of southern Italy and Sicily – were as hostile to Byzantine Christians as they were to Muslims. Even Venice, which assisted the Byzantines against the Normans, did so only in return for major trade concessions within the empire. In the east the declining Abbasid empire, which had failed to stop Byzantine advances in the late tenth century, was replaced by a new and powerful force, the Seljuk Turks.

Under Toghrul Beg the Seljuks had by the mid-eleventh century conquered most of the eastern areas of the Abbasid empire and were nearing Baghdad. In the capital the Sunni Abbasid caliph was under the control of the Shiite Buyids, but the latter were overthrown by the Seljuks in 1055. The Abbasid caliph was retained as a religious leader by the Sunni Seljuks, but Toghrul Beg had supreme power as the new sultan. His nephew and successor, Alp Arslan, next led the Seljuks against their remaining major enemies, the Christian Byzantine empire and the Shiite Fatimid caliphate based in Egypt. The Seljuks raided Armenia, destroying its capital Ani in 1064. The Byzantines permitted many Armenians to migrate to new settlements in the Taurus mountains, which would one day become the state of Cilician Armenia. By 1068 Armenia had been overrun by the Seljuks and in 1070 their raids almost reached the Aegean coast of Anatolia.

In 1071 Emperor Romanus IV Diogenes decided to retake Armenia from the Turks while their main army was busy fighting the Fatimids in Syria. The emperor received bad news as he left Constantinople to embark on his campaign. Bari, the last Byzantine possession in Italy, had fallen to the Normans. Moreover, the Byzantine army assembled for the advance into Armenia was a mere shadow of the powerful force that Emperor Basil II had commanded fifty years earlier, with most of its troops being mercenaries. These even included contingents from both the empire's chief enemies: the Turks and the Normans. The Byzantine provincial troops from the themes of Anatolia were more reliable than the mercenaries, but they were poorly equipped. Most of the army was infantry, with a large baggage train, so the emperor's forces moved only slowly. In contrast, once he had been informed of the Byzantine advance, Alp Arslan led his army quickly from Syria to Armenia. Most of his warriors were mounted archers, unencumbered by any baggage train.

Still believing that Alp Arslan was far away, Romanus captured the town of Manzikert, near Lake Van, from the Turks in August 1071. The emperor had failed to send out scouts and was taken by surprise when Alp Arslan's horsemen suddenly appeared near Manzikert. Nevertheless, Romanus deployed his army and advanced on the enemy. Soon his battle line began to break up as troops pursued bodies of Turkish cavalry making feigned retreats, and then springing surprise attacks on their pursuers. The horse archers deluged the Byzantine infantry with showers of arrows, steadily wearing down their resistance. Finally Romanus gave the command for an orderly retreat, but his forces soon began to flee. The commander of the Byzantine rearguard, Andronicus Ducas, was both a relative and an enemy of the emperor. Instead of covering the retreat, he led his men away and rode for Constantinople to assist in the appointment of a new emperor. The mercenaries had been equally useless. The Turkish contingent deserted to Alp Arslan on the night before the battle, and the Norman heavy cavalry refused to fight at all. Romanus stayed with his doomed Byzantine infantry, until he was wounded and taken prisoner by the Turks.

Manzikert was perhaps the most decisive disaster in Byzantine history, being ever after referred to by the empire's chroniclers as 'the dreadful day'. The Byzantine empire was to survive in an increasingly shrunken form for almost another four centuries, experiencing several periods of apparent revival, but the defeat at Manzikert led to the most important disruption of the Byzantine state since the Arab invasions of the seventh century. To the later crusaders it seemed that the Byzantines had forfeited on the battlefield their title as protectors of Christendom. Manzikert justified the intervention of the west.

The Seljuk Turks made no immediate use of their great victory, but by the end of the 1070s their raiders had occupied most of Anatolia. A relative of the Turkish leader was permitted to set up the sultanate of Rum (Rome), which covered most of Anatolia. The loss of that area was a great blow to the Byzantines, since it had been the principal recruiting ground for their army. In the chaotic years after Manzikert, others as well as the Turks tried to set up their own states in Anatolia. Roussel de Bailleul, the leader of the Norman contingent at Manzikert, made a failed attempt at establishing his own Norman dominion, but the Armenians were more successful in setting up their own Christian state in Cilicia.

The Seljuks reached the peak of their power under Malik Shah (1072–92), but after his death their empire began to fall apart, dividing into separate states and contesting factions. As in Iberia and Sicily earlier in the century, this Muslim disunity gave the Christians their chance to make significant advances. But those advances would not be made this time by the Byzantines. For the first time, western Christians advanced into the Middle East as a major military force, a force that was as alarming to the Byzantines as it was to the Muslims.

SEA POWER AND SICILY

From the very beginning of the eleventh century, western Christendom began to exert its sea power against the Muslims. In 1004 the Venetians defeated a Muslim fleet off Bari in the Adriatic Sea and in the following year the Pisans achieved a similar success off Messina in Sicily. In 1016 the Genoese and the Pisans combined to retake Corsica and Sardinia from the infidel. War was later carried directly to Muslim lands, with Pisan attacks on the Algerian city of Bone in 1034 and on

Palermo, the capital of Sicily, in 1063–4. In 1087 Pope Victor III helped organize a successful attack on Mahdia in Tunisia by a Christian fleet that included Genoese, Pisan and Amalfitan ships. During the First Crusade Genoa and Pisa sent ships to assist the crusaders and were rewarded with trading bases in the ports that were taken. Venice was somewhat sidetracked from the struggle against Islam by its involvement in the conflict between Normans and Byzantines in the 1080s. Only in 1100 did a Venetian fleet go to Palestine and assist crusaders with the capture of Haifa, where they were rewarded with a trading base.

The eleventh century had witnessed the spread of western Christian naval power out of the Tyrrhenian and Adriatic seas and throughout most of the Mediterranean Sea. Most Muslim fleets had been defeated, with only the Fatimid navy of Egypt surviving for a little longer, until its decisive defeat by the Venetians off Ascalon in 1123. However, these maritime advances would have been seriously hampered if Sicily had remained in Muslim hands, dominating as it does the central Mediterranean and the narrowest point of the west-to-east sea route through that sea. The Byzantines had made one last attempt to recapture the island from the Muslims between 1038 and 1040, but had eventually failed. It was left to a new force, the Normans, to recapture the island, with some Genoese and Pisan naval assistance, and allow Christian shipping free movement through the Mediterranean.

Several centuries earlier, Vikings had settled in the part of northwest France that became known as Normandy, but these Normans did not restrict their warlike activities to that area. The Norman conquest of England in 1066 is well known, but the creation of a Norman state in southern Italy and Sicily has attracted less notice, although it was of considerable importance for the Christian–Muslim struggle. Originally coming to southern Italy as mercenaries in the early decades of the eleventh century, by 1050 the Normans were seizing land for themselves. Pope Leo IX organized a coalition against them, but at the battle of Civitate in 1053 the Normans crushed the coalition army.

Although this victory put the Normans in a stronger position, their growing success over the next twenty years was due to a number of factors. First, after the failure of their Sicilian expedition in 1040, the Byzantines were forced by the growing Seljuk Turk menace in the east to give less and less attention to their possessions in southern Italy. Second, from 1059 the papacy and the Normans became increasingly close allies. The Normans provided the military muscle to back the pope in dealing with their common enemies: the Byzantines, the Muslims and the western emperor. Third, the Muslim rulers of Sicily began to fight among themselves, providing an opportunity for Norman intervention from 1060 onwards. Finally, the Normans came to be dominated by two outstanding and long-lived warriors, Robert Guiscard of Hauteville and his younger brother Roger. They gave a continuity of leadership and unity of command to the Normans that their enemies could not match. Robert Guiscard in particular became, as his epitaph later noted, 'the terror of the world', a warrior who made popes, Muslim emirs and Byzantine emperors tremble.

The two brothers initially fought to subdue Apulia and Calabria in southern Italy as their own possessions. Their principal enemies were the Byzantines, but in 1060 their interest shifted to Muslim Sicily. A rebellious Muslim ruler asked for Norman assistance against his enemies, which gave the Normans their chance to gain a foothold on the island, taking Messina in 1061. The brothers then made an alliance with Ibn Tamnah, the emir of Syracuse, and helped him defeat rival Muslim forces near Enna. Then Robert Guiscard had to return to Italy, the emir of Syracuse died, and Roger found himself besieged in Troina during the winter of 1062–3. His besiegers were not just the Muslims, but also Greek inhabitants of Sicily who had little love for the anti-Byzantine Normans. Roger managed to break the siege and later in 1063 inflicted a heavy defeat on the Muslims at the battle of Cerami. This success allowed the Normans to advance on the Muslim capital, Palermo, which was already under attack from the Pisan fleet. The Normans, however, were forced to withdraw without making a serious attack on Palermo, and for the next few years the conflict in Sicily seemed to reach a stalemate.

Sicily was nominally subject to the Zirid sultan in Tunisia, who had his capital at Mahdia. The sultan sent troops from North Africa to assist the local Muslim emirs in Sicily in their struggle against the Normans, but disputes soon broke out between Sicilian and North African Arabs. Roger sought to exploit these divisions. In 1068 he advanced from Troina, defeated the North African Arabs at the battle of Misilmeri, and tried to take Palermo, only to fail once again. Another stalemate developed and Roger was recalled to Italy to assist Robert Guiscard in the siege of Bari, the last Byzantine possession in Italy. Bari fell in 1071 and both brothers then went to Sicily, determined to take Palermo.

Applying the land and sea blockading tactics that had worked so well at Bari, Robert Guiscard and Roger eventually forced Palermo to surrender in January 1072. The capture of the great Muslim metropolis was a major boost to Norman prestige. At this time Palermo was, with the single exception of Constantinople, the largest and richest city in the world under Christian government. It was the first major Muslim city in the Mediterranean to fall to the Christians during the eleventh century. Before that century was over it would be joined by Toledo in Spain, taken in 1085, and Jerusalem, stormed in 1099. But once again other concerns delayed the completion of the Norman conquest of Sicily, especially Robert Guiscard's war against the Byzantines in the Balkans during the first half of the 1080s.

Despite the capture of Palermo in 1072, the Norman hold on Sicily was far from secure, being chiefly restricted to the north and north-east of the island. Between 1072 and 1074 Roger built castles to consolidate his hold on the areas in Norman possession, and in 1075 he negotiated a treaty with the sultan in Tunisia, which led to the withdrawal of North African troops from Sicily. Nevertheless, Muslim resistance in the island continued and found an able leader in Ibn el Werd, the emir of Syracuse. Called Benarvet by his Christian opponents, the emir was a match for Roger, and towns such as Catania, Trapani and Taormina changed hands several times during the next ten years. Roger was often recalled to the mainland by events in southern Italy, giving the emir chance to regain ground in Sicily and raid across the Strait of Messina. During the autumn of 1084 he ravaged Calabria, carrying off the nuns of Reggio to decorate the harems of Syracuse.

Roger was now ready to launch a major offensive against Syracuse. By the end of 1084 he was building a new fleet and in May 1086 began a sea blockade of Syracuse, while sending an army to besiege the port from the land side. In October 1086 Syracuse fell to the Normans. The last Muslim stronghold in Sicily, Noto, fell in 1091, the same year that the Normans took possession of the island of Malta. Roger now controlled all of Sicily, and after the death of Robert Guiscard in 1085 he took over southern Italy as well, being known as Roger I, the 'Great Count'. He was generally lenient in his treatment of his new Muslim subjects in Sicily and included Muslim troops in his army, finding them particularly useful for suppressing Christian rebels in southern Italy. Until his death in 1101, Roger also made determined efforts to expand his fleet so that it might rival those of Pisa, Genoa and Venice. His successor, Roger II, persuaded the pope to make him a king in 1130, and he used the Sicilian fleet to capture Muslim ports on the nearby North African coast between 1146 and 1153. For a time the Christians controlled both sides of the Sicilian Narrows, but by 1160 the Muslims had recaptured all the lost ports.

SPAIN: CHRISTIAN ADVANCE AND MUSLIM REACTION

One rebellious Muslim leader gave the Normans their chance to get into Sicily. In Spain during the first half of the eleventh century Muslim rulers so divided and weakened al-Andalus that it seemed that the Christians might overrun the whole area. After the death of Almanzor's son in 1008, the ineffectual Umayyad caliph in Córdoba had no strong leaders to support his cause. Civil wars broke out among the Muslims, and the Córdoba caliphate came to an end in 1031. Al-Andalus broke up into the realms of the so-called *taifa* (party) kings, originally about thirty in number, but later reduced to about six larger states.

Muslim disunity was compounded by declining military strength. The Umayyad caliphs had come to rely largely on imported troops, either Slavs from eastern Europe who became Mamluk (slave) soldiers or Berber mercenaries from North Africa. After the year 1000 the supply of Slavs began to decline, while, with the collapse of central authority, the Berbers became increasingly unreliable, even sacking the city of Córdoba at one point. The *taifa* state of Denia enjoyed some naval success, seizing the Balearic Islands, but its efforts to take control of Sardinia were defeated by the Genoese and Pisan fleets in 1016. In general, the *taifa* states became increasingly defenceless.

The Iberian Christians had internal disputes of their own, but by 1050 they were ready to take advantage of the military weakness of Muslim *taifa* states. In the tenth century the Christian states had been compelled to pay tribute to the Muslims, but in the middle decades of the eleventh century the position was reversed. The originator of this levy was Ferdinand I, King of León and Castile from 1037 to 1065. By the end of his reign he was taking annual tribute (known as *parias*) from the Muslim states of Toledo, Badajoz and Saragossa, and occasional tribute from Seville and Valencia. His son Alfonso would even add distant Granada to the list of tributaries.

Tribute-taking might be expected to make the Christians reluctant to occupy their Muslim neighbours for fear of killing the goose that laid the golden eggs. However, territorial advances were also made. From 1055 Ferdinand I of León and Castile launched an offensive that won him the lower valley of the River Douro. He captured the city of Coimbra in 1064 after making a special pilgrimage to Santiago de

Compostela to pray for the assistance of St James. Further east, the advance of the kingdom of Aragon faltered after its king died leaving only a minor as heir. Pope Alexander II stepped in to organize an expedition against the city of Barbastro, near Saragossa. His papal order sanctioning the campaign and the presence of French and other foreign knights in the attacking force were precursors of later practices in the Crusades. Barbastro fell in the same year as Coimbra, but the death of Ferdinand of León and Castile in 1065 held up further Christian territorial advances.

There was a bitter succession dispute among Ferdinand's sons, which gave the Muslims some respite. Castile went to the eldest son, Sancho, and León to his brother Alfonso, but the two soon came to blows. Sancho was victorious in 1072, partly thanks to the efforts of his supporter Rodrigo Díaz de Vivar, known as El Cid ('the lord'). Alfonso was sent into exile in Moorish Toledo, only to return in the same year, after Sancho was murdered. Now undisputed king as Alfonso VI, he came to terms with El Cid, who agreed to support him. However, such good relations did not last and in 1081 Alfonso banished El Cid from the kingdom. It is a measure of how much frontier realities overlaid a supposedly clear-cut religious divide that El Cid next found employment with the Muslim king of Saragossa, fighting both his Muslim and Christian rivals.

Alfonso also exploited Muslim rivalries and installed a puppet ruler in Toledo. The ruler then offered to hand Toledo over to Alfonso if he would assist him in gaining control of Valencia. The king was happy to accept the offer. In May 1085 Alfonso took over the *taifa* state of Toledo. This was perhaps the biggest Christian success since the Reconquista had begun more than 350 years earlier. At a stroke, Alfonso's kingdom had increased in size by roughly one-third, and he was able to begin the Christian colonization of the lands between the River Douro and the River Tagus. The city of Toledo itself was the ancient capital of the Visigoths and the seat of the primate of the Spanish Church. For a monarch like Alfonso VI, who, from 1077, had begun to make clear his hegemonic pretensions in the Iberian peninsula by styling himself 'Emperor of all the Spains', the conquest of Toledo was an act imbued with immense symbolic significance.

The loss of Toledo finally forced the *taifa* kings to take concerted action. Conscious of their own weakness, they appealed to the new Muslim power in North Africa to come to their aid. In North Africa a Berber fundamentalist sect, the Murabittin, known to Christians as the

Almoravids, had taken control. Their leader, Yusuf ibn Tashufin, took his army across to al-Andalus and defeated Alfonso at the battle of Sagrajas near Badajoz in October 1086. The Christian reverse led Alfonso to become reconciled with El Cid, while in 1087 Odo, Duke of Burgundy, led a force of French knights into Spain to fight the infidel. Yusuf, however, had already withdrawn to North Africa. The Almoravids then returned to Iberia in force and in 1090 Yusuf made an attack on Toledo. He retook much of the territory lost to the Christians, but not the city itself.

The Almoravid leader felt the remaining *taifa* states had failed to support him in his efforts. Declaring them not to be true Muslims, Yusuf conquered most of the *taifas* in the west and south of al-Andalus between 1090 and 1094. El Cid had once again fallen out with Alfonso VI and gone into exile. He now devoted his efforts to securing the Moorish kingdom of Valencia for himself. In 1094 he finally took control of Valencia and when the Almoravids tried to intervene he inflicted the first defeat on them at the battle of Cuarte. Although still maintaining links with Alfonso, El Cid reigned in Valencia as an independent prince. He died in 1099 and in 1102 the Christians withdrew from Valencia, which then fell to the Almoravids. In 1110 Yusuf's son captured Saragossa, the last *taifa* state in al-Andalus. A strong and united Muslim power had now been re-established in al-Andalus, posing a serious threat to the Iberian Christians. Nevertheless, even if the Reconquista had suffered a setback, it was far from over.

THE FIRST CRUSADE, 1096–9

Although dramatic events were taking place in Iberia in the 1090s, most of western Christendom was looking towards the Middle East, where the First Crusade was seeking to liberate the Christian holy sites in Jerusalem from the Muslims. Why this military pilgrimage took place at this time and in this form has been a matter of much scholarly debate. Jerusalem had been in Muslim hands for more than four centuries, and in the past Christians had felt no burning desire to liberate it, being apparently content if Muslim rulers allowed pilgrims access to the Christian sites. By the start of the eleventh century Jerusalem was in the hands of the Fatimid dynasty of Egypt, and in 1009 Caliph al-Hakim ordered the destruction of the Church of the Holy Sepulchre and other Christian churches in the holy city. The damage was considerable, but the response of Christendom to this provocation was decidedly muted, with the Byzantine emperor, Basil II, renewing his truce with the Fatimids rather than embarking on a new war with them. Money was raised to pay for reconstruction, but not until the 1040s were the churches rebuilt under the terms of a Byzantine-Fatimid agreement. After 1071 Jerusalem was held by the Seljuk Turks, only to be regained by the Fatimids a year before the crusaders reached its walls in 1099.

Thus there seemed to be no new danger to the Christian sites in Jerusalem that might justify the expedition to the east. The immediate justification for the First Crusade was that it was in answer to requests from the Byzantines for assistance in fighting the Seljuk Turks. Yet the defeat at Manzikert and its terrible consequences took place in 1071, and despite many pleas no major western aid was sent for more than 25 years. Indeed, when something of a Byzantine military revival began in the 1080s under Emperor Alexius I Comnenus, the Byzantines were deflected from fighting the Muslims by the need to resist invading Christian Normans in the Balkans. Nor were the Byzantines asking for the kind of mass movement that eventually reached them. They merely wanted contingents of western knights such as those that had already given support to the Iberian Christians in the 1060s and '80s. Byzantine pleas for help would probably still have been ignored had there not been powerful forces at work in western Europe favouring an expedition to the east.

The papacy had been growing in power during the eleventh century and the popes had already been involved in organizing holy war against the Muslims in Spain. When Pope Urban II issued his call for an expedition to the east in 1095, he no doubt hoped it would be an orderly affair under papal control. Like the Byzantines, the pope was probably surprised by the movement that was actually created. One aim of the Church was to stop knights fighting each other in western Europe. Christians, like Muslims, had a basic belief that co-religionists should not fight each other, although in reality this was a frequent occurrence. The knights were to redirect their warlike energies against the infidel in the east, religious motives mingling with a secular desire to win new lands for themselves.

Such a desire should not be confused with a wish to convert the inhabitants of those lands. The Crusades were not an attempt at the mass conversion of Muslims into Christians. Unlike the Muslim jihad, the aims of the crusaders were essentially limited. They wished to liberate and defend the Christian holy sites in Palestine, not to engage in a holy war with universalist aims. That the First Crusade has been associated with such apocalyptic aims is due to the fervent popular response it evoked. To the cool calculations of the papacy and the warlike instincts of the knights was added a popular religious fervour that helped to make this crusade such a unique event. The depth of popular religious emotion surprised many contemporaries, and although it led to some terrible events, such as the massacre of Jews in the Rhineland before the crusaders departed, it did inspire many Christians to join the great armed pilgrimage to the east.

Pope Urban did not want a crusade led by kings, since this would reduce papal control of the expedition – in any case, he was on bad terms with the rulers of France and Germany. The pope's appeal for leaders went largely to important nobles, although some of them had royal connections. The Normans, who had served as the military arm of the papacy in Italy, were to have a major presence among the leaders of the crusade, including Normans from both Normandy itself and southern Italy. Pope Urban tried to discourage Spanish nobles and French lords near the Pyrenees from joining the crusade – they would be better employed opposing the growing menace of the Muslim Almoravids in Iberia.

Apart from the papal legate, Bishop Adhémar of Le Puy, the crusade's principal commanders were a group of French, Flemish and Norman lords, some with royal connections. Count Raymond IV of Toulouse led the largest contingent. Other groups of crusaders were led by Godfrey de Bouillon, Duke of Lorraine, and his brother, Baldwin of Boulogne; by Hugh, Count of Vermandois and brother of the King of France; by Duke Robert of Normandy, brother of the king of England; and by Bohemond of Taranto and his nephew Tancred, who led the Normans of southern Italy. The quarrels of these nobles did not assist unity of command, nor did their strained relations with the Byzantines, yet this crusade was to be more successful than any of those that followed it. Fervent Christians would assign their success to God's favour, but the reality would seem to be that Muslim disunity as a consequence of the collapse of the Seljuk Turk empire gave the western Christians their chance to advance deep into Muslim territory and take Jerusalem.

Yet the opportunity offered by Muslim disunity should not detract from the uniqueness of the crusade and the long-lasting impact it would have on western relations with both the Muslims and the Byzantines. As far as the Muslims were concerned, the crusade was a shock because it penetrated to the very heart of the Islamic lands. For most

Muslims, holy war with the Christians was something that took place on distant frontiers. Now the western Christians were to invade the Islamic heartland and seize Jerusalem, the third holiest Muslim city after Mecca and Medina. To Christians the crusade was also a novel venture. Recapturing lost Christian territory was not a new thing, as seen by Christian advances in Iberia and Sicily in the west and on the Byzantine frontiers in the east. But to mount a vast armed pilgrimage, sanctioned by the pope and backed by all of western Christendom, with the aim of retaking and defending the Christian holy sites in Palestine, was certainly a major innovation. Whatever the secular motives of many participants, the religious fervour of many crusaders cannot be denied. They had a clear aim, to retake Jerusalem, and they were ready to make any sacrifice to achieve that goal.

Given the growing Christian dominance of the Mediterranean Sea during the eleventh century, many crusaders might have been expected to travel to Palestine by sea. The number of crusaders was so great, however, that it would have overwhelmed available transport and there was as yet no provision for the large-scale carrying of horses by sea. The role of Christian shipping in the First Crusade would largely be to provide supplies for the crusaders once they had reached the Holy Land. In any case, since the ostensible reason for the crusade was to aid the Byzantine empire, the main rendezvous point for the crusaders would be its capital, Constantinople. For most crusaders this city could be reached most easily by taking the land route across the Balkans.

The so-called People's Crusade, led by Peter the Hermit and Walter Sansavoir, preceded the main crusader forces and arrived at Constantinople in August 1096. The Byzantines were horrified by this collection of poor pilgrims, with only a few knights and soldiers among them. The unmilitary horde was quickly shipped over to Anatolia, where most of the crusaders were massacred by the Turks. Only a few escaped, including Peter the Hermit, and they began to spread tales of Byzantine betrayal that would serve to increase existing hostility between Byzantines and westerners. The main crusader contingents reached Constantinople by the spring of 1097, but Emperor Alexius detained them until their leaders had promised to restore to him any former Byzantine territory that they liberated. All the crusade leaders eventually gave their word, although Bohemond of Taranto, an old Norman foe of the Byzantines, held out as long as possible.

In May 1097 the crusaders crossed over to Anatolia and laid siege to the city of Nicaea. Kilij Arslan, the sultan of Rum, attacked the besiegers, but was repulsed. However, when Nicaea surrendered in June, its commander gave it up to the Byzantines. This infuriated the crusaders who had hoped to pillage the city. The crusaders pushed on across the often barren interior of Anatolia, suffering a shortage of food and water. Kilij Arslan attacked them again at Dorylaeum in July, but after a desperate struggle the Turks were eventually driven off.

In September 1097 the crusaders reached Christian territory once again when they passed through Cilician Armenia. In October they began the siege of the great city of Antioch, which had been taken from the Byzantines by the Seljuk Turks in 1085. The siege would last until June 1098 and would be a pivotal event in the history of the First Crusade; indeed, some contemporaries called the crusade the 'Antioch War'. Similarly, many Muslims initially saw the crusaders as just Frankish mercenaries intent on recapturing Antioch for the Byzantines, and failed to appreciate their wider aims.

Antioch was strongly fortified and held by a large Turkish garrison commanded by Yaghi-Siyan. The crusaders did not attempt a direct assault on the city, preferring to starve out the defenders by a blockade. Towards the end of 1097 a Muslim relief force under Duqaq of Damascus was repulsed by the Christian besiegers, and in February 1098 a relief force under Ridwan of Aleppo met a similar fate. In March a Christian fleet appeared off the coast and brought the starving besiegers much-needed food and other supplies. The crusaders now tightened the blockade of Antioch and Bohemond began secret negotiations with Armenian Christians within the city. The Armenians arranged that in early June a tower in the city walls was betrayed to the crusaders and they swarmed into Antioch. While the crusaders sacked much of the city, Yaghi-Siyan withdrew the garrison into the citadel.

Then a large army under Kerbogha of Mosul approached Antioch, and the crusaders found themselves in a devastated city exhausted of supplies, caught between Kerbogha outside the walls and Yaghi-Siyan above them in the citadel. There seemed to be no way out for the Christian warriors and their morale slumped. Then, providentially, a relic that was said to be the 'Holy Lance' thrust into Christ's side at the Crucifixion was found buried in the cathedral of St Peter in Antioch. The discovery was seen as a sign of God's favour and inspired the crusaders to launch a desperate sortie on 28 June 1098, which precipitated the 'great battle' of Antioch. Kerbogha's superior army was apparently taken by surprise and routed after a bitter struggle. During the battle the crusaders claimed to have seen a heavenly host led by the military saints George and Demetrius in the skies above them.

After the surprise victory over Kerbogha, Yaghi-Siyan surrendered the citadel and all of Antioch belonged to the crusaders. They promptly began to argue among themselves. Bohemond held the citadel and claimed to be the new ruler of Antioch, much to the fury of Raymond of Toulouse, who considered himself to be the leader of the crusade. Such disputes held up the expedition, and it was not until the last months of 1098 that the crusaders began to move south from Antioch. The quick siege and brutal sack of Marat-an-Numan convinced other cities to aid the crusaders with money and supplies as they advanced. By taking a largely coastal route the crusaders kept in touch with their supply ships offshore. They finally entered Fatimid territory and on 7 June 1099 reached Jerusalem.

The defences of Jerusalem were weaker than those of Antioch, but the Fatimid Egyptian garrison repulsed the first crusader assaults on the walls. Then a Christian fleet arrived at the port of Jaffa and provided the besiegers with timber, nails and other equipment to build siege engines, in particular two large siege towers. On 15 July 1099 the crusaders used the towers to break into Jerusalem at two points. They then sacked the holy city, massacring all its Muslim and Jewish inhabitants.

Godfrey de Bouillon was made ruler of Jerusalem with the title 'Advocate of the Holy Sepulchre', but once again the leaders of the crusade began to squabble amongst themselves. As in the past, only a new Muslim threat restored a united Christian front. Al-Afdal, the Fatimid vizier and effective ruler of Egypt, led a large army from Egypt to Ascalon, where he awaited his fleet. His intention was to defeat the crusaders and retake Jerusalem, but they moved too quickly for him. Gathering their forces in August 1099, the crusaders surprised the Fatimid army outside the walls of Ascalon and inflicted a crushing defeat. This victory secured the crusaders' grip on Jerusalem and made possible the conquest between 1100 and 1124 of the rest of the Syrian coastline, although Ascalon itself was not finally taken until 1153.

The victors carved out new Christian territories in the conquered lands. Godfrey de Bouillon changed his title to King of Jerusalem and ruled the most southerly of the crusader states. To the north, Raymond of Toulouse ruled the county of Tripoli, Bohemond of Taranto the principality of Antioch, and Baldwin of Boulogne the county of Edessa. In addition, the Armenians had their Christian state in Cilicia, while the Byzantines had used the success of the crusaders to regain some of their lost territories in Anatolia. The Christians seemed to have won a great success in the east, their capture of Jerusalem crowning their other successes in Sicily and Spain during the eleventh century. Now they could only wait and see how the Muslims would react to these Christian triumphs.

5

MUSLIM REACTION: VICTORY OVER OUTREMER, DEFEAT IN SPAIN, 1100–1300

REVIVING THE JIHAD

In the years immediately following the First Crusade, the Muslims did not seem greatly bothered by the loss of Jerusalem and the setting up of Christian states in Syria and Palestine. Some Muslim scholars saw this Christian success as part of a wider religious struggle throughout the Mediterranean region, with Christians achieving similar success against Muslims in Sicily and Spain. Such writers called on Muslim rulers to revive the jihad and drive out the Christians, but in the early twelfth century those rulers were more likely to be fighting each other than the infidel.

Muslim disunity allowed the crusader states, known collectively to western Christians as Outremer ('overseas'), almost thirty years in which to establish themselves. This did not mean, however, that the crusaders were never defeated. Roger of Antioch, for example, was defeated and killed at the battle known as 'The Field of Blood' in 1119. Yet such Muslim successes were not followed up and there was no overall authority to coordinate a Muslim counter-offensive. Even in the south, the Fatimids failed to make any sustained attack on the crusaders. After their failure to save Tyre, which fell to the Christians in 1124, the Fatimids retained only one port on the coast of Syria and Palestine. This was Ascalon, which remained a thorn in the crusader side, being the only Fatimid naval harbour north of Egypt and a base for raids into the interior, even up to the walls of Jerusalem at one point. From 1136 the crusaders sought to isolate Ascalon by building a chain of castles around it, but they would not finally conquer it until 1153.

Even after securing all but one of the coastal cities, Outremer in 1124 remained a fragile construction. Most of the original crusaders had gone home after the capture of Jerusalem in 1099 and there had been comparatively little immigration to the new states from western Europe.

The Catholic rulers of Outremer treated their Orthodox and other eastern Christian subjects only a little better than they did Muslims, which hardly encouraged Christian solidarity. The crusader states had no fleets of their own, and almost from the beginning they became heavily dependent on the Italian maritime states for their sea communications and naval defence. The capture of Tyre, for example, would have been very difficult without the assistance of a Venetian fleet that defeated the Fatimid fleet off Ascalon in 1123 and blockaded Tyre during the siege in 1124. As a reward, the Venetians obtained control of part of the captured port as their exclusive trading centre.

The rulers of Outremer parcelled out their land to feudal vassals, but those subordinates could not provide enough troops for large field armies. Warfare on the frontiers of Outremer was usually a matter of raids and of holding on to castles, with the Christians avoiding major battles if possible. Pilgrim knights might offer to fight for a season while visiting the Holy Land, but they were not a long-term solution to Outremer's chronic shortage of military manpower. The crusader states could not survive without continued support in men and money from western Christendom, and the most effective way in which this was provided was via the institutions known as the military orders. Made up of knights who were part-warrior and part-monk, the military orders were a unique crusader creation that was to provide a permanent Christian military establishment in the Holy Land.

The first of these creations was the Order of the Temple of Solomon in Jerusalem, whose members were better known as the Knights Templar. Originally they were just a small group of warriors formed around 1119 to escort Christian pilgrims on the road from Jerusalem to Jericho, calling themselves the 'Poor Knights of Christ'. They received their new name when the king of Jerusalem gave them a building on the Temple Mount as their headquarters. In 1124 the founder of the order, Hugh de Payns, went back to France and sought recognition for his order from the pope. This was duly obtained, and the rule of this military-religious organization was prepared by Bernard, Abbot of Clairvaux. Bernard saw the Templars as a 'new knighthood', who would fight not for selfish ends but for the defence of Christendom. Knights flocked to join the new order, so that when Hugh returned to Palestine in 1130 he took with him some 300 knights. By the time of the Second Crusade there would be nearly 600 Knights Templar in the Holy Land, supported by several thousand sergeants of the order and other troops. The Templars also received many donations of land in western

Europe to provide wealth that would support their military efforts in Outremer, and also Iberia.

The second of the great international military orders had much older roots than the Templars. This was the Order of the Hospital of St John in Jerusalem, whose members were known as the Knights Hospitaller. The order's original function was to provide a hospital for Christian pilgrims visiting Jerusalem, and it had carried on this task since the second half of the eleventh century. This function would always be retained by the order, but during the twelfth century the Hospitallers increasingly undertook a military role as well. This task was not taken on deliberately to rival the Templars, but seems to have been assumed because of the desperate need for resident troops in Outremer. As with the Templars, the Hospitallers were to become a military-religious organization directly subject to the pope, and they too received donations of land in western Europe from pious benefactors. Although originally slow to build up their military forces, the Hospitallers received their first castle to garrison (one of those surrounding Ascalon) in 1136, some years before the Templars were allocated theirs (in the principality of Antioch). By 1168 Hospitaller forces had grown considerably, allowing them to send 500 knights on an expedition to Egypt in that year.

The military orders provided a professional core around which the armies of Outremer could be built, but Christian survival depended most of all on Muslim disunity, which began to end in the 1120s. In 1127 Imad al-Din Zengi, a Seljuk officer, seized control of Mosul and in the following year took Aleppo. In 1138 he added Homs to his dominions and in 1139–40 laid siege to Damascus. Its Muslim ruler called for assistance from the Christian king of Jerusalem and Zengi was forced to withdraw. Zengi revived the jihad against the Christians and achieved a major success towards the end of 1144, when his forces captured Edessa and overran much of the crusader state of which it was capital. Zengi was murdered in 1146, but his son, Nur al-Din Mahmud, continued his struggle against the Christians.

When news of the fall of Edessa reached western Christendom in 1145, Pope Eugenius III called for a new crusade, and the fiery religious orator Bernard of Clairvaux spread that message from country to country. Unlike the First Crusade, major royal figures came forward to lead the crusaders: King Louis VII of France and Conrad III, King of the Germans. Conrad and Louis marched their armies to Constantinople in the autumn of 1147, but found the Byzantine emperor, Manuel I Comnenus, reluctant to assist their expedition. English and Flemish crusaders headed for the Mediterranean by sea and stopped off in Iberia on their way to help the Portuguese king capture Lisbon from the Muslims. This was to be one of the few successes associated with the Second Crusade.

The crusaders began to cross Anatolia in October 1147, but Conrad's army ran into a Turkish ambush near Dorylaeum and was heavily defeated. Pleading illness, Conrad returned to Constantinople. The remnants of the German army joined the French, who were making their way along the coast road to Adalia. Winter conditions, Turkish harassment and Byzantine failure to provide supplies wore down the crusaders. Their force narrowly escaped destruction in a Turkish attack at Mount Cadmus in January 1148 and morale began to collapse. The crusaders were rallied by the Templars, who imposed strict discipline, and finally reached Adalia. Louis then took part of the army on to Outremer by sea, but those troops left to continue by land were mostly lost crossing the Taurus mountains.

Giving up the idea of trying to recapture Edessa, Louis and Conrad, who had rejoined the crusade, consulted with the king of Jerusalem at Acre in June 1148. It was decided to attack Damascus, even though its ruler had up to then been an ally of the Christian states. The siege of Damascus in July ended in ignominious failure and the crusade fell apart, the leaders returning to the west. The mutual recriminations that ensued were to sour relations between the west and the crusader states for a generation.

The failure of the Second Crusade was to have serious consequences for Outremer. Nur al-Din had been neither confronted nor defeated. In 1149 he killed Prince Raymond of Antioch at the battle of Inab and sent his head to the caliph in Baghdad. After Nur al-Din took Damascus in 1154 he controlled most of Syria and was acknowledged as the leading opponent of the crusader states. The failure of the Second Crusade caused deep disenchantment with the whole crusading movement in western Europe, and the chances of Outremer receiving major assistance from the west in the near future diminished. The rulers of the crusader states could only look to local sources of support, chiefly a somewhat revived Byzantine empire.

THE COMING OF SALADIN

By 1160 Christians and Muslims had achieved something like a balance of forces in Syria and Palestine, and both now saw Egypt as the crucial area of confrontation. The Shiite caliphate of the Fatimids in Cairo was on the verge of collapse and a succession struggle seemed inevitable. Although, given his limited forces, there was no question of his conquering Egypt, the king of Jerusalem did hope to install a compliant Muslim government that would pay him tribute. In 1163 King Amalric of Jerusalem invaded Egypt and in the following year Nur al-Din sent his Kurdish vassal Shirkuh with an army to assist the Egyptians against the Christians. Shirkuh also took with him his nephew, Salah al-Din bin Ayyubid, better known to the Christians as Saladin. After a number of campaigns, the Christian armies finally withdrew from Egypt in 1169 and Shirkuh died soon afterwards. Saladin took over his uncle's position as Nur al-Din's representative in Egypt. In 1171 he abolished the caliphate based in Cairo, and the Abbasid caliphate in Baghdad was left supreme, although real power lay with Nur al-Din. Saladin soon began to treat Egypt as his own possession, and Nur al-Din was preparing to lead an army against his wayward vassal when he died in 1174.

Saladin's shaky grip on power was legitimized by his claim to be continuing the traditions of Zengi and Nur al-Din in waging jihad against the Christians. More sceptical Muslims saw him as an opportunistic adventurer. It is certainly true that between 1174 and 1186 Saladin spent 33 months fighting fellow Muslims and only 13 months campaigning against the Christian states. Yet by subduing most of the Muslim territories bordering Outremer, Saladin was creating a united Egyptian/Syrian state that could attack the Christians with overwhelming power.

If the Muslims were growing in unity and strength, the crusader states were beset by internal faction and growing external isolation. One group of barons led by Raymond of Tripoli clashed with another group that included Reynald de Chatillon and was supported by the Master of the Templars, Gérard de Ridefort. This latter group supported Guy de Lusignan, who eventually became king of Jerusalem in 1186, although Raymond of Tripoli initially refused to do homage to him. In addition, Outremer's external support began to weaken. In 1176 the Byzantine emperor, Manuel I Comnenus, suffered a crushing defeat by the Seljuk Turks of Rum at Myriocephalon in Anatolia. After Manuel's death in 1180, the Byzantine empire ceased to be a major force in the region. As for western Christendom, occasional small expeditions of crusaders came to Outremer, but they could provide no major support for the crusader states in face of the growing threat from Saladin.

Despite the declining position of Outremer, there was one Christian leader who never wavered in his determination to attack the Muslims. Reynald de Châtillon had become lord of the castle of Kerak, south-east of the Dead Sea, in 1175. The fortress held an important strategic position at what might be called the hinge of Saladin's emerging Egyptian/Syrian state. From Kerak Reynald could attack the caravan route from Egypt to Syria and the route from Damascus to the Muslim holy cities of Mecca and Medina. Reynald later seized the port of Aqaba and in 1182 sent a raiding squadron into the Red Sea. He intended that the ships would prey on the pilgrim trade and then put men ashore to attack Mecca and Medina. Saladin sent troops to oppose the raiders, and their last remnant was captured (and executed) only a few miles from Medina. This was the closest the Christians ever came to attacking the two holiest cities of Islam, and their near success was a major embarrassment for Saladin.

Twice Saladin tried to capture Reynald's castle at Kerak, but each time he failed. Finally in 1187, during a time of Christian-Muslim truce, Reynald launched a treacherous attack on a Damascene caravan (said to include Saladin's sister) that was passing his lands. Being now prepared for a final confrontation with the Christians, Saladin used this attack as an excuse to go to war. Saladin's army invaded Christian territory and laid siege to Tiberias in Galilee. King Guy of Jerusalem assembled all available forces to mount a relief expedition. Unfortunately, the king listened to unwise advice from men like Reynald de Châtillon and Gérard de Ridefort, the Templar master, and fatally mismanaged the battle of the Horns of Hattin in July 1187. The Christian army was crushed and many men, including King Guy, were taken prisoner. Reynald de Châtillon was executed, as were the knights of the military orders, although the Templar master was spared. Saladin now began to sweep across Outremer compelling castles and towns to surrender. Even his prisoners helped in this: King Guy persuaded Ascalon to surrender and the Templar master ordered Gaza to do so. Jerusalem resisted for a short time, but on 2 October 1187 Saladin returned the city to Muslim control after nearly a century of Christian occupation. Saladin had brought the revived jihad to a triumphant conclusion.

THE THIRD CRUSADE

The response of western Christendom to such a traumatic event as the loss of Jerusalem was suitably impressive. King Richard I (the Lionheart) of England, King Philip II of France, and the Holy Roman Emperor, Frederick I, all took the cross and became the principal leaders of the Third Crusade. It was not, however, likely to reach the Holy Land quickly, so immediate Christian survival depended on local forces. A recently arrived crusader, Conrad of Montferrat, had repulsed Saladin's attempts to capture Tyre, while Italian ships kept the port supplied and beat off attacks by Saladin's fleet. In 1189 Saladin unwisely released King Guy and the Templar master. They immediately went to Tyre and by August 1189 the Christians were besieging Muslim-held Acre. Saladin attacked the Christians, but his army was repulsed by Conrad and Guy, the Templar master dying in the battle. The Muslim leader then settled down to besiege the Christian besiegers of Acre and to see what aid they would receive from abroad.

Frederick's army came by land from Germany, but after the emperor was drowned crossing a river in southern Anatolia, the army fell apart and only a small contingent reached Acre in late 1190. The kings of France and England brought their forces by sea, with Richard finding time to take Cyprus from the Byzantines in a quick campaign. Arriving in 1191, the French and English helped to bring the siege of Acre to a successful conclusion. The French king then went home, but left most of his forces under Richard's command. Moving south from Acre, Richard's army repulsed an attack by Saladin at Arsuf in September 1191 and went on to occupy Jaffa. In December Richard marched on Jerusalem, but bad weather forced him to turn back at Beit Nuba, only 20 miles from the holy city, in January 1192. Guy de Lusignan had now given up the position of king of Jerusalem and bought Cyprus from Richard as his new domain. The crown was to be offered to Conrad of Montferrat, but he was murdered by the Assassins, and Henry of Champagne became the new king.

The Assassins were Ismailis, an offshoot of Shiism, who had come to inspire terror among both Muslims and Christians. The sect had come into being in the eleventh century and came to hold fortresses in Persia and Syria. It was their skill in murdering political leaders that made the Assassins so feared, although their victims were more usually Muslim than Christian. As ever, killing those said to be untrue to Islam had a higher priority than killing mere infidels. Several times the

Assassins tried to kill Saladin. Their murder of Conrad was for a very prosaic reason: he had seized a ship carrying some of their goods and refused to return the cargo. It was not a blow against Christendom; indeed, at one time the Assassins in Syria had paid tribute to the Templars in return for protection against other Muslims. The Assassins continued their terrorist activities until the Mongols destroyed their Persian strongholds and the Mamluk sultan Baybars their Syrian fortresses during the thirteenth century.

Having settled who should have the crown of Jerusalem, Richard set out from Ascalon in June 1192 in an attempt to recapture the holy city. Again he turned back at Beit Nuba, probably because he realized that even if he took Jerusalem, he would be unable to hold it with his reduced forces. Also Saladin was nearby with a large army and had poisoned the springs around the city. Saladin followed up Richard's retreat by attacking Jaffa, but the English king rushed to the port and, despite being heavily outnumbered, drove off the Muslim army. When Richard left the Holy Land in October 1192, Christian control of a strip of coastal Palestine and Syria had been achieved, but the Third Crusade had failed in its principal aim of retaking Jerusalem. Acre now became the capital of what remained of the kingdom of Jerusalem.

After the Third Crusade the sea route to the east became of primary importance for later crusaders. The land route to the Holy Land across Anatolia had become too risky and difficult. In any case, the strategic target for the Christians now shifted to Egypt, which was most easily reached by sea. Egypt was the principal power base of the Ayyubid empire, and remained so even after the divisions that followed the death of Saladin in 1193. An indirect strategy now appealed to the Christians, with a maritime descent on Egypt to seize cities that might be used as bargaining chips to be exchanged for Jerusalem and other Christian sites in Palestine. This strategy, 'the way of Egypt', was to be particularly important for crusaders in the first half of the thirteenth century. Cyprus, now ruled by the Lusignan family, provided a secure offshore base where Christian forces could be assembled for attacks on Egypt.

Saladin had made some attempt to revive Muslim sea power, but his forces had been defeated. The Christians remained dominant at sea in the Mediterranean for most of the next 300 years. One of the disadvantages of the maritime option for later crusaders, however, was that it put them too much into the power of the Italian maritime cities, which had their own ambitions. This would be shown most clearly during the

Fourth Crusade, when the Venetians played a major part in redirecting the crusaders against their own enemies, the Christian Byzantines, leading to the sack of Constantinople in 1204.

SPAIN: TOWARDS CHRISTIAN VICTORY

If by the 1190s the position of the Christians in Outremer was at best precarious, that of those in Iberia seemed equally difficult, with new Muslim forces at work in the peninsula. Yet for much of the twelfth century the Christian kingdoms had made slow but steady progress in their reconquest of Muslim territory. Even during the floodtide of Almoravid success, King Alfonso VI of León-Castile had managed to capture the fortress town of Medinaceli in 1104. In May 1108, however, a Leónese-Castilian army was annihilated by the Almoravids at Ucles, east of Toledo. Alfonso's son and heir, the Infante Sancho, died in the battle and this led to political problems after Alfonso's own death in 1109. A succession dispute and predatory neighbouring Christian states reduced the power of León-Castile for a generation.

However, if one Christian state was in temporary decline, another, Aragon, came forward to take its place as the leader of the *Reconquista*. King Alfonso I (the Warrior) of Aragon led a Christian counter-attack in the valley of the River Ebro. In December 1118, supported by a contingent of French knights who had fought in the First Crusade, he took the city of Saragossa after a seven-month siege. This was the first major loss suffered by the Almoravids and the most important Christian success since the capture of Toledo in 1085. Alfonso I followed up this victory by taking Tudela in 1119 and defeating the Almoravids at the battle of Cutanda in 1120. The Aragonese ruler made a daring raid down the east coast of Iberia in 1125, reaching as far south as Malaga. He collected Christian families from al-Andalus and brought them back to be colonists in the Ebro valley. In retaliation for this, the Almoravids deported many Christians from al-Andalus to Morocco in 1126. Alfonso I continued his efforts to clear the Muslims out of the Ebro valley, but in July 1134 he was defeated by the Almoravids at Fraga and he died in the following September.

With the demise of such a successful Christian warrior, some Muslim revival might have been expected, but instead the decline of Almoravid power continued. They lost North Africa to a new Berber sect called the Muwahhids (known as Almohads to the Christians); faced growing Muslim revolts in al-Andalus, which began a second

The Iberian Peninsula in the 12th and 13th centuries.

period of *taifa* states; and suffered further Christian attacks. In 1139 Afonso Henriques defeated the Almoravids at Ourique and in 1143 the pope recognized him as the ruler of the new kingdom of Portugal. In 1147, with the aid of crusaders on their way to the Second Crusade, he took the city of Lisbon from the Muslims.

By the mid 1140s al-Andalus had fragmented into more than a dozen small Muslim states, which the Almoravids could no longer control. Militarily weak, these states were soon being raided by the Christians. In 1146 Alfonso VII of Castile even managed to capture the city of Córdoba, but could not hold it for long. In the following year, in alliance with a Genoese fleet, he captured Almeria, perhaps the most important port in al-Andalus at that time. This gain he would hold on to for a decade. In 1148 Ramon Berenguer IV, count-king of Barcelona and Aragon, captured Tortosa at the mouth of the River Ebro and went on to take Lerida and Fraga in the following year, ending the Muslim presence in the Ebro Valley. By 1151 Alfonso VII and Ramon Berenguer were discussing how they should divide up al-Andalus between them.

Their plans, however, were premature. From 1148 onwards the Almohads moved steadily into Iberia, conquering the Muslim *taifa* states and forcing the last of the Almoravids to take refuge in the Balearic Islands. The new Almohad threat forced the Christians onto the defensive, and their rulers sought to expand the role of the military orders in protecting their increasingly exposed frontiers with the Muslims. The international orders, the Templars and the Hospitallers, had already established themselves in the Iberian Christian states, but found a warmer welcome in Aragon and Portugal than in Castile. From 1160 the Christian rulers began to set up native military orders to garrison strongholds and safeguard their borders. In Castile the order of Calatrava was founded in 1158, that of Santiago in 1170 and that of Alcantara in 1175. In Aragon the order of Mountjoy and in Portugal the order of Avis were also established in the early 1170s. The native orders were soon given greater favour than the international orders, which were subject to the pope, and they played a major role in the future history of Christian–Muslim conflict in Iberia.

Almohad pressure was not continuous but varied according to whether the Almohad ruler was available to campaign in Iberia or was called away by events in North Africa. While trying to take Santarem from the Portuguese in 1184, the Almohad leader Yusuf I was killed, and by 1190 the Portuguese, with assistance from crusaders on their way to the Third Crusade, had captured most of the Algarve, in the south of Portugal. Then the new Almohad leader, Abu-Yusuf Yaqub, attacked the Portuguese in 1191 and soon recaptured all the territory they had gained south of the River Tagus. He then went on to defeat King Alfonso VIII of Castile at the battle of Alarcos in 1195, and it seemed that once again Iberian Christians were at the mercy of a resurgent Islam.

Distracted by further troubles in North Africa, however, the Almohad ruler agreed a truce with the Christians in 1197. The papacy was now keen to halt fighting between the Christian rulers of Iberia and to rekindle the flame of crusade. Diplomatic efforts to build a Christian coalition were intensified in 1211 when the Almohad ruler, Muhammad al-Nasir, captured the headquarters of the order of Calatrava at Salvatierra in La Mancha. Pope Innocent III declared a crusade and Alfonso VIII of Castile, Pedro II of Aragon and Sancho VII of Navarre agreed to support it. The Archbishop of Toledo, Rodrigo Jimenez de Rada, was sent to France to drum up support. By the spring of 1212 the Christian coalition was in place. Despite the desertion of most of the French crusaders after the capture of Calatrava in June, Alfonso VIII and his allies continued to advance. In July 1212 at Las Navas de Tolosa they inflicted a decisive defeat on the Almohad army under Muhammad al-Nasir. This victory was to be the turning point of the *Reconquista*, after which both the Almohad empire and Moorish al-Andalus were steadily to disintegrate.

Divisions among the Christians, however, were to prevent them exploiting their victory for some years. After 1224 Almohad authority broke down, with al-Andalus fragmenting for a third and final time into *taifa* states. It was not until the 1230s that the Christians were ready to make major advances, with the kings of Portugal, Aragon and Castile agreeing on zones of operations. The capture of Silves in 1249 effectively completed the reconquest of Portugal. The king of Aragon, James I (the Conqueror), took the Balearic Islands from the Moors (1229–35) and then gradually overran the wealthy *taifa* state of Valencia (1232–45), the city of Valencia itself falling in 1238. Ferdinand III of Castile moved down the valley of the River Guadalquivir, capturing Córdoba in 1236, Jaén in 1246 and Seville in 1248. The *taifa* state of Murcia came under Castilian control in 1243–4. By 1250 Granada was the only Muslim state left in Iberia, but it was forced to pay tribute to Castile. Improbably, Granada was not to fall to the Christians for more than 200 years, thus delaying the final completion of the *Reconquista*.

Nevertheless, the achievements of the Iberian Christians by 1250 were considerable and much admired in the rest of western Christendom. At a time when Outremer seemed on the verge of extinction at the hands of either the Muslims or the new force of pagan Mongols, the Christians had achieved major successes in Spain and Portugal, which were to prove lasting.

CRUSADERS, MONGOLS AND MAMLUKS

The Fourth Crusade of 1202–4 hardly merits inclusion in a history of Christian–Muslim conflict. Although intended to attack Egypt, it was sidetracked, chiefly by the Venetians, into an attack on the Byzantines. Constantinople was sacked in 1204, a Latin emperor was set up there, and the victors divided the spoils – mostly territories and islands in Greece and the Aegean Sea – among themselves. The Byzantines eventually recovered Constantinople in 1261, but the Byzantine empire was by then just a shadow of its former glory. That it was no longer an obstacle to Muslim resurgence was due to the actions of fellow Christians and not the infidel.

After the cruel farce of the Fourth Crusade, Pope Innocent III called once more for a crusade against the Muslims. In 1217 the king of Hungary and the Duke of Austria brought crusaders to the Holy Land, but initial operations achieved little. The Hungarian king went home, but new crusaders, from Germany and Flanders, then arrived. They agreed to join the king of Jerusalem in a seaborne attack on Egypt. Damietta was taken at the end of 1219 and it was hoped to exchange it for Jerusalem. The Sultan of Egypt, al-Kamil, offered favourable terms for a settlement, but the papal legate, Pelagius, ordered an advance on Cairo in 1221. This failed and the crusaders were forced back to Damietta, where they accepted a treaty to allow their peaceful withdrawal from the country. The Fifth Crusade had ended in a humiliating defeat.

The Holy Roman Emperor, Frederick II, who was also ruler of Sicily, had intended to go on the Fifth Crusade, but did not do so. He had taken the cross back in 1215 and his failure to go on a crusade further strained his already difficult relations with the papacy. Papal chroniclers were to portray Frederick as being too pro-Muslim, indeed of being a secret Muslim himself. Nevertheless, it was in his reign that the last Muslims were expelled from Sicily in 1223, a final remnant being moved to Lucera in southern Italy where they lived under Frederick's special protection. Like his Sicilian predecessors, Frederick had Muslim troops in his army and maintained close relations with the Muslim rulers of North Africa, but this did not make him any less a Christian ruler.

When Frederick finally went on crusade in 1228 he had already been excommunicated by the pope, but had inherited the claim to be king of Jerusalem. The Sultan of Egypt, still al-Kamil, felt threatened by Muslim rivals in Syria and was ready to negotiate with Frederick. By the treaty of Jaffa in 1229 the Muslim ruler handed over Jerusalem to Christian control, but with the city's defences demolished and Muslims retaining control of their holy sites. Only a narrow corridor was allowed to give access to Jerusalem for the Christians. Frederick came to the holy city and had himself declared king of Jerusalem, only to return to western Europe soon afterwards. Both Muslims and Christians claimed to be outraged by the deal between Frederick and al-Kamil, but neither side took any action to overturn it. As a result, the Christians resumed a tenuous hold on Jerusalem – for once won by negotiation rather than war.

Frederick's visit to the Holy Land did much to boost the fortunes of a new military order. A hospital of St Mary of the Germans was said to have been founded in Jerusalem in the early twelfth century and some of its members later aided German troops at the siege of Acre in 1190. These brethren were later militarized as the Teutonic Knights of St Mary's Hospital in Jerusalem, and the order was recognized by the pope in 1198. Although the Teutonic Knights took a major part in the crusades against pagan Slavs in the Baltic area, they also wished to expand their presence in Outremer. Frederick gave the order his support, partly to spite the Templars and the Hospitallers who were generally hostile to the emperor. The three military orders became increasingly powerful in the crusader states during the thirteenth century. With the Christians now restricted to just a coastal strip, there were few feudal lords left to provide troops. More and more castles were handed over to the military orders to garrison, and the whole military strategy of Outremer was now one of passive defence, unless a major crusading expedition arrived from western Europe.

Christian control of Jerusalem proved short-lived, for in 1244 the Khwarazmian Turks seized the city, smashing Christian holy sites and the tombs of the Christian kings, and returned Jerusalem to Muslim control, which would be unbroken until 1917. The Khwarazmian Turks, fleeing from the Mongols, went on to ally with the Ayyubid ruler of Egypt. His Syrian rivals were supported by the Christians of Outremer, and the two sides met at the battle of La Forbie, near Gaza, later in 1244. The Syrians and their Christian allies suffered a crushing defeat, with the knights of the Christian military orders suffering particularly heavy losses. Fortunately for the Christians, the Egyptian ruler did not follow up his victory with a major attack on Outremer.

When news of the loss of Jerusalem and the decimation of the Christian forces at La Forbie reached western Europe, the pope sent out a call in 1245 for a new crusade. Most rulers in the west failed to respond with more than promises, and it was only King Louis ix of France (St Louis) who took the cross. He arrived in Cyprus in 1248 and in the following year landed in Egypt, capturing Damietta. Louis then advanced to Mansurah, only to be defeated and taken prisoner. After paying ransom and giving up Damietta, Louis was allowed to go to Acre, where he spent four years trying to organize further attacks on the Muslims. Little came of his efforts and in 1254 he returned to France, leaving behind some French troops to support the defence of what remained of Outremer.

The Christians were in need of defenders, since by the 1250s two new forces were at work in the Middle East. Most important were the Mongols, who had first entered the area in the 1220s, but began to push west in force from 1240. In 1258 they sacked Baghdad and finally brought the Abbasid caliphate to an end. The pagan Mongols were a far greater threat to the continued existence of Islamic civilization than the Christians had ever been. It seemed they were invincible until they came up against the second new force at work in the region.

The Ayyubid sultans of Egypt had, like many Muslim rulers, recruited slave soldiers, known as Mamluks. In Egypt at this time they were chiefly Turks, and they used the opportunity afforded by Louis' attack on Egypt in 1249–50 to seize power from their Ayyubid masters. The Mamluks were to be the saviours of Islam in the Middle East, halting the Mongol advance with their victory at Ain Jalut in September 1260. This victory also gave them control of the former Ayyubid territories in Syria. For the first time since the days of Saladin, the Christians of Outremer found themselves surrounded by a united Egyptian/Syrian state.

THE END OF OUTREMER

The Christians of Outremer found themselves in a difficult position. Some were ready to support the Mongols against the Muslims, and there were even hopes that the pagan Mongols might be converted to Christianity. Others, seeing the Mongols as the greater danger, were ready to assist the Muslims. In 1260 the Mamluks halted the Mongol advance, but the struggle between the two sides continued on the borders of Syria for many years to come. Not until the 1290s did the Mongols in the Middle East convert to Islam, and that did not greatly reduce their aggressive tendencies. The Mamluks were always fearful of a Mongol–Christian alliance linked to a new crusade coming from western Europe, so it seemed sensible that they should remove the weaker of their two enemies, the Christians of Outremer.

Shortly after the battle of Ain Jalut in 1260, al-Zahir Baybars seized power as Mamluk sultan. Baybars was to deploy the increased Muslim skill in siege technique against the defences of Outremer. Expert builders of stone-throwing machines and adept at undermining walls, the Muslims were not to need more than six weeks to reduce any of the great crusader castles to submission. Baybars's policy would be to refortify inland towns and castles taken from the Christians, but to demolish the defences of all captured ports so that new crusaders from Europe would not have bases on the coasts of Palestine and Syria. In 1265 Baybars captured Caesarea and Haifa, and in the following year he took the fortress of Safad from the Templars. In 1268 the sultan captured Jaffa and then Antioch, ending its long political and economic importance. Ascalon was destroyed in 1270 and in 1271 Baybars took the fortress of Krak des Chevaliers from the Hospitallers. The sultan next planned to attack Tripoli, but he was distracted when a crusading force reached Acre from western Europe.

Even before the loss of Antioch, King Louis of France was planning another crusade, and he obtained promises of assistance from his brother, Charles of Anjou, now king of Sicily, and Prince Edward of England (later Edward I). It was claimed that Louis decided to launch an initial attack on Tunis because he had learned that its ruler was ripe for conversion to Christianity. More likely the operation was a favour to his brother, the new ruler of Sicily, after which the crusaders would move on to the Holy Land. Soon after Louis attacked Tunis in 1270, however, he died of disease and his crusade largely collapsed. Nevertheless, Prince Edward led a small force of crusaders to Acre, where he tried to arrange an alliance with the Mongols against the Mamluks. This plan failed, and, having narrowly survived an assassination attempt – probably ordered by Baybars – he departed for England in 1272.

Edward had agreed a ten-year truce with Baybars, so the Mamluk ruler campaigned elsewhere up to his death in 1277. His successor, Kalavun, beat off another Mongol invasion and then marched against the Christians. In 1281 he took Tripoli and demolished its defences, leaving Acre as the last major Christian stronghold. In late 1290 Kalavun died while preparing to attack Acre. His son, al-Ashraf Khalil, took over and Acre was stormed in May 1291. Most members of the Christian military orders who were in the city died fighting. The remaining Christian outposts along the coast were soon taken, and after nearly 200 years the Christian crusader states deep in Muslim territory had been destroyed, except for the offshore base of Cyprus, still protected by Christian sea power.

The end of Outremer represented a serious defeat for the Christians, since if the Christian–Muslim struggle in the Holy Land was seen as a trial by battle, then God seemed to have decided in favour of the Muslims. Such a view was clearly unacceptable to western Christendom, which took comfort from the fact that Christian arms had been victorious in Iberia, reconquering almost all the peninsula. The loss of

Outremer was not accepted as final, and plans were laid for new crusades. With the rise of the Ottoman Turks in the fourteenth century, however, crusading began to be less a matter of trying to regain the Holy Land and more one of defending Christian Europe from growing Muslim attack.

6

RISE OF THE OTTOMAN TURKS,
1300–1500

FRONTIER WARRIORS

Many Turkish tribes, fleeing the onslaught of the Mongols, found their way to Anatolia, where they were given protection by the Seljuk sultans of Rum. In 1243 the Mongols reached Anatolia and defeated the sultan of Rum at the battle of Kose Dagh, after which he became their vassal. In the second half of the thirteenth century Anatolia divided into a number of small Muslim states that flourished in the space between the Christians to the west and the Mongols to the east. One such petty state, in north west Anatolia, was the realm of the Ottoman Turks, who took their name from their first major leader, Osman.

Ottoman territory was on the Muslim–Christian frontier, alongside the remnants of the Byzantine empire. The Ottomans saw themselves as *ghazis*, holy warriors in the struggle against the Christians, and for much of their history a commitment to the jihad was to remain important to their rulers. The Ottoman ruler Orhan captured Bursa in 1326, and it became the first Ottoman capital. Defeating the Byzantines at the battle of Pelekanon in 1328, Orhan went on to capture Nicaea in 1331 and Nicomedia in 1337. Ottoman expansion was chiefly aimed at the Christians, but they did in 1345–6 conquer one neighbouring Muslim state, Karesi, which brought their lands up to the shores of the Dardanelles. The obvious next step was to cross over into Europe.

It is a sign of the fluid nature of frontier relations, even on a religious divide, that it was the Christians who assisted the Ottomans to enter Europe. Orhan helped John Cantacuzene in his struggles to become Byzantine emperor and was rewarded with a fortress on the European side of the Straits. The Ottomans secured a more important base on the European shore when they occupied the town of Gallipoli, on the Dardanelles, in 1354. Then the Ottomans began to spread across Thrace.

The arrival of the Ottoman Turks in Europe caused no major concern among the Christians. The Muslim states of Anatolia that had provoked a Christian reaction were Aydin and Menteshe in the southwest of the region. This was because they had developed navies that preyed on Christian shipping and challenged Christian command of the sea, one of the few advantages that remained to them in the Christian–Muslim struggle after the fall of Outremer.

CRUSADE AT SEA

Many refugees from Outremer, including the military orders, had gone to Cyprus. It was to offer, under its Lusignan kings, a base from which Muslim ports and shipping could be attacked, but only one of the military orders took the crusade to sea. Indeed, after 1291 all the military orders had to re-examine their military position. They had been given great wealth by benefactors in western Christendom in order to protect the crusader states in the Holy Land. They had become the principal defenders of Outremer and they had manifestly failed in their task. There were few calls for the abolition of the military orders, but many people wanted them amalgamated into a single order before a new crusade was launched to regain the Holy Land.

Resisting the calls for amalgamation, the military orders retained their independence and went on to new destinies. The Teutonic Knights deserted the Mediterranean and concentrated all their efforts on the war against the pagan Slavs in the Baltic region. The Templars began to develop a fleet of their own and made some raids on Muslim ports, but their great wealth, partly due to their lucrative secondary function as bankers to Christian pilgrims, attracted the attention of Philip iv of France. In 1307 the king supported allegations that the Templars had engaged in witchcraft and other heinous sins. In France the knights were arrested and their property seized. In 1312 the pope was persuaded to dissolve the Order of the Temple and in 1314 the last Templar grand master was burnt at the stake in Paris. The wealth of the Templars was supposed to be passed to the Hospitallers, but much of it stuck to royal fingers in France and elsewhere. In Portugal Templar riches were used to fund a new military order, the Knights of Christ, which would later link the Christian–Muslim conflict to European maritime exploration.

During the 1290s the Hospitallers had begun naval operations against the Muslims, launching raids and giving assistance to Cilician Armenia, and by 1299 the office of admiral, usually filled by an Italian, had been created within the order. In the early years of the fourteenth century, the growing problems of the Templars and royal hostility in Cyprus convinced the Hospitallers that they would be safer if they had their own territory, like the Teutonic Knights in Prussia. In 1306 the Hospitallers attacked the island of Rhodes, which was still held by the Byzantines. By 1310 the knights had secured control of Rhodes and the rest of the Dodecanese islands off the south-west coast of Anatolia. Rhodes was to provide an excellent base for naval attacks on Muslim territory and shipping, and it would remain the order's home for the next 200 years.

As already noted, the raiding was not all one way. The 'sea ghazis' of Aydin and Menteshe fought the knights from Rhodes among the islands of the Aegean Sea. The pope encouraged the creation of the first crusading league in 1332 to pursue a naval war against the infidel, and in 1334 the league's fleet obtained its first naval victory over the Turks in the Gulf of Adramyttium. The greatest success of the crusading league, however, was achieved in 1344 when its forces captured Smyrna, the ruler of Aydin's principal port. The Hospitallers were to provide most of its garrison up to 1402, when it was sacked by Tamerlane. The Christian naval operations could not, however, save Cilician Armenia, which was finally overrun by the Muslims in 1375, its last king escaping to Rhodes.

The Mamluk empire of Egypt and Syria was slow to develop any naval capacity, and so it was often at the mercy of Christian seaborne attacks. After the fall of Outremer, the papacy had banned western Christians from trading with the Mamluks, but the prohibition was soon ignored by the Venetians and Genoese. Even a more limited embargo, relating to the sale of military equipment to the Mamluks, had little practical effect. Generally the Italian maritime cities preferred peaceful trade to war with the infidel, but if a major Christian maritime attack was imminent they were usually ready to join it.

When Peter I, King of Cyprus, led his seaborne crusade against Egypt in 1365, his fleet included Cypriot, French, Hospitaller, Venetian and Genoese contingents. Alexandria was taken and sacked, but later given up when the Mamluks began a counter-attack. Even after this incursion, the Mamluks were slow to build up their naval strength. Only in the 1420s did they create a fleet powerful enough to attack Cyprus and force its king to become a Mamluk vassal, ending the use of his island by Christian corsairs. In the 1440s the Mamluks sent their fleets as far as Rhodes, but their attempts to capture that base for Christian corsairs was a failure.

Generally the Christians preserved their superiority at sea in the Mediterranean during the fourteenth century and well into the fifteenth. It was on land that the Muslim threat began to grow in the second half of the fourteenth century, with the Ottoman Turks making major advances in the Balkans.

THE OTTOMANS IN EUROPE

Gallipoli, the first major Ottoman base in Europe, was temporarily lost to a crusade led by Amadeus of Savoy, a relative of the Byzantine emperor, in 1366, but the Ottoman occupation of Adrianople in 1369 restored their position in Europe and also gave them a new capital. The Ottoman sultan Murad I set out to conquer the Balkans, and his victory at the River Maritsa in 1371 won him most of Bulgaria and Macedonia. Soon Bulgaria, Serbia and even the remnants of the Byzantine empire were forced to accept Murad as their overlord. In 1388, however, the Christian states in the Balkans revolted against Ottoman rule and the sultan had to march against them.

In June 1389 Murad brought an army of Serbs and Bosnians, under Prince Lazar of Serbia, to battle near Pristina in Kosovo. Known as the first battle of Kosovo, this hard-fought encounter left both the opposing royal commanders dead and their armies decimated. Traditionally, the battle has been viewed as a major Serb defeat that ended the greatness of their medieval state, yet it can also be viewed as a draw. The sultan's son, Bayezid, had to withdraw after the battle to the Ottoman heartlands to ensure his orderly succession to the throne, while a Serb state would survive for more than 50 years, albeit usually as a vassal of the Ottomans. Only after he was secure on the throne did Bayezid I return and reduce the Serbs, Bulgars and other Balkan Christians to obedience.

Murad I has been credited with beginning the transformation of the Ottoman army from a band of frontier warriors into a highly disciplined military machine, with Europe's first permanent military establishment at its centre. That core was principally made up of janissaries (meaning 'new troops'), a very professional force of slave soldiers, mostly infantry, who were the sultan's own troops. The bulk of the army continued to be composed of free-born mounted warriors, but these *sipahis* became increasingly bound to the sultan because they were supported by income from landed estates (*timars*) granted to them by the sultan. A force of slave soldiers as part of the sultan's household was nothing new in Islamic history, but the novelty of the janissaries lay in their mode of recruitment.

Although zealous Muslims, the Ottomans, at least in the first centuries of their empire, may have ruled over more Christian subjects than Muslims. Only after the Ottoman conquest of the Mamluk empire in the early sixteenth century did their dominions become predominantly Muslim. In Murad I's time the centre of gravity of the Ottoman empire lay in the Balkans. The *devshirme* system was instituted, by which a levy of young boys was taken from Christian villages. The boys were then converted to Islam and trained as military slaves, with the best of them being creamed off to become high officials in the sultan's palace. They combined professional skill with complete loyalty to the sultan.

During the fifteenth century the janissaries developed further, eventually giving up their bows in favour of firearms, while specialist artillery and sapper units were created to support them in battle and siege. During the reign of Mehmed II the number of janissaries was said to have risen from 5,000 to 10,000. No west European ruler of that period could maintain a personal, household force on any remotely comparable scale. Nor could any west European ruler assemble an army of 80,000 – composed of janissaries, *sipahis* and volunteer irregulars – as Mehmed did for his siege of Constantinople in 1453. After 1458 the Hungarian king Matthias Corvinus did attempt to establish a large military force on a permanent footing in imitation of the Ottomans, but his expensive 'black army' (from the colour of its armour) was disbanded soon after the king's death in 1490. About that time the beginnings of a professional army in western Europe were being created by the Valois kings of France.

The janissaries were to become a legendary corps in the Ottoman army and one of the main reasons for its success. In the late fourteenth century, however, the janissaries were at an early stage of development. When Bayezid I moved from the Balkans to Anatolia in the early 1390s to campaign against the remaining independent Muslim states in that region, the chief forces he took with him derived from Christian sources were the contingents provided by his Christian vassals. Nevertheless, they assisted him in successfully imposing his will on the Muslim states. By 1395 Bayezid was back in the Balkans, pushing up to the River Danube and threatening the borders of Hungary.

Aware of the growing Ottoman threat, King Sigismund of Hungary had been active for several years in trying to obtain support in western Europe for a crusade against the Muslim invaders. The papacy gave its approval for the crusade, and because there was a period of truce in the long war between England and France, many western knights were ready to take the cross. The biggest western contingent was made up of French and Burgundian knights. When finally assembled on the southern border of Hungary in 1396, the crusader army was said to have been one of the largest ever to take the field against the infidel. A fleet made up of Venetian, Genoese and Hospitaller ships entered the Black Sea and sailed up the Danube to assist the crusaders.

King Sigismund favoured a defensive strategy against the Ottomans, but his western allies insisted upon an offensive. Two small fortresses were taken and their Turkish garrisons massacred before the crusaders began a siege of Nicopolis, the chief Ottoman stronghold on the Danube. In September 1396 Sultan Bayezid appeared with a large army and the crusaders formed their battle line to prevent him relieving the fortress. The Franco-Burgundian knights launched an undisciplined charge against the Turks. After some initial success, the knights were surrounded and defeated and the rest of the crusader army fled, with the Turks in hot pursuit. King Sigismund escaped to a Venetian ship in the Danube and took the long way home to Hungary via Constantinople. As the Venetian ships passed through the Dardanelles, the Turks displayed the noble prisoners taken at Nicopolis on the beach at Gallipoli.

The crusade that ended so disastrously at Nicopolis was the last time the western Europeans would send a major army to oppose the Ottomans for several centuries. When they did so again during the sixteenth century Hungary would have been conquered by the infidel and the Turks would be approaching the gates of Vienna. After his great victory in 1396, Bayezid had another Christian city on his mind. He intensified his blockade of Constantinople and had hopes of finally capturing it. However, the Byzantines were to survive once again, finding salvation in an unlikely quarter.

Bayezid's campaigns in Anatolia had brought him up against client states of Timur Leng (known to Christians as Tamerlane) and had eventually provoked this great Turco-Mongol warlord to intervene against the Ottomans. At the battle of Ankara in July 1402 Tamerlane crushed Bayezid's army and led the sultan away into permanent captivity. Tamerlane went on to storm the Christian-held city of Smyrna, in part so that he could still the criticisms of pious Muslims that by attacking the Ottomans he was destroying the principal fighters against the infidel. Throwing the Christians out of Smyrna gave the campaign of Ankara some retrospective justification as a holy war. Tamerlane then went on to re-establish the small Muslim states in Anatolia. The Ottoman empire was further weakened by a long and bitter succession struggle between Bayezid's sons, which ended only in 1413, when Mehmed I achieved final victory. Once again, a collapse of Muslim unity gave the Christians a breathing space, but they did little to prepare their defences for the eventual resumption of the Ottoman advance in south-east Europe.

OTTOMAN REVIVAL AND THE FALL OF CONSTANTINOPLE

Murad II, who succeeded his father in 1421, attempted to capture Constantinople in 1422, but was repulsed. Murad had more success in the Balkans, capturing Thessalonica in 1430 and steadily pushing the Christians back. The Byzantine emperor became so desperate that in 1439 he agreed with the pope that the Eastern and Western Churches should be reunited in return for military aid from western Europe. However, the emperor's Orthodox Christian subjects refused to heal the schism of 1054 by a surrender to the pope. In any case, no western troops were forthcoming, and by 1440 the Ottomans seemed about to invade Hungary.

The Hungarians were fortunate to find a worthy leader in John Hunyadi, the governor of Transylvania, who repulsed the first Ottoman attacks. The Hungarians possessed field artillery that assisted in their defence, but the Ottomans soon made efforts to acquire their own guns. Hunyadi then invaded Ottoman territory and by the end of 1443 he had driven the Turks out of much of Serbia, Bosnia and Bulgaria. This success encouraged the Albanians to rise in revolt, and their resistance continued for several decades under the leadership of the formidable Scanderbeg. Originally a Christian called George Kastriotis, he converted to Islam and held a command position in the Ottoman army under the name Iskander Beg. When his people rose up, Scanderbeg (a corruption of his Muslim name) switched sides and led the Albanian resistance until his death in 1468, after which the Ottomans finally took control of Albania.

In 1444 the Hungarians launched their own crusade aimed at driving the Ottomans out of the Balkans. However, after some early clashes a truce was agreed with Murad II. Then the Christians learned that the sultan had decided to abdicate in favour of his young son, and it was felt such an opportunity to attack a potentially weakened enemy could not be ignored. The papal legate persuaded the Christian leaders that it would not be a sin to break the truce, and the crusaders took up arms once more. Murad reacted by reassuming his powers and crushing the crusader army at the battle of Varna, in which both the Hungarian king and the papal legate were killed. Hunyadi was lucky to survive the Varna disaster, and he was made governor of Hungary and guardian of its new young king in 1446. Leading another invasion of Ottoman territory in 1448, Hunyadi sought to coordinate his operations with those of Scanderbeg. Yet this proved impossible, and Hunyadi was again defeated by Murad at the second battle of Kosovo.

By 1450 the Ottoman Turks had ensured that they, not the Hungarians, would dominate the Balkans, but their empire was still not a major power. The Mamluk sultanate of Egypt and Syria seemed to many observers to be of greater importance, not least because it held the three holiest cities of Islam: Mecca, Medina and Jerusalem. By the time Selim I became Ottoman sultan in 1512, great changes had taken place. The Ottoman empire had acquired an imperial capital, Constantinople, and its territories in both the Balkans and Anatolia were much bigger. The Ottoman army had been brought to such a peak of excellence that it was probably the most efficient military force in the world at that date, ready to subdue the Mamluks and make the Ottoman empire the dominant Islamic state. In addition, the Ottomans had established themselves as a naval power for the first time, providing a serious Muslim challenge to Christian control of the Mediterranean for the first time in centuries.

The principal architect of this great change in Ottoman fortunes was Mehmed II, who had succeeded Murad II in 1451. Not yet twenty, at first he was underestimated by his potential Christian foes because of his youth. This misapprehension did not last long. The Ottomans had already taken a keen interest in gunpowder weapons, whether siege guns, field artillery or handguns, during the wars with the Hungarians in the 1440s. In 1452 Mehmed took that interest further when he commissioned a German gunner to produce some huge cannon for him. The first of these weapons were mounted in a new fortress the sultan built on the shores of the Bosphorus, some miles to the north of Constantinople. Mehmed intended to control the passage of ships to and from the Black Sea; to make his point, his guns swiftly sank a Venetian ship that refused to stop for inspection. Access to the Black Sea, a vital source of supplies for Constantinople, was now under Ottoman control.

During the winter of 1452–3 Mehmed was preparing to launch a major attack on Constantinople. The Byzantine emperor, Constantine xi Palaeologus, began desperate defensive preparations in the city, while Mehmed assembled a large fleet at Gallipoli to cut the Byzantines off from the Aegean Sea. In March 1453 the Ottoman fleet moved into the Sea of Marmara and approached the sea walls of Constantinople. In Thrace, Mehmed's army, said to number 80,000 men, moved up to the land walls and from April the sultan's giant siege guns began to bombard them. The Byzantine emperor could muster barely 7,000 defenders to man 14 miles of city wall, and the ships of the Byzantine navy, only ten in number, hardly dared venture beyond the chain protecting their anchorage in the Golden Horn. Some Venetians, Genoese and other foreign volunteers aided the defence, but other Genoese in the suburb of Galata across the Golden Horn attempted to remain neutral throughout the coming Christian–Muslim struggle.

The land walls that had survived so many sieges in the previous 1,000 years began to crumble under the fire of Mehmed's siege guns. The defenders hoped that Venice would send a fleet to save them, but weeks passed with no sign of any relief force. A few supply ships did manage to fight their way through the Ottoman fleet to reach the safety of the Golden Horn. They were too little too late, but their success in breaking the blockade infuriated the Ottoman sultan. Mehmed ordered that some of his ships should be dragged across land and launched onto the upper waters of the Golden Horn. There was now no safe place for Christian shipping and the Turks might have launched an attack on that part of the city wall along the Golden Horn where the soldiers of the Fourth Crusade broke into the city in 1204. In fact, the final Ottoman assault on 29 May 1453 was launched against the crumbling land walls, with the sultan's janissaries leading the attack. Taking off his insignia, Emperor Constantine xi joined his soldiers in the last desperate resistance. His body was never found. By the end of the day Mehmed had achieved the centuries-old Muslim dream of capturing Constantinople. Ever after he would be known as Mehmed the Conqueror.

The fall of Constantinople marked the final collapse of the Roman empire after some 1,500 years of existence in one form or another. Who was to inherit its legacy? Mehmed ii staked his claim by adding *Rum Kayseri* ('Roman Caesar') to his titles and by trying to add former Roman/Byzantine territories to his empire, even preparing to invade Italy at the end of his life. However, the real heirs of the Orthodox Christian tradition of the Byzantine empire were to be found elsewhere. In 1472 Zoe-Sophia, a niece of the last Byzantine emperor, married Ivan iii, Grand Prince of Muscovy. As part of her dowry she brought him the

Palaeologi emblem of the double-headed eagle and, it was thought, the spiritual heritage of Byzantium.

After 1480 the Russians began to throw off the rule of their Mongol (Tatar) conquerors, who had converted to Islam. Removing the 'Tatar yoke' was a slow process, but by the 1550s Czar Ivan the Terrible, Zoe-Sophia's grandson, was able to begin the conquest of Muslim territory. By the end of the seventeenth century Russia would be the most important Orthodox Christian state, and its rulers believed they had a mission to free their co-religionists in the Ottoman empire from the Turkish yoke. Moscow was to be the 'Third Rome', inheritor of the traditions of both Constantinople and the first Rome, and Russia was to be an implacable foe of Islam.

In 1453, however, all this lay in the distant future. Mehmed II sought to follow up his success at Constantinople by further advances in the Balkans, but encountered difficulties when he attacked Belgrade in 1456. The Franciscan friar John of Capistrano inspired the defenders of the city while John Hunyadi brought up a relieving army that defeated the Ottoman sultan and captured several of his giant siege cannon. Hunyadi died soon afterwards, but left Hungary secure for the moment. The Ottoman sultan then turned to the destruction of the last remnants of the Byzantine empire, overrunning the Morea in southern Greece in 1460 and taking Trebizond on the southern shore of the Black Sea in 1461. Steadily the Ottomans advanced along the shores of the Black Sea, and with the submission of the khan of the Crimean Tatars in 1475, the Black Sea was effectively an Ottoman lake.

Ottoman activities in Greece and the Aegean Sea led to clashes with Venice, and war between the two powers took place between 1463 and 1479. Earlier in the century the Venetians had been much superior at sea to the Ottomans, crushing the infant Ottoman fleet in a battle outside the Dardanelles in 1416, but now the Turks made great efforts to build up their fleet. The Ottomans avoided open battle, but the coordinated advances of their army and fleet brought successes, with the Venetians losing Negroponte, their most important island posses-sion in the Aegean, in 1470. A peace was eventually agreed, and the Venetians hoped to achieve a lasting commercial relationship with the Ottomans that might avoid further wars.

In 1480 Mehmed II had sought to remove one of the most annoying Christian naval bases, the island of Rhodes, still held by the Hospi-tallers. The sultan's attack was unsuccessful, so he then turned to a possible invasion of Italy. The Turks captured the Italian port of

Otranto, at the entrance to the Adriatic Sea, and panic swept across Italy, the pope even considering a hasty departure from Rome. Mehmed died in 1481, however, and the Christians recaptured Otranto. For the moment the threat of an Ottoman thrust into the very heart of western Christendom had been removed.

Bayezid II followed Mehmed the Conqueror, but he had to fight a civil war with his brother Jem to secure his position. Jem escaped and took up residence with the Hospitallers on Rhodes. Jem's survival made Bayezid reluctant to go to war with the Christian powers, since they might use his brother to create divisions within the Ottoman state. Bayezid, however, did undertake a campaign against the Christians of Moldavia to establish his reputation as a *ghazi*, a politically essential task, before engaging in an inconclusive war with the Mamluks in Syria. Bayezid also took an interest in naval matters and laid the foundations of Ottoman sea power.

In the century after the occupation of Gallipoli in 1354 the only sea passage vital to the Ottoman empire was the Straits (the Dardanelles and the Bosphorus) that divided its Asian and European territories. The situation changed after the conquest of Constantinople in 1453. That great city received most of its food and other supplies by sea from territories around the Black and Aegean seas. It became essential for the Ottomans to control the sea lanes in those areas, and Mehmed II had largely achieved that by the time of his death. To expand their maritime control further, the Ottomans would need a fleet capable of sustaining more distant operations and of taking on Venice, which was still the dominant sea power in the Adriatic and the eastern Mediterranean.

Bayezid II built up such a war fleet, and after Jem's death in 1495 he felt free to take a more aggressive line with the Christian powers. In 1499 the sultan went to war with Venice, and by coordinating the operations of his army in Greece with the advance of the Ottoman galley fleet, Bayezid achieved considerable success. Venetian fortresses on the south and west coasts of the Morea and in the Gulf of Corinth were taken, and, for the first time, the Ottomans defeated the Venetians in sea battles, such as Zonchio in 1499. Venetian difficulties led the pope to organize an international coalition, including France and Spain, to assist them against the Turks. Coalition forces had some success in the Ionian Islands, but the Ottomans struck back by capturing Durazzo in the Adriatic from the Venetians. When peace was made in 1503 the Ottomans kept most of the fortresses they had taken from the Venetians. More important, Bayezid had established the Ottoman empire as a major naval power. After centuries of Christian domination in the Mediterranean, the Muslims now seemed capable of gaining the upper hand at sea.

By the 1490s the Ottomans could look back on an impressive record of achievement in land warfare against the Christians, and they were developing an increasing competence in naval warfare as well. If the Muslim threat was increasing in south-east Europe, however, the Muslim presence in south-west Europe, in the Iberian peninsula, was being finally extinguished. The religious fervour that inspired the Portuguese and the Spanish in the *Reconquista* was then to launch them into new efforts against the Muslims, first in North Africa and then, more importantly, by maritime ventures that would reshape the whole context of the Christian–Muslim struggle.

THE FALL OF GRANADA AND NEW FRONTIERS

After the great successes of the Christian reconquest of Iberia in the first half of the thirteenth century, the area near the Strait of Gibraltar became a new focus of conflict. Granada, the only remaining Muslim state in Iberia, was nearby and ready to cooperate with Morocco, just across the strait, in hopes of starting a Muslim reconquest of Iberia. In addition, a stretch of water whose principal use in the past had been to link Muslim Spain with Muslim North Africa now became part of a major Christian trade route from the Mediterranean to north-west Europe. After 1250 trade between the two most advanced economic areas of western Christendom, Italy and Flanders, went increasingly by sea through the Strait of Gibraltar, and the old land trade routes across the Alps declined in importance. It was now vital to Christian rulers not only to keep the Muslims out of Iberia, but also to secure control of the strait for the safe passage of Christian shipping.

In 1259 Alfonso x of Castile took the Muslim enclave of Cádiz, and in the following year a crusading expedition raided Morocco. In the years 1264–6 the Muslim populations of Andalusia and Murcia revolted against their Christian masters and received some support from Granada and Morocco. Castile and Aragon cooperated to crush the revolt and many Muslims were expelled from Christian territory. A Moroccan army landed in Iberia in 1275 and raided up the Guadalquivir valley. After defeating a Christian force at Ecija the Moroccans withdrew to their own country. However, the Granadans passed control of the ports of Tarifa and Algeciras to the Moroccans so that they would have bases in Iberia from which to launch further attacks on the Christians.

Another Moroccan incursion occurred in 1282, but in 1291 the Castilians captured Tarifa. In 1309 Castile and Aragon launched a joint attack on Granada, causing its ruler to renew his alliance with Morocco. Christian attacks on Algeciras and Almeria were repulsed, but they did take Gibraltar, only to lose it in 1333.

In 1340 the Moroccan ruler Abul Hasan led an expedition to Iberia, where, in alliance with Yusuf I of Granada, he besieged Tarifa. Alfonso XI of Castile, assisted by Portuguese forces and an Aragonese fleet, as well as crusaders from northern Europe, defeated the combined Muslim armies at the River Salado, near Tarifa, in October 1340. During 1344 Alfonso, aided by foreign crusaders, including an English contingent, took Algeciras from the Muslims. In 1349 the king tried to recapture Gibraltar with the aid of Aragonese forces, but the siege was abandoned at the onset of the Black Death, which killed Alfonso in March 1350.

Gibraltar did not finally come into Christian hands until 1462. Nevertheless, Alfonso XI's efforts had been sufficient to end the Moroccan threat. Christian–Muslim clashes continued on the borders of Granada for decades, but Christian divisions and distractions enabled the Muslim state to survive until almost the end of the fifteenth century. Only at the start of the 1480s did the Christians begin the final campaign to conquer Granada.

The marriage of Ferdinand of Aragon to Isabella of Castile in 1469 had laid the basis for a more united Spanish state, allowing the mobilization of considerable forces against the Muslims. Most of the local troops came from Castile, while large contingents of foreign, mostly Swiss, mercenaries were recruited. The pope offered crusading privileges and volunteers came from all over Christendom to join the crusade against Granada. The Englishman Edward Woodville, for example, was to play a prominent part in the capture of Loja in 1486. A Muslim attack on the frontier town of Zahara in December 1481 was used as the occasion to declare war on the Granadans, and the Christians made their first conquest in February 1482, taking the town of Alhama. Yet if there were any hopes that Christian victory would be quick and easy, they were soon to be disappointed. A bitter and bloody ten-year war of attrition had begun.

The Christians were aided by the outbreak of civil war within Granada. In July 1482 the reigning emir was driven from the city of Granada by his son Abu Abdullah, who was known to the Christians as Boabdil. The ousted father withdrew to Malaga, from where he waged war on both his son and the Christians, defeating the latter's attack on Malaga in 1483. That year also saw Boabdil defeated and captured by Christian forces at Lucena. He was eventually allowed to go free after swearing an oath of vassalage to Ferdinand and Isabella, and returned to Granada to continue the civil war with his relatives. The Christian forces, which enjoyed superiority in both financial and military resources, including artillery, steadily ground down Muslim resistance. Ronda fell to them in 1485, Malaga in 1487 and Almeria in 1489. Finally, the city of Granada was besieged from April 1491 and in the following November terms of surrender were agreed. On 2 January 1492 Boabdil handed over Granada to Ferdinand and Isabella, and soon he and 200,000 other Muslims had emigrated to North Africa. After nearly 700 years of struggle the *Reconquista* was finally at an end.

In victory the Christians were to prove far from magnanimous. After their successes in the thirteenth century, they had been fairly generous in their treatment of the Jews and Muslims who had come under their rule. By the fifteenth century, however, there was growing Christian hostility to both groups. In the same year that Granada fell, the Jews of Castile and Aragon were ordered to become Christians or leave the country. By 1498 the same bitter choice had been offered to all the Jews of Spain and Portugal. The Muslims fared little better. The activities of the Inquisition provoked a Muslim revolt in Granada in 1499–1501, and after it was suppressed there were calls for the Muslims to be expelled. Between 1502 and 1526 all Spanish Muslims were ordered to convert (becoming Christianized Moors or *moriscos*) or leave the country. Both Jews and Muslims went to Muslim states, especially in North Africa, carrying with them a hatred of Iberian Christians that would persist for centuries and strengthen such manifestations of militant Islam as the Barbary corsairs.

The struggle with Islam was one of the basic conditioning factors of the Christian Europe that emerged during the medieval period. On the level of individual nations, the centuries-long *Reconquista* had left an indelible impression on the national characters of the Portuguese and the Spanish. Expelling the Muslims from Iberia was not enough. Their crusading zeal compelled them to follow the beaten Muslims into North Africa and even beyond the seas.

As well as the fall of Granada, the year 1492 saw the discovery of the Americas by Columbus. This was to become the focus of Spanish maritime endeavours, and voyages to the east that would directly challenge Islam were by papal order left to the Portuguese. The immediate target for the Spanish after the completion of the *Reconquista* was North Africa. From 1497 the Spanish spread eastwards along the North African coasts, seizing ports and strong-points including Melilla, Mers el Kebir,

Oran, Algiers and Bougie. Often 'occupation' meant no more than controlling a fortification commanding the harbour, but it still gave the Spanish control of the locality. In 1510 Pedro Navarro seized Tripoli in Libya for Spain, but was then defeated when he tried to capture the island of Djerba. Nevertheless, there was talk that King Ferdinand of Aragon and his kinsmen Manuel I of Portugal and Henry VIII of England might lead a crusader army across North Africa to Jerusalem. Henry VIII in fact sent a contingent of English archers to Cádiz to join in Ferdinand's proposed crusade against Tunis, but that expedition never took place. For the moment the Spanish advance in North Africa had come to a halt.

The original impulse for Portuguese overseas expansion seems to have been to carry the crusade against the Muslims from Iberia into North Africa. Morocco was the principal target, with the Portuguese taking Ceuta in 1415 and Tangier in 1471. A more general interest in maritime exploration, however, supported by Prince Henry the Navigator, master of the Knights of Christ, encouraged ships to venture further down the west coast of Africa during the fifteenth century. One aim was to see if a direct sea route could be found to India and China. Such a route would avoid dependence on the existing trade routes that passed through the Muslim Middle East and would give Christian Europeans direct access to the spices and other goods that came from the east. Bartolomeu Dias rounded the Cape of Good Hope in 1488, and in 1497 Vasco da Gama, a Knight of Christ, set out for India. In east Africa he found a Muslim pilot who was willing to guide him on the final stage of his voyage to India, where he reached Calicut in 1498. A new age of world history was about to open, with the Christian Europeans spreading across the seas of the world, but its impact would not be immediate. First the Christians of Europe would have to survive a new and more powerful Muslim threat from the Ottomans, on both land and sea.

7

OTTOMAN CHALLENGE:
THE SIXTEENTH CENTURY

NEW LANDS AND NEW ENEMIES

By 1520 the Ottoman empire was clearly one of the world's great powers, comparable to Ming China or the Habsburg empire of the Holy Roman Emperor Charles v in Christian Europe. The Ottoman claim to be the greatest Muslim state was strengthened by the conquest of the Mamluk empire in 1516–17. This brought not only Egypt and Syria under Ottoman rule, but also the Muslim holy cities of Mecca, Medina and Jerusalem. The Mamluks had maintained descendants of the Abbasids as puppet caliphs in Cairo, although few other Muslim states recognized them. The Ottomans took over this claim to the caliphate from the Mamluks. However, when Muslim leaders in places as far apart as Spain, Russia, India and Sumatra appealed to the Ottoman sultan for support, it was more because of his military power than any claim to be the spiritual leader of all Muslims.

The Ottomans were not the only great Muslim empire of the sixteenth century. That period also saw the rise of Safavid Persia, the most powerful Shiite state for centuries, and of the Mughal empire in India. Safavid Persia was a particular challenge to the Ottomans. In the past they had been able to concentrate largely on their war with the Christians, but as staunch Sunnis the Ottomans felt bound to oppose the new Shiite state in Persia. If the Protestant Reformation was to shatter the unity of Christian Europe during the sixteenth century, the conflict between Sunni Ottomans and Shiite Safavids was to produce almost comparable disorder in the Islamic world. Like their Byzantine predecessors, the Ottomans faced the possibility of war on two fronts: against the Christians in south-east Europe and against the Shiites along the Persian frontier. Ottoman expansion in the Middle East was also to bring them into new zones of conflict with the Christians, notably North Africa and the Indian Ocean.

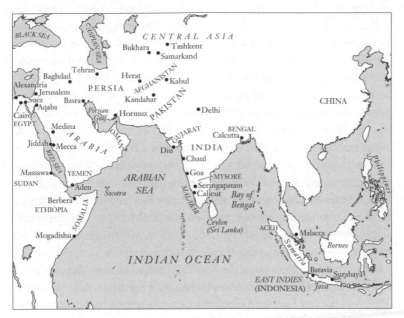

Central Asia and the Indian Ocean in the 16th century.

The appearance of the Portuguese in the Indian Ocean around 1500 had provoked a Muslim response from both local Muslims, such as the ruler of Gujarat, and from the Mamluk sultan in Cairo. A Mamluk fleet was sent to support the Gujaratis on the west coast of India, and their joint force destroyed a Portuguese squadron at Chaul in 1508. The Portuguese 'governor of India', Francisco de Almeida, avenged his son's death at Chaul by destroying the Mamluk-Gujarat fleet at Diu in 1509. Soon afterwards he was replaced as governor by Afonso de Albuquerque, who led a series of successful operations in the following years. He captured Hormuz, at the entrance to the Persian Gulf, in 1509, Goa in India in 1510, and Malacca in the East Indies in 1511. All were Muslim cities, and it was now clear that the centuries-old Christian–Muslim conflict had found a new theatre of operations. The aim of the Portuguese was to control the main ports on the spice trade route to the Middle East and Europe. Hormuz closed off the route through the Persian Gulf, but the capture of the island of Socotra was insufficient to seal the entrance to the Red Sea. In 1513 Albuquerque attacked Aden, a more suitable base for this task, but was repulsed. The failure of this and later attempts to close the Red Sea gap allowed the spice trade through the Muslim Middle East to survive for a longer period.

Worried by the growing Portuguese success in the Indian Ocean and aware of their own weakness in naval matters, the Mamluks sought aid from the Ottoman sultan. This was provided in 1515, when shipbuilding timber and naval commanders were sent so that joint Mamluk-Ottoman squadrons could be fitted out. Rather incongruously in 1516–17, when the Ottomans were actually conquering the Mamluk empire, joint Mamluk-Ottoman naval operations were still taking place against the Portuguese. In 1517 a Portuguese squadron under Lope Soarez de Albergaria entered the Red Sea and attacked a Mamluk fleet under an Ottoman commander at Jiddah. This was the port for Mecca, and the Portuguese assault was the most serious Christian threat to the two holiest cities of Islam since the ships sent by Reynald de Châtillon raided the area in the late twelfth century. No doubt inspired by their duty to protect the cities, the Muslims beat off the Portuguese attack and the Red Sea remained under their control.

The Ottoman conquest of the Mamluk empire meant that the conflict with the Portuguese in the Indian Ocean now became a direct concern. This duty further increased when the Ottomans took Iraq from the Persians and reached the Persian Gulf at Basra. In 1538 the Ottomans sent an expedition to India to aid local resistance to the Portuguese, but its attack on Diu was repulsed. More importantly, the expedition left an Ottoman garrison at Aden to reinforce Muslim control of the entrance to the Red Sea. In the Persian Gulf the Ottomans tried to break through to the Indian Ocean by capturing the Portuguese base at Hormuz, but their attack in 1552 was defeated. During the 1560s the sultan of Aceh in distant Sumatra asked for Ottoman aid in his struggle against the Portuguese in the East Indies. Some Ottoman ships, men and cannon eventually reached Aceh, but the sultan's attacks on Malacca were unsuccessful.

The Portuguese searched for the legendary 'Prester John', the supposed Christian king in the east, who might help them in their fight against the infidel. All they found were the Christians of Ethiopia, more in need of help than able to provide it. From the 1520s a jihad led by Ahmad Gran conquered most of Ethiopia, but in the 1540s the Portuguese sent musketeers to aid the embattled Christians. Ahmad Gran turned to the Ottomans for firearms, but he was killed by Portuguese troops in 1543. The Ethiopian Christians had retaken most of their country by 1555, even though the Ottomans established a garrison at Massawa on the Red Sea coast nearby.

If conquest of the Mamluk empire brought the Ottomans new maritime concerns in the Indian Ocean, it also led them into North Africa and a new confrontation with the Christians. Strongly entrenched in Egypt, Ottoman influence spread westwards along the North African coast, bringing them into direct conflict with the Spanish for the first time. The naval struggle between the Ottomans and the Venetians in the eastern Mediterranean now became merged with a wider naval war against the Spanish in the central and western Mediterranean. Charles of Habsburg had become king of Spain in 1516 and Holy Roman Emperor, as Charles v, in 1520. An heir to old crusading traditions, Charles was ready to fight the Ottomans in the Mediterranean, but the Habsburgs were to meet the Turks for the first time in Hungary.

SUCCESS FOR SULEIMAN

Sultan Selim i had spent most of his reign fighting other Muslims: first the Safavid Persians, then the Mamluks. It seemed incumbent upon his son and successor Suleiman (called 'the Magnificent' by Christians and 'the Lawgiver' by Muslims) to revive the jihad against the Christians. In 1521 Suleiman captured Belgrade, which had defied the conqueror of Constantinople, Mehmed ii, and so opened the way to further advances in the Balkans. In 1522, however, Suleiman moved against another Christian bastion that had repulsed the great Mehmed: the island of Rhodes, still held by the Hospitallers. After a long siege the knights agreed to the sultan's lenient terms and withdrew to Crete at the start of 1523.

After these two successes against the Christians, Suleiman decided to attack the kingdom of Hungary, which had since the late fourteenth century acted as 'the shield of Christianity'. Rather than waiting in his capital Buda to be attacked, King Louis ii of Hungary led his army south and faced Suleiman's forces at Mohács in August 1526. The Hungarian army was no longer the professional force that Matthias Corvinus had put together in the previous century. It had reverted to a feudal levy, with armoured cavalry as its principal strike force. King Louis led his cavalry in a series of attacks on the enemy, at first achieving some success against the Ottoman light cavalry. Then the Hungarian knights ran into a line of Ottoman artillery, backed by janissary infantry with firearms. The attackers were steadily cut down and when the Ottoman cavalry counter-attacked, the Hungarian army collapsed and fled, King Louis being killed during the rout. Suleiman's army then advanced to Buda and sacked the Hungarian capital. Among the booty carried away were the two giant siege guns that the Hungarians had taken from Mehmed the Conqueror at Belgrade in 1456.

Suleiman did not intend to occupy Hungary permanently. Instead, he aimed to set up a puppet ruler who would be his vassal. However, the dead King Louis had been married to a Habsburg princess and his brothers-in-law were Emperor Charles v and Ferdinand, the ruler of Austria. Ferdinand laid claim to the crown of Hungary, but most of the Hungarian nobles who had survived the slaughter at Mohács supported John Zápolya, who was the candidate backed by Suleiman. Ferdinand, elected king by a minority group of nobles, refused to accept this situation and attacked the client king.

This action provoked Suleiman to launch a campaign against Austria. In May 1529 the Ottoman sultan led his army north from Constantinople, but bad weather delayed its march and it only reached Buda in August. The advance into Austria was similarly held up by the weather and many large siege guns were abandoned along the way. Ferdinand had fled to Bohemia and the defence of his capital was left to Nicholas, Graf von Salm. Suleiman began his siege of Vienna late in September, but lacking much of his siege artillery he had to rely on his sappers to bring down the walls. Several mines were exploded under the walls and desperate assaults were made, but the Austrians continued to hold out. After only a few weeks Suleiman decided it was too late in the year to continue the siege, and withdrew his army before the onset of winter.

Ferdinand still refused to accept the settlement that the Ottomans had imposed on Hungary, so in 1532 Suleiman set out once again to attack Vienna. This time, however, Ferdinand's brother Emperor Charles v roused western Europe and assembled a large army, including Spanish, Italian and German troops, which he led towards Vienna. It was the first large western European army to oppose the Ottoman Turks since the one that had been destroyed at Nicopolis in 1396. Faced by these numerous Christian forces, Suleiman decided that discretion was the better part of valour and withdrew his army without attacking the Austrian capital. There were, however, limits to the emperor's support for his brother, and in 1533 Ferdinand was forced to accept a compromise peace with the Ottomans. John Záploya was to rule Transylvania and most of Hungary as a vassal of the Ottomans, while Ferdinand was to pay tribute to the sultan for the small part of Hungary he retained. In not much more than a decade Suleiman had achieved a number of major successes against the Christians in eastern Europe and had come close to capturing Vienna. His achievements were not solely due to Ottoman power and skill, for the Habsburgs faced considerable problems on other fronts.

The rise of Protestantism led to conflict within Germany, but Charles v's chief problem in the west was his long-running conflict with Francis i of France. The French had been perhaps the most consistent supporters of crusading against the Muslims during the medieval period, but in 1535 Francis was to take the revolutionary step of agreeing a secret alliance with the Ottoman Turks against his Christian enemy, the Habsburgs. Protestantism was one threat to the unity of Christendom, but another was the new, secular approach to international relations that Francis exemplified. Some of the emerging nation states of Europe were increasingly ready to put their own interests before those of a wider Christian community.

Suleiman could assist the French by tying down Habsburg forces on the Hungarian frontier, but the increasing strength of Ottoman sea power also allowed him to act directly in support of the French in the central and western Mediterranean.

BARBARY PIRATES AND BARBAROSSA

The ports of Muslim North Africa had equipped corsairs to attack Christian coasts and shipping long before the sixteenth century. However, the expulsion of Muslims from Iberia after 1492 provided new recruits for this trade who had additional reasons for hating the Christians. These seaborne holy warriors came to be known to the Christians as the Barbary pirates, 'Barbary' being derived from the name of the Berber inhabitants of these coasts. In fact, Berbers were to provide few of the pirates, most of whom were to come to North African ports from other areas, such as Iberia and Anatolia, while many were Christian renegades, either converted slaves or exiles from their homelands. At the start of the sixteenth century the setting up of Spanish strongholds in various North African ports did something to curb the pirates, but then a new force arrived in the shape of the Barbarossa brothers.

Originally from the island of Lesbos in the Aegean Sea, the brothers had gained considerable experience of raiding the Christians before they took control of Algiers in 1516. Aruj, the elder brother and the first to be known as Barbarossa ('red beard'), was killed by the Spanish in 1518; control of Algiers passed to his brother Khizr, who also inherited Aruj's nickname. With the Spanish threat growing, the new Barbarossa decided to submit to the Ottoman sultan, Selim I, and received a force of janissaries from his new overlord. Barbarossa and his captains raided widely in the western Mediterranean during the following years, aiming chiefly at Spanish targets. In 1530 the Spanish gave Malta and Tripoli (in Libya) to the Hospitallers, who had been without a permanent home since leaving Rhodes in 1523. The knights turned these places into major bases for Christian corsairs (pirates in the eyes of Muslims), waging a holy war against Barbarossa and his men.

In 1532 Andrea Doria, a Genoese admiral in Spanish service, seized several fortresses on the Greek coast and thwarted Ottoman attempts to retake them. This development worried Sultan Suleiman and he brought Barbarossa to Constantinople to overhaul the Ottoman fleet. Now 'Kapudan Pasha', the highest Ottoman naval post, Barbarossa led the Ottoman fleet westwards in 1534. After raiding southern Italy he took his force to Tunis, where the pro-Spanish Muslim ruler was quickly overthrown. Emperor Charles V retaliated by organizing a crusade, which he personally led against Tunis in 1535. Barbarossa was defeated and Tunis sacked. The Christians returned the ruined city to their puppet ruler, but retained a garrison in the strongpoint of La Goletta, which controlled the harbour. Charles V had restored the Habsburg cordon across the central Mediterranean. This cordon included Sicily, Malta, Tunis and Tripoli, and it hindered major penetrations into the western Mediterranean by the Ottoman fleet, although it could not stop raiding from bases like Algiers.

In 1537 the Ottomans set out to secure the entrance to the Adriatic Sea with a view to a possible invasion of Italy. Barbarossa ravaged the Italian coast, but Suleiman's siege of the Venetian-held fortress on Corfu was a failure. Barbarossa returned to the area in the following year, but although he defeated Andrea Doria's fleet at the battle of Preveza, there was no chance of capturing Corfu. It seemed that Suleiman had no more chance of crossing the Strait of Otranto to invade Italy than Mehmed II had in 1480–81. The Venetians had been involved in the war with the Ottomans only reluctantly and took the opportunity to make peace with their trading partners in 1540.

Barbarossa remained at Constantinople, but his lieutenants based in Algiers continued their attacks on Christian coasts and shipping. In 1541 Charles V decided to deal with the Algiers problem once and for all, and accordingly he assembled a large fleet and army. Unfortunately, the force sailed late in the year and a severe storm destroyed most of it soon after reaching Algiers.

In 1543 Barbarossa led an Ottoman fleet westwards to cooperate with the French against the Habsburgs. After raiding the Italian coast, Barbarossa assisted the French in capturing Nice, which was then sacked, seemingly by the French rather than the Turks. Barbarossa and his fleet spent the winter of 1543–4 in Toulon, from which all the Christian inhabitants had been temporarily removed. In 1544 the Ottoman fleet returned home after the usual raids on Italy. Such an open association of the French with the Turks caused outrage in much of Christian Europe.

When Barbarossa died in 1546, the Ottoman fleet controlled the eastern Mediterranean, while the Barbary pirates continued to exert pressure in the western part of that sea. The Habsburg barrier or cordon in the central Mediterranean continued to exist, however, and no concerted Ottoman effort had yet been made to remove it. This was to come after 1550, but for the moment Suleiman was drawn back to the Hungarian frontier.

HUNGARIAN STALEMATE AND RUSSIAN VENTURE

The puppet king of Hungary set up by the Ottomans died in 1540, and Ferdinand of Habsburg showed every intention of trying to secure control of the whole kingdom. This was unacceptable to Suleiman, who invaded Hungary in 1541 and for the first time began to rule it directly as an Ottoman province. War dragged on until 1547, when Ferdinand recognized Ottoman control over most of Hungary. The Habsburg ruler sent his forces into Transylvania in 1551, prompting a strong Ottoman response in the following year, which led to their capture of Temesvar. The war continued until 1562, but like most of the previous conflicts in the area it was largely a matter of raids and the occasional siege. Neither side seemed ready to risk a potentially decisive encounter on the battlefield. In part this was because both sides were distracted by conflicts elsewhere. For the Habsburgs this was often war against enemies such as the French; for the Ottomans it was usually war against the Persians.

After Ferdinand died in 1564 the war was renewed in Hungary. Suleiman in person led his troops to besiege Szigetvár in 1566, but the Croatian commander of the garrison, Nikola Zrinski, kept up a determined resistance. The sultan died in his tent before the city fell, while Zrinski and his men were all killed in a last desperate sortie. After Suleiman's death the Hungarian front saw no major campaigning for more than twenty years. Both sides were prepared to accept a stalemate.

A new element came into Ottoman strategic calculations when the growing Russian state defeated and absorbed the Muslim khanates along the river Volga in the middle of the sixteenth century. The Mongols (or Tatars as they were called by the Russians) of the Golden Horde had made the Russian principalities their vassal states in the thirteenth century. Then the formerly pagan Tatars had adopted Islam, further estranging them from their Christian subjects. During the fifteenth century the Russian states began to unite under Muscovy and were determined to throw off the 'Tatar yoke'. In the same period the Golden Horde began to break up. First it split into the khanates of Kazan and the 'Great Horde'; then later the khanates of Astrakhan and the Crimea went their separate ways. Around 1475 the ruler of the Crimean Tatars became a vassal of the Ottoman sultan, but the other khanates tried to retain their independence. However, as the princes of Muscovy began to increase pressure on the khanate of Kazan, its ruler declared himself a vassal of the Ottomans in 1524, only to be overthrown by a more pro-Russian khan soon afterwards.

In 1533 Ivan IV 'the Terrible' became ruler of Muscovy and was the first to call himself 'czar' ('caesar') in recognition of his family's claim to the inheritance of the Byzantine empire. From 1545 Ivan made determined efforts to take Kazan and finally did so in 1552. He then sent his armies southwards and they took over the khanate of Astrakhan in 1556. Complete control of the River Volga down to the Caspian Sea opened up new routes for Russian soldiers and traders. To the east, across the Ural mountains, lay Siberia, with only a few weak Muslim Tatar states to oppose a Russian advance, while to the south new trading links to Persia and India might be established.

Ivan the Terrible's success brought his dominions to the north shore of the Caspian Sea and they were not far distant from the Black Sea, posing a possible threat to Ottoman control there. Mehmed Sokollu, the Bosnian-born grand vizier of Selim II, reacted to the Russian advance by proposing the construction of a canal from the River Don to the River Volga. This would allow Ottoman fleets to move from the Black Sea to the Caspian. Then they could either attack the Russians or cross to the southern shores of the Caspian to attack the Persians. In 1569 an Ottoman force was sent to the steppes to begin construction of the canal, but the project soon failed due to Russian attacks.

A more damaging Muslim response to the Russian advance was the great raid on Moscow in 1571 by the Crimean Tatar khan Devlet-Girei. Czar Ivan fled to Vologda, much of Moscow was burnt, and many of its inhabitants were carried away into slavery by the Tatar horsemen. In the following year, however, an invading Tatar army was heavily defeated at Molodi. Nevertheless, the Russians made no further advances towards the Black Sea. Instead they moved eastwards, beginning the conquest of Siberia in the 1580s.

Mehmed Sokollu's canal project aimed at halting the Russian advance was matched by his scheme to build a Suez canal that would allow Ottoman fleets to move easily from the Mediterranean to the Red Sea and the Indian Ocean. This capability would not only permit Ottoman action against frequently rebellious provinces like Yemen, but would also allow more effective operations against the Portuguese in eastern seas. While at least some attempt was made to start building the Don–Volga canal, however, the Suez canal was never begun. These canal projects were imaginative, but centuries ahead of their time; in the mid-sixteenth century, realistic Ottoman maritime plans were fixed firmly on the Mediterranean.

CONFLICT AROUND THE CORDON

In 1550 the eastern Mediterranean was largely under Ottoman control. The Genoese still had a tenuous hold on Chios, while the Venetians possessed the more important islands of Crete and Cyprus. The Italians, however, were more interested in commerce than in war. Their islands were not bases for Christian attacks on the Ottoman empire, and peaceful trade was the chief occupation. In the western Mediterranean the Barbary corsairs held some ports along the coast of North Africa, most importantly Algiers. Although their attacks on Christian coasts and shipping were a constant nuisance, they could not have a major impact on the wider Christian–Muslim conflict without the presence of the main Ottoman fleet from Constantinople. To reach the western Mediterranean, such an imperial fleet would first have to break through the Habsburg cordon in the central area of that sea. Holding Naples, Sicily, Malta and various North African ports, the Habsburgs and their naval allies aimed both to keep the Ottoman main fleet in the eastern Mediterranean and to curb the activities of Muslim corsairs. The Spanish Habsburgs had the advantage that most of their warships were provided by the Italians, whose bases were close at hand, while the Ottoman fleet had to come all the way from Constantinople.

Bases were the key to strategy on both land and sea in the Christian–Muslim conflict at this time. From bases on the Ottoman borders the holy warriors (*ghazis*) of the frontier could raid enemy territory and extend Islamic control. However, they could not take major enemy fortresses without the help of an imperial expedition from Constantinople. Once a new base had been taken it would be used by *ghazi* raiders to further extend Muslim territorial control. Major battles with the enemy were to be avoided as far as possible. On land this process involved Suleiman leading his army up from Constantinople for a campaign, taking some Christian fortresses by siege, and then leaving them to the local *ghazis* for use as new bases. At sea the Ottoman fleet would bring troops and siege guns from Constantinople to aid local corsairs in attacking a Christian-held port. Once it was taken it would be handed over to the 'sea ghazis' as a new base. Such bases were particularly important in the galley warfare that dominated the Mediterranean in the sixteenth century. Galleys had only a limited range because of their inability to carry large supplies of food and water, so they always had to operate near friendly bases where they could be resupplied.

The central Mediterranean was to become the principal battleground for Christian–Muslim naval warfare, with ports regularly changing hands between the competing sides. The Spanish Habsburgs were always trying to strengthen their defensive cordon while the Muslims tried to dismantle it and break through. In 1550 Andrea Doria brought the Christians new bases by capturing Mahdia and Monastir on the Tunisian coast. The Muslim reply in 1551 was to besiege Tripoli in Libya, which was held by the Hospitallers. Eventually the knights were forced to yield, but the French ambassador, who was with the besieging forces, persuaded the Turks to grant them lenient terms. The Ottomans were annoyed at the ambassador's conduct, given that France was supposed to be their ally, and the Turks also noted that Frenchmen were well represented among the Hospitallers. In the next few years the Ottomans built on their success at Tripoli by making several forays into the western Mediterranean in cooperation with the French, but they never wintered there as Barbarossa had done in 1543–4. The recapture of Bougie on the Algerian coast in 1555 was another Muslim success.

After King Philip II of Spain agreed a peace with France in 1558, he had more time and resources to contribute to the war against the Ottomans in the Mediterranean. Tripoli had been developed into a major base for Muslim corsairs, and its recapture was suggested by the Spanish viceroy in Sicily in 1559. The king agreed to the expedition and forces were assembled at Syracuse, consisting of a fleet of 90 ships commanded by Gian Andrea Doria, great-nephew of Andrea Doria, with 12,000 troops commanded by the Duke of Medinaceli, Viceroy of Sicily. The expedition sailed in December 1559, only to be forced back by storms. Setting off again in March 1560, the force headed initially for the island of Djerba, which was to be used as a base from which to attack Tripoli.

Unfortunately, the delays in despatching the expedition had allowed news of it and its targets to reach Constantinople. The Ottoman fleet, under Piali Pasha, embarked troops and sailed westwards. In May 1560 the Ottomans surprised the Spanish force at Djerba, defeated their fleet, and blockaded the army on the island. Doria and Medinaceli escaped, but 10,000 troops were eventually forced to surrender to the Turks. The prisoners were led in triumph through the streets of Constantinople on their way to slavery. Djerba was one of the worst defeats suffered by Spain during the sixteenth century.

Yet the Ottomans largely failed to exploit their victory at Djerba. A Muslim attempt to recapture Oran in 1563 was repulsed, and by 1564 the Spanish fleet had regained its former strength. In 1565 Sultan Suleiman decided to launch a major attack on the island of Malta, the last stronghold of the Hospitallers. It was not only an important base for Christian corsairs that could provide similar facilities for the Muslims, but it might also be a place where forces could be assembled for an invasion of Sicily or Italy. The Ottoman fleet, still commanded by Piali Pasha, was to take an army of 40,000 men, under Mustapha Pasha, to attack Malta. North African corsairs such as Dragut were to provide additional forces.

The Hospitaller Grand Master, Jean de la Vallette, had only about 600 members of the order with which to oppose the invaders. The Reformation had further increased the Latin domination of the Hospitallers. Probably most of the knights were French, like the Grand Master, and most of the rest Spanish, Portuguese and Italian. There were some Germans, but the English contingent had shrunk to a single knight, Oliver Starkey, who was de la Vallette's secretary. Spanish and other foreign soldiers made up another contingent on the island, while the local Maltese population provided a militia force. In all the Christians had only 8–9,000 defenders. The Hospitaller forces were concentrated in defence positions around the Grand Harbour, with the three principal fortresses being St Elmo, Senglea and Birgu. The knights hoped that the Spanish viceroy in Sicily would quickly come to their aid, but they were to be disappointed.

The Ottoman forces landed on Malta in May 1565 and initially concentrated most of their efforts against the fort of St Elmo, bombarding and assaulting it for almost a month. Towards the end of June it was finally overrun and nearly all its garrison killed, but there were many Turkish casualties, with the old corsair Dragut among the dead. The Ottoman army then turned its full attention on Senglea and Birgu, which resisted attack after attack. By the end of August battle casualties and losses from disease had badly weakened the Ottoman army and its commanders were thinking of giving up the siege. Their minds were finally made up by the belated arrival in early September of a relief force of 11,000 men under the viceroy of Sicily, Garcia de Toledo. The Ottoman fleet and army departed after suffering a famous defeat that inspired all of Christendom. As many as 20,000 men of the Ottoman forces may have died, while the defenders may have lost as many as 5,000, including 250 knights. After their victory the Hospitallers built a new, heavily fortified city by the Grand Harbour and named it after their master: Valletta.

Although repulsed at Malta, the Ottomans regained control of Tunis in 1569, and it seemed the taking and retaking of bases around the cordon might go on indefinitely. At Christmas 1568 the Spanish received a major shock at home when Moriscos (Christianized Moors) revolted in the Alpujarras mountains of southern Granada. The rebels proclaimed their true allegiance to Islam and hoped for assistance from the Ottomans, or at least the Barbary corsairs, but little help came. By the spring of 1570 there were said to be 4,000 Turkish and Berber volunteers fighting alongside the 30,000 rebels. Don Juan of Austria, an illegitimate son of Charles v, was given command of the Spanish troops suppressing the rising, and by November 1570 peace had largely been restored. The insurrection, in which as many as 60,000 people lost their lives, left bitter memories and a deep distrust of the Moriscos. The complete expulsion of the Moriscos was proposed in 1582, but Valencian nobles objected because they made up such a large part of their agricultural labour force. Such economic arguments were eventually worn down by the deep hostility of the Spanish Church and people to the 'enemy within'. Between 1609 and 1614 the Morisco population was finally expelled: almost 300,000 people out of a total Spanish population of eight million were deported to Muslim lands.

Suleiman's successor, Selim II, was ready to act against the Christians, but not in faraway Spain. The Venetian-held island of Cyprus presented a much nearer target. The Venetians were keen to avoid war with the Ottomans, largely for commercial reasons, and had only reluctantly gone to war with the sultan in the late 1530s for a short period. Nevertheless, the Ottomans attacked Cyprus in 1570. Nicosia fell quickly, but Famagusta was to hold out until the following year. Pope Pius v now encouraged the formation of a holy league to fight the Turks, and its combined fleet assembled at Messina in Sicily in the autumn of 1571. The fleet was made up of more than 200 galleys, with the largest group of over 100 coming from Venice. Of the remainder, 63 came from Spanish-controlled Italy (Sicily, Naples, Genoa), and only 14 from Spain itself. The pope provided twelve. The Hospitallers could provide only three galleys, having lost half their fleet to Muslim corsairs the previous year. The new military order of the Knights of St Stephen, founded in Tuscany in 1562 to fight the Muslims at sea, eclipsed the Knights of Malta by contributing five galleys. Don Juan of Austria, fresh from his victory over the Morisco rebels, was given overall command of the fleet.

The last Venetian resistance on Cyprus had ended back in August, and the Ottoman fleet had moved westward, operating at the southern end of the Adriatic Sea. Don Juan now led the Christian fleet out to find the enemy, and battle was joined near Lepanto on the western coast of Greece on 7 October 1571. The Ottoman galley fleet, under Ali Pasha, had slightly more ships than the Christians, but the latter had twice as many guns aboard their ships. Altogether more than 100,000 men took part in the battle. Ali Pasha hoped to defeat the wings of the Christian galley line and then concentrate his forces against the Christian centre, but this plan was largely unsuccessful. Christian firepower sank many Turkish galleys, but more were captured in fierce boarding battles. Almost the whole Ottoman fleet was sunk or captured, with only a small group of ships escaping.

In this the last and greatest battle between galley fleets, the Christians lost twelve galleys and 10,000 men. The Turks had 113 galleys sunk and 117 captured, losing more than 30,000 men, including their fleet commander. Some 12,000 Christian galley slaves were liberated from the Turkish ships. The victory at Lepanto was welcomed all over Christian Europe, even among Protestants. For much of the sixteenth century there seemed a real danger that the Muslims would become dominant at sea throughout the Mediterranean, a situation that had not existed for centuries. Now it seemed that Christian sea power had reasserted its superiority.

Lepanto was undoubtedly the greatest defeat suffered by Ottoman arms since that at Tamerlane's hands at the battle of Ankara in 1402. It was also the first great Christian victory over the Ottomans, not just in the sixteenth century, but since the Ottoman Turks had first entered Europe in the fourteenth century. Had the battle been fought on land and in the presence of the sultan, the consequences of Lepanto might have been as dire for the Ottoman empire as those that followed the defeat at Ankara. A defeat at sea, however, no matter how crushing, could never be fatal to such a great land power.

The Christians rejoiced, but Lepanto quickly proved not to be quite such a decisive victory as they had initially hoped. The Ottoman grand vizier, Mehmed Sokollu, restored the Ottoman fleet to its former size within twelve months, and the Christian victors soon fell out among themselves. The Venetians wanted to retake Cyprus, but the Spanish were interested only in strengthening the central Mediterranean cordon. The Venetians made peace with the Ottomans in 1573, the same year the Spanish captured Tunis, but the Ottomans showed their continued strength by retaking the city in 1574.

Soon it became clear that there was just as much of a stalemate between Habsburgs and Ottomans in the Mediterranean as there was on the Hungarian plain. Truces were made and renewed as the protagonists found their forces were required elsewhere, with the Spanish becoming embroiled in the Dutch revolt and the Ottomans embarking on a long war with the Persians. The Spanish had largely preserved their central Mediterranean cordon and no Ottoman fleet ever again passed into the western Mediterranean, but the Barbary corsairs had survived and would continue to torment Christian shipping for centuries to come.

The Ottomans had posed a major threat to Christian Europe on both land and sea for much of the sixteenth century. At times, such as the siege of Vienna in 1529, it seemed that the Turks might break through into the very heart of the continent, but that had not happened. Christian fleets and armies, usually provided by the Spanish or Austrian Habsburgs, had blunted the Ottoman challenge, and by the last quarter of the century both sides were prepared to accept a stalemate. The question now was whether the Ottomans could gather their strength for a renewed offensive or would the strategic initiative pass to the Christian side?

LAST CRUSADE AND AMERICAN INVASION

The overseas empire in Africa, Asia and South America brought great material benefits to the Portuguese crown, but interest in Morocco never abated. That country was never part of the Ottoman empire, and so perhaps appeared an easier target for the old crusading zeal against the Muslims. For most of the sixteenth century, however, the clashes between the Portuguese and the Moroccans, still called Moors by the Christians, were largely confined to the coast, with forts won and lost between the two sides. Then King Sebastian came to the throne of Portugal in 1557 and developed a passionate interest in the idea of a crusade against the Moors.

In 1578 an opportunity arose for Sebastian to intervene in Morocco. He hoped to set up a puppet Muslim ruler in the interior of the country, and to do so he organized what is often seen as the last old-style crusade against the Muslims. Pope Gregory XIII approved the expedition and granted crusader privileges. It was a largely Portuguese venture, but some foreign troops did join the expedition. A Catholic Englishman, Thomas Stucley, was on his way with troops to Ireland where he intended to join Irish rebels in the fight against his heretic fellow countrymen. However, the chance of joining a crusade against the infidel proved more attractive than war against heretics, especially to a man like Stucley who had fought at the battle of Lepanto. His contingent joined the 20,000-strong crusader army. Unfortunately, the whole project turned out to be a disaster. King Sebastian led his men into the Moroccan interior and clashed with a Moroccan army of 50,000 under Abd al-Malik. The battle of Alcazarquivir took place in August 1578 and resulted in a crushing defeat for the Christians. King Sebastian, Thomas Stucley and perhaps half the crusader army were slaughtered.

The death of the childless King Sebastian led to serious problems concerning the Portuguese royal succession. The result was that in 1580 the crown of Portugal passed to King Philip II of Spain, and for the first time since the Visigothic kingdom nearly eight centuries earlier the entire Iberian peninsula was under one ruler. This situation was not to last, because Portugal regained its independence in 1640, but for the moment the enemies of Spain such as the English and the Dutch were only too happy to attack Portuguese targets as well as Spanish ones.

The English sought friendly relations with the enemies of Spain and Portugal, including the Muslim ones. The Levant Company established trading relations with the Ottomans, and when in 1593 an English galleon delivered the English ambassador to Constantinople, the local inhabitants marvelled at the ship's many guns and the fact that it had sailed thousands of miles to reach their city. Such an ocean-going warship seemed much more powerful than the galleys on which Muslim naval power was largely based.

The English also established good relations with the Moroccans, and it was the ocean-going capacity of their ships that led the Moroccans to propose a joint expedition against the Spanish of a rather novel kind. In 1603 the ruler of Morocco, Ahmad al-Mansur, wrote to Queen Elizabeth 1 of England proposing that Moroccan and English troops, using English ships, should together attack the Spanish colonies in the West Indies, expel the Spanish and colonize those lands themselves. The Moroccan leader thoughtfully pointed out that since the Moors were more used to heat than the English, they would make better permanent colonists. Elizabeth's reply is not recorded. She, like the Moroccan ruler, died during 1603 and her successor, King James 1 of England, proved pro-Spanish and anti-Muslim. It would not be until almost four centuries later that militant Islam struck a decisive blow in the Americas.

8

OTTOMAN REVIVAL AND DECLINE, 1600–1815

SAVED BY THE GRAND VIZIERS

According to some historians, the death of Suleiman the Magnificent in 1566 marked the end of the greatness of the Ottoman empire. From then until its disappearance some 350 years later the empire was said to be in terminal decline. The end of the Ottomans was never inevitable, however, nor was a serious decline in Muslim power obvious until well into the eighteenth century. The Ottoman empire in Europe did not reach its greatest extent until the 1670s, and Ottoman forces came close to capturing Vienna in 1683. Even in the first half of the eighteenth century the Ottomans were still capable of inflicting humiliating defeats on both the Austrians and Russians. While recognizing that from 1700 onwards Christian Europe became less and less afraid of the Ottoman Turks, one should beware of giving too early a date for the beginning of their empire's decline. In the late sixteenth century, if any great power seemed on the verge of collapse it was not the Ottoman empire but France, torn apart as it was by religious civil wars.

Nevertheless, there were signs of decay in the political and military structure of the Ottoman empire after 1600. The Ottomans had ruthlessly centralized government in their empire, and all power was concentrated in the hands of the sultan – consequently, too much depended on the character of one man. The first ten Ottoman rulers up to Selim II had all shown leadership skills in varying degrees. After the death of Suleiman the Magnificent in 1566, few sultans had strong characters and even fewer led their armies in the field. The power lost by the sultans began to be taken up by the janissaries and the *ulema* (religious leaders). These groups were ready to depose and even murder sultans of whom they disapproved, Sultan Osman II being the first to die in 1622, and this factionalism could lead to paralysis at the heart of Ottoman government. Usually only a gifted grand vizier (chief minister), such as Mehmed Sokollu in the late sixteenth century, could restore Ottoman strength. That the Ottomans achieved further advances against the Christians in the mid-seventeenth century was largely due to a remarkable series of grand viziers from the Koprulu family, who dominated Ottoman affairs for most of the period 1656–91.

The military pillars of the Ottoman state, the slave janissaries and the free-born *sipahis*, also declined after 1600. The *devshirme*, the levy of Christian boys, was made only a few times after 1600 and janissaries were increasingly recruited from ordinary Muslims, not slave converts. These Muslims soon obtained the right to pass on janissary status and privileges to their sons with a consequent decline in quality and discipline in the corps. The number of janissaries grew rapidly, from perhaps 20,000 in 1566 to nearly 40,000 in 1610. The janissaries began to interfere in politics and put their privileges before their duty and military efficiency.

Another reason for the expansion of the janissary corps was related to the changing nature of warfare. In the armies of Christian Europe troops increasingly consisted of infantrymen armed with firearms, while cavalry became less important. The Ottoman army, true to its nomad origins, had largely been made up of horsemen, but now it became necessary to boost the number of janissaries, most of whom were firearm-equipped infantry. They were a salaried force paid by the central exchequer, so it seemed sensible to reduce the number of *sipahis*, the *timar*-holding cavalry. The horsemen had received the income from their lands in return for service in war. To the central government it was desirable that the lands should be given to tax farmers who could extract the maximum income and pass money to the administration to pay infantrymen. Not only did the number of *sipahis* fall, but many of those who lost their land turned to banditry, damaging public order in the provinces.

In the long run, these changes were to undermine Ottoman military power, but for much of the first half of the seventeenth century the Christian–Muslim conflict seemed largely suspended on the European front. The Ottomans and the Austrian Habsburgs began the so-called Long War in 1592, but its longevity was not matched by intensity or decisiveness. The Ottomans were unable to exploit their victory at Mezokeresztes in 1596 and disputes between the rulers of Transylvania, Wallachia and Moldavia distracted the major protagonists. Michael the Brave, Prince of Wallachia, defeated the Turks at Calugareni in 1595 and for a short time ruled Transylvania and Moldavia as well as his own state. The Habsburg–Ottoman war ended in 1606 with only a few border outposts changing hands. The Turks clashed with the Poles in the Ukraine in 1620–21, but for the most part the Christian powers were distracted by the Thirty Years War and France's struggle to restore its fortunes and replace Spain as the leading Christian power. Daring raids around the Black Sea by seaborne Cossacks exposed a decline in Ottoman naval capability, but were eventually overcome. Similarly, early Persian successes in new border wars were reversed in the 1630s, Baghdad being recaptured in 1638. In some areas, however, Ottoman power was no longer exercised. The Barbary corsairs were increasingly left to their own devices and in the Indian Ocean the Portuguese now had more to fear from European rivals like the Dutch than from the Ottomans.

Christian–Muslim conflict was to be revived in the eastern Mediterranean during the 1640s. The Venetians still held the island of Crete, which was near the vital Ottoman sea route from Constantinople to Egypt, but did their best not to annoy the Turks. Unfortunately, Christian corsairs licensed by the Hospitallers to sail out of Malta were less circumspect. In 1644 one such raider seized an Ottoman vessel bound for Alexandria with a rich cargo and important passengers. The prize was taken to Crete so that the booty could be divided up. Although the Venetians were not actively involved in this incident, Sultan Ibrahim decided this was a good excuse to attack Crete and remove the last Christian possession in the eastern Mediterranean. In 1645 an Ottoman force of 400 ships and 60,000 men invaded the island. Many of the Orthodox Christian inhabitants were not unhappy to see their Catholic masters replaced by more tolerant Muslims. By the start of 1648 all of Crete had been subdued except the capital, Candia. The port was besieged, but few could have foreseen that it would turn out to be one of the longest sieges in history, dragging on for more than twenty years.

When the Ottomans had attacked Venetian-held Cyprus in 1570 it caused the immediate formation of a Christian holy league against the Turks and led to the battle of Lepanto. The reaction in Christian Europe to the attack on Crete in 1645 was decidedly muted. The pope did not call for a crusade to aid the Venetians, and western European states took a largely pragmatic view of the conflict, putting their own interests before religious considerations. Nevertheless, over the long years of the siege foreign volunteers and mercenaries from Italy, France and Germany joined the Venetian defenders on the ramparts of Candia at various times, as did a contingent from the Hospitallers. In 1669 the Venetian commander, Francisco Morosini, decided that the fortress could no longer hold out, so he negotiated its surrender to the Turks.

By the time Candia finally fell, it was reckoned that 30,000 Christian troops had been killed or wounded in its defence, 96 sorties had been made against the besiegers, 53,000 tons of gunpowder had been used, and more than 270,000 cannon balls fired.

That Candia held out for so long was largely due to the decline in the Ottoman navy that had taken place since its glory days in the previous century. The Venetian navy was strong enough to keep Candia supplied while disrupting Turkish maritime communications with their forces in Crete. Both sides now had galleons as well as galleys in their fleets, but the Venetians had made a more successful transition to the square-rigged sailing galleon carrying a large battery of guns. In 1649 the Venetians beat an Ottoman fleet near Smyrna and in 1651 had a similar success off Naxos. The Ottoman fleet was steadily driven out of the Aegean Sea, and by 1656 Venetian naval power was so dominant that it threatened to close the Dardanelles and starve Constantinople. An attempt by the Ottoman fleet to break the blockade was defeated, leading to a revolution in the capital and the appointment of Albanian-born Mehmed Koprulu as grand vizier. In 1657 he organized the recapture of the islands of Tenedos and Lemnos, thus depriving the Venetians of bases near the Dardanelles and ending the blockade. As well as pursuing a more vigorous war against Venice, the grand vizier also took action against the ruler of Transylvania, a rebellious vassal of the Ottomans. By the time of Mehmed Koprulu's death in 1661 Transylvania was once again under Ottoman control.

Mehmed Koprulu was followed by his son Ahmed, who reacted to Austrian meddling in Transylvania by invading Austrian territory in 1663. In a larger campaign in 1664, it seemed that the Turks might threaten Vienna, but they were defeated at the battle of St Gotthard. Despite their victory, the Austrians were keen to make peace and gave the Turks lenient terms in a treaty agreed soon after the battle. Unusually, the victorious Christian army at St Gotthard had included a large contingent of French troops. Since the time of Francis I back in the sixteenth century, France had been an important ally of the Ottomans because of their mutual hatred of the Habsburgs. This situation was soon restored once the young Louis xiv obtained greater control of French foreign policy.

Having finally snuffed out the last Christian resistance on Crete in 1669, the Ottomans then turned their attention to war in the Ukraine. Some of the free Cossack communities of the Ukrainian steppes had asked for Ottoman assistance in resisting the advances of the Poles and

Russians. The Ottomans, aided by their Crimean Tatar vassals, were happy to answer this call, invading the Ukraine in 1672. Defeating the Poles, the Ottomans soon captured Kamienic Podolski, the chief city of Podolia. The Polish military leader John Sobieski then won several victories over the Turks and was elected king of Poland in 1674. Nevertheless, the annual Turkish campaigns began to wear down Christian resistance and in 1676 Sobieski made peace with the Ottomans, giving them the territory of Podolia. The Ottoman empire had now reached its greatest territorial extent in Europe.

Just before the settlement with the Poles, the Cossack allies of the Ottomans went over to the Russians, and the Turks continued to campaign against these two adversaries for several more years. By 1681 developments in Hungary demanded that the Ottomans make peace with the Russians. Kara Mustapha, brother-in-law and successor of Ahmed Koprulu, made some territorial concessions to the Russians, but kept Podolia. Between 1645 and 1680 the Ottomans had taken both Crete and a large part of the Ukraine from the Christians, while the latter had taken no territory from them. The Ottoman ability to campaign in the Ukraine every year from 1672 to 1680 showed that Turkish military capacity was still a formidable force, but it was soon to face its greatest challenge.

TO VIENNA AND BACK

In 1678 the French had been trying to stir up a revolt among the Hungarians in Habsburg territory, but their efforts had ended when they made peace with the Austrians. The Ottomans then began to stir the pot of Hungarian discontent, eventually recognizing the rebel leader as 'Prince of Middle Hungary'. With the French still posing a threat in the Rhineland, Emperor Leopold I was reluctant to see Austria go to war with Ottomans. However, French agents encouraged Kara Mustapha to march on Vienna by promising that France would not aid Austria. In the summer of 1683 the grand vizier led an army of more than 100,000 men into Austrian territory and was further reinforced by contingents from the Ottoman vassal states of Transylvania, Wallachia, Moldavia and the Crimea. It was one of the largest armies the Ottoman Turks had ever sent against the Christians, far outnumbering the Austrian force of 33,000 men under Charles, Duke of Lorraine, which initially opposed it.

Leopold begged for support from other Christian states and Pope Innocent XI pressed all Catholics to unite in opposition to the Turks.

German and Polish forces began to assemble with the aim of assisting the Austrians, but the Turks were making rapid progress. Leaving covering forces to contain untaken fortresses on the Austrian frontier, Kara Mustapha made directly for Vienna, from which Leopold fled in early July and went to Passau in Bavaria. The defence of Vienna was left to Graf Ernest Rudiger von Starhemberg, who burnt the suburbs of the city to deny cover to the Ottomans. Vienna was surrounded by the Turks on 16 July and the besiegers were soon making assaults on its defences. Lacking heavy siege guns, the Ottomans relied on undermining the defences and achieved some success. Casualties were high on both sides, caused by battle and disease, but the Turks made steady progress. On 4 September, with the Turks almost on the point of breaking through, Starhemberg ordered distress rockets to be fired to urge the relief army to action.

A relief army of perhaps 60,000 Austrians, Germans and Poles had been assembled by the end of August, with the Polish king John III Sobieski in overall command. Early in September the army began to advance through the wooded hills near Vienna, but Kara Mustapha, although informed of the enemy movements, made little preparation to resist attack. In particular he failed to remove artillery from his siege works to use against the approaching Christian army. On 12 September 1683 Sobieski's forces attacked the Ottomans and defeated them at the battle of the Kahlenberg just outside the city. Vienna was saved and the Turkish forces fled to their own territory, where Kara Mustapha received the usual reward for such a major defeat: strangulation by the sultan's executioners.

In 1684 the pope forged a holy league with the Austrians, the Poles and the Venetians to continue the war against the Ottomans. Although it was an Orthodox Christian state, Russia became associated with this Catholic league in 1686. This was perhaps the most formidable Christian coalition the Ottomans had yet faced. Although the members of the league failed to coordinate their operations to any great degree, the disciplined weight of their forces proved a serious challenge to the Turks, who had to spread their forces across a number of fronts, stretching from southern Greece via Hungary to the eastern Ukraine. Nevertheless, Ottoman resistance was to make Christian advances slow work. An Austrian attack on Buda in Hungary was defeated in 1684, and it was not until 1686 that the city was finally captured. Then the tempo of the Christian advance picked up. In August 1687 Austrian forces under Charles of Lorraine defeated the Ottoman grand vizier Suleiman

Pasha at the battle of Harkány. After this defeat the Ottoman field army mutinied and was inoperative for months. By the end of 1688 Transylvania and most of Hungary were in Austrian hands and they had taken Belgrade from the Turks. In the following year the Austrians pushed as far south as Skopje in Macedonia and in 1690 they advanced to Bucharest in Wallachia. It seemed the Ottomans might be driven completely out of the Balkans.

Unfortunately for the Austrians, they now had to divert troops to western Europe to fight the French, in what became the war of the League of Augsburg. This was to drag on for most of the 1690s, giving the Ottomans an opportunity to rebuild their forces under yet another Koprulu grand vizier, Fazil Mustapha, who soon launched a successful counter-offensive. By the end of 1690 the Turks had regained all the territory they had lost south of the River Danube, reoccupied Belgrade and reasserted their authority in Transylvania. The reconquest of Hungary now seemed possible, but in 1691 the Ottoman army was defeated by an Austrian force under Louis William, Margrave of Baden, at the hard-fought battle of Slankamen. A third of the Austrian army was killed or wounded, but Turkish losses were even higher, with Grand Vizier Fazil Mustapha among the dead.

An Austrian attempt to recapture Belgrade failed in 1693, and from 1695 Ottoman fortunes seemed to revive once again under the energetic new sultan Mustapha II. As the war against Louis XIV of France was winding down, however, the Austrians could transfer new forces to the Ottoman front, along with their increasingly successful general Prince Eugène of Savoy. In 1697 Eugène surprised Sultan Mustapha at Zenta while the Turkish army was crossing the River Tisza. The Turks were slaughtered, supposedly suffering 30,000 casualties to Eugène's 300, and the sultan was lucky to escape with his life. The victory established Prince Eugène's military reputation and made the Ottomans desperate for peace.

In contrast to the earlier wars between the Austrian Habsburgs and the Ottomans, the years between 1683 and 1697 saw no fewer than fifteen major battles. Of these, the Ottomans won two, one was indecisive, and twelve were won by the Christian forces. Gone were the days when war between the two sides was largely a matter of sieges and raiding. The Turks clearly no longer had sufficient military skill to achieve victory over the Christians in field battles. The Ottoman armies still had numbers and often reckless courage on their side, but they now lacked the order, discipline and military technique that had once made the janissaries the terror of Christian Europe. They also suffered from poor leadership, with men like Fazil Mustapha and Mustapha II as rare exceptions. While the military genius of Prince Eugène would overwhelm almost any enemy, even less gifted commanders like Charles of Lorraine and Louis William of Baden could inflict major defeats on the Ottomans.

The victories over the Ottomans were not all on the Hungarian front. After several attempts, Peter the Great, Czar of Russia, captured the fortress of Azov, near the Black Sea, from the Turks in 1696. A Greek revolt in the Morea helped the Venetians to expel the Turks from that area in the years 1685–7. The Venetians then advanced into Attica and attacked Athens in 1687. The Turks withdrew to the Acropolis, where they stored their ammunition in the Parthenon. A Venetian mortar bomb blew up the ammunition store, reduced the Parthenon to the ruins we see today, and forced the Turks to surrender. Later Venetian attacks on Euboea in 1689 and Crete in 1692 were defeated, while their capture of Chios in 1694 was reversed the following year.

The Austrian, Russian and Venetian successes taken together forced the Ottomans to make peace in 1699. By the treaty of Karlowitz the Ottomans ceded Transylvania and most of Hungary to Austria, Podolia to Poland, and the Morea to Venice. A truce was agreed with Peter the Great soon afterwards, with the Russians keeping Azov. For the first time in their history the Ottoman Turks had been comprehensively defeated by Christian forces and compelled to hand over large territories to their enemies. The only comfort for the Ottomans was that these lands were Christian majority areas, so comparatively few Muslims came under infidel rule. In general, at the start of the eighteenth century, the outlook for the Ottomans was grim.

A chance to take revenge on at least one of their Christian enemies was offered to the Ottomans in 1708. Charles XII of Sweden was at war with Peter the Great and in that year the Swedes invaded Russia. The Cossacks of the Ukraine supported the invaders, but the Ottomans and their Crimean Tatar vassals remained aloof. The Swedes were defeated by Peter at Poltava in 1709 and Charles XII fled to Ottoman territory, where he eventually persuaded the Turks to declare war on Russia. Perhaps overconfident after his success at Poltava, Peter led a Russian army into Moldavia in 1711 and called on Balkan Christians to rise up against the Turks. His call was largely ignored and the Ottoman army surrounded the Russians on the River Pruth. Unable to escape, the czar came to terms with his enemy. The subsequent treaty was remarkably lenient, with the Russians merely having to give up Azov, and there were accusations that Turkish officials had been bribed by the Russians.

Encouraged by their success against Czar Peter, the Ottomans went to war with the Venetians at the end of 1714. The Orthodox Christian inhabitants of the Morea had grown tired of their Catholic masters, so they gave little assistance to the Venetians when the Turks overran the area in 1715. This further Ottoman success alarmed the Austrians, and a new war broke out between the two sides in 1716. In August of that year Prince Eugène inflicted a major defeat on the Ottomans at Peterwardein and then went on to capture Temesvár. In 1717 Eugène was besieging Belgrade when a huge Turkish army arrived to relieve the city. The prince escaped from his difficult position by launching a surprise attack on the new arrivals and completely routed them. Belgrade surrendered soon afterwards, and was retained by the Austrians at the treaty of Passarowitz in 1718. The treaty also gave the Banat of Temesvár and territories south of the Danube to Austria, but the Turks were not required to return the Morea to Venice.

The Austrians had been suspicious of the Russians in the past, but the two states grew closer during the 1730s. In 1736–7 they launched a joint attack on the Ottomans. For the Austrians it proved a disastrous venture and they suffered defeats at the hands of the Turks. The Russians made some progress along the northern shores of the Black Sea, but all their attempts to seize the Crimea failed. France encouraged Austrian suspicions of the Russians and helped the Turks to obtain the favourable treaty of Belgrade in 1739. The Austrians had to give up Belgrade and all their gains at Passarowitz, while the Russians retained only Azov, which had to be demilitarized.

Thus the situation facing the Ottomans – which in 1699 had seemed so hopeless – had by 1740 improved a good deal. Both Austria and Venice had suffered losses at the hands of the Turks, while Russia had made only minor gains. However, Ottoman success at the peace conferences was increasingly due less to their own strength and more to the diplomatic intervention of other powers who preferred a weak Ottoman empire to the growing power of Austria and Russia. Christian solidarity had largely disappeared in international relations. It was not the balance between Christian and Muslim states that mattered, but the balance of power between all states, whatever their religious convictions. As Ottoman military power began its steady decline after 1740, the Turks became more and more dependent on the diplomatic support of other, usually Christian, states.

THE BRITISH AND MUGHAL INDIA

The 1740s were to witness crucial changes in the impact of the Christian European powers on the Muslim Mughal empire in India. By the mid-seventeenth century the Dutch and then the English had eclipsed the Portuguese as the predominant European power in Indian seas. The Europeans were chiefly interested in trade and had little impact on internal political developments in India. During the 1680s the English East India Company rashly embarked on a war with the Mughals, but was forced to make a humiliating peace in 1690. The English had sent 300 soldiers to India to fight this war at a time when the Mughal emperor could easily field an army of 100,000 men.

Although the Mughal emperor and his nobles were Muslims, the survival of the empire depended on the continued submission of the majority Hindu population of India and the cooperation of vassal Hindu rulers. Aurangzeb, the last of the so-called Great Mughals, followed a more strictly Islamic policy than his predecessors and increasingly alienated his Hindu subjects. After Aurangzeb's death in 1707, the Mughal empire began to decline. A number of Muslim and Hindu successor states began to emerge, although they still paid nominal allegiance to the Mughal emperor in Delhi, and the British East India Company obtained imperial recognition of its trading and other privileges in 1717.

By the 1740s the power of the Mughal emperor was declining steadily, while the British East India Company was now embroiled in a bitter conflict with its French trading rival both on India's coasts and further inland. Europeans had always had superiority at sea over the native Indian states, but now they began to build up substantial military power on land as well. Both the British and the French assembled large armies of their own Indian troops (known as 'sepoys') and enlisted additional military help from allied Indian states. By the mid-1750s the British were beginning to gain the upper hand over their French rivals, and some Indian rulers became concerned about the growing British power. In 1756 the Nawab of Bengal seized Calcutta from the British and the East India Company sent an army under Robert Clive to recapture the trading post.

At the battle of Plassey in June 1757 Clive defeated the Nawab of Bengal. Soon the British had taken control of his state, once one of the richest provinces of the Mughal empire. Now a coalition of Indian rulers, including the current Mughal emperor, Shah Alam II, tried to halt further British advances, but their forces were defeated at the battle of Buxar in 1764. The following year the Mughal emperor recognized British control of Bengal, and the Company accepted his nominal position as their overlord. In fact, Mughal power in northern India had come to an end.

The principal Muslim resistance that the British encountered in India during the second half of the eighteenth century came from the state of Mysore in southern India. A Muslim soldier called Haidar Ali Khan seized control of the state in 1761 and assisted the French in their struggles with the British. In the first two Mysore wars (1767–9 and 1780–84), Haidar and his son Tipu Sultan held the British to a draw, although Tipu's destruction of a British force at the first battle of Polilur (1780) was the worst defeat inflicted upon them by Indian forces up to that date. Haidar died in 1782, and his successor Tipu sent an embassy to the Ottoman sultan in 1785 to alert the Islamic world to British designs on India's Muslim powers. The embassy also sought to effect a political and commercial alliance, and to elicit from the sultan, as the successor of the caliphs, recognition of Tipu's status as a legitimate Islamic sovereign. The Ottoman sultan proved unhelpful, and a Mysore embassy to its old ally France in 1787 also had little result, although French experts were brought back to help modernize Tipu's army.

The third Mysore war (1790–92) was declared and largely conducted by Lord Cornwallis, trying to recapture the military reputation he had lost at Yorktown in 1781 by surrendering to the Americans and French. Tipu was eventually driven back to his capital, Seringapatam, and forced to agree terms by which he gave up much of his territory. However, the British continued to view Tipu with suspicion. After Napoleon landed in Egypt in 1798 and talked of going on to India, Tipu's fate was sealed. Richard Wellesley, Earl of Mornington, provoked the fourth Mysore war in 1799 and sent a British army (including his brother Arthur, later Duke of Wellington) against Tipu. Seringapatam was stormed and Tipu died in the fighting, the last major Muslim opponent of the British conquest of India.

In 1803, during a war against the Hindu Mahrattas, General Lake's British army seized Delhi and took control of the Mughal emperor. Now renamed the king of Delhi, the former emperor became a pensioner of the East India Company and his realm did not extend much beyond his residence, the Red Fort in Delhi. But if the emperor's powers were being circumscribed, so were the Company's, as it fell more and more under the direct control of the British government and parliament. In 1813, during negotiations for the renewal of its charter, the Company was forced to give way to the demands of the Evangelical movement in England and abandon its long-standing refusal to allow Christian missionaries to operate in its Indian territories. For the next four decades Christian missionary activity increased in India, offending both Muslims and Hindus, and it was one of the reasons that those two groups cooperated in the great rebellion of 1857 in the Bengal army, known to the British as the Indian Mutiny. The king of Delhi was briefly restored to his position as Mughal emperor by the rebels, but British victory led to his final deposition in 1858. Yet this was really just homage to an already long-dead past. The Mughal empire had died in the eighteenth century, when the Ottoman empire had also been struggling to survive the increasing power of its Christian enemies.

RUSSIAN VICTORIES

Between the 1740s and the 1760s both Austria and Russia lost interest in the Turks, concentrating instead on the wars in central Europe provoked by Frederick the Great of Prussia. For 30 years the Ottomans had peace on their European frontiers. This seemed to be an opportunity to modernize the Turkish armed forces in preparation for the inevitable renewal of Christian attacks. Unfortunately, the Ottoman government proved unable to carry even this limited modernization very far. Russia's increasing intervention in the affairs of Poland forced the Ottomans to take an increasingly belligerent stance against the Russians. When war finally broke out in 1768, the Turks faced a hard struggle against an increasingly superior enemy.

Under Catherine II the modernization of the Russian army, which had been begun by Peter the Great, made further progress. Peter had eased the path to modernity by destroying the old military class, the *streltsi*, towards the end of the seventeenth century. Ottoman military modernization continued to be obstructed by the conservatism of the janissaries, whose power was only broken by Mahmud II in 1826. Although the Russians had initially been heavily dependent on foreign military advisers, by Catherine's reign their numbers were declining and the native Russian officer corps was increasingly skilled in modern warfare. In particular, Russian generals at last succeeded in mastering the logistics of moving a large European army across the vast and empty steppes.

A sign of growing Russian military confidence was the decision in 1769 to send warships to the Mediterranean to attack Ottoman territory there. It was a bold move for a navy that had little experience of mounting long-distance operations. The outward voyage from the Baltic was made easier when the Russian warships were allowed to re-supply at British ports on the way. Arriving in March 1770, the Russian squadron established a base at Navarino in the Morea. In July the Russian force of nine ships of the line, under Admiral Orlov, attacked a Turkish fleet of sixteen ships of the line near the harbour of Chesme between Chios and the Anatolian mainland. Shortly after the ships leading the opposing lines opened fire on each other they both exploded, killing most of those on board. This caused most disorder in the Turkish fleet, which fled into the bay of Chesme and anchored under protecting gun batteries. In a night fireship attack several days later the Russians set most of the Ottoman fleet ablaze and destroyed it. Chesme was the greatest Ottoman defeat at sea since Lepanto in 1571. Although British naval officers in the Russian service played an important part in the success, they did so under Russian command and with Russian-manned ships. Like the Russian army, the navy was now increasingly modernized and outgrowing any need to depend on foreign instructors. The same could not be said for the Ottoman fleet, for whatever the quality of its ships, leadership was poor and skill in modern naval warfare lacking. This was clearly shown by the Russian ability to dominate the eastern Mediterranean in the following years, with operations in the Aegean Sea, off the coast of Egypt, and along the Lebanese coast, including the capture of Beirut in 1773.

In the land war Russian forces under General Rumiantsev defeated the Turks at the battles of Larga and Kagul in 1770 and advanced to the Danube. Rumiantsev had less success in 1771, but other Russian forces invaded and occupied the Crimea during that year. Russian advances then ceased for a time as troops were drawn away to assist in the first partition of Poland (1772) and to suppress the Pugachev revolt (1773–5) within Russia. Only in 1774 did the Turkish war regain priority. Rumiantsev sent forces across the Danube, defeated the Turks at Kozludzhi and threatened to advance towards Constantinople.

The Ottomans now made peace by the treaty of Kutchuk Kainardji, and it proved a turning point in the story of Turkish decline. The Ottoman frontier was pulled back to the River Bug and the Crimea was given 'independence'. In fact, this grant meant little, and the Crimea was formally annexed by Russia in 1783. For the first time the Ottomans had been forced to hand over a Muslim population to Christian rule. The Russians also obtained navigation rights for their ships on the

Black Sea and permission for them to pass through the Straits (the Bosphorus and the Dardanelles) into the Mediterranean. The Ottoman domination of the Black Sea, which had lasted since the late fifteenth century, was now at an end.

There was also a clause in the treaty that the Russians chose to interpret as giving them the right to act as protector of Orthodox Christians within the Ottoman empire. France had claimed such a general right with regard to Catholics in the empire since the sixteenth century, while Austria claimed to be protector of the Catholic inhabitants in Ottoman areas of the Balkans. As Turkish power declined, such rights as protectors were to be exploited by the Christian powers to interfere even more in the internal affairs of the Ottoman empire.

Grigori Potemkin had distinguished himself as a cavalry general during the Russo-Turkish war, and, after being Catherine the Great's lover for a time, he became virtual co-ruler with her for the rest of his life. Potemkin's particular role was to expand and develop 'New Russia', the lands taken from the Ottomans and their vassals along the northern shores of the Black Sea. Potemkin also encouraged Catherine in the so-called Greek project. Emboldened by success in the war of 1768–74, the czarina now dreamed of liberating Constantinople and creating a new version of the Byzantine empire, with her grandson as its ruler. An Austrian alliance was needed if this plan was ever to become a reality, and after Joseph II became sole ruler of Austria in 1780 he made a secret agreement with Catherine.

In 1787 Catherine made a triumphant tour of 'New Russia', and this provoked the Ottomans into declaring war on Russia in the hope of regaining the Crimea. As a first step, the Turks sought to take control of the Liman, as the estuary of the River Dnieper was known. On one side of the Liman was the Turkish fortress of Ochakov; on the other the Russian fortress of Kinburn. General Suvorov beat off several Ottoman attacks on Kinburn in 1787, and in the following year Russian naval forces won control of the Liman in a series of battles. The American naval hero John Paul Jones was a commander on the Russian side, but left Catherine's service soon afterwards. Potemkin, the Russian commander-in-chief, then began a siege of Ochakov, but the fortress was not finally taken until the very end of 1788.

Conflict with Sweden in the Baltic prevented the Russians from sending a fleet to the Mediterranean to fight the Turks as they had done during the previous war, but Joseph II honoured his treaty with Catherine and joined the war, thus forcing the Turks to divide their forces. The 'hinge' of the Austro-Russian front was in Moldavia, and it was here that the Ottomans chose to attack in 1789, hoping to drive their enemies apart. However, Russian forces under Suvorov and Austrians under Coburg cooperated to defeat the Turks at Fokshany and Rymnik. Before the end of the year the Austrians had captured Belgrade and advanced into Wallachia, while the main Russian army under Potemkin had reached the mouth of the Danube.

The Turks seemed to be in a difficult position, but the death of Joseph II in early 1790 gave them some relief. Emperor Leopold II, the new ruler of Austria, was more worried about the situation in revolutionary France than continuing the Turkish war. He quickly made peace with the Ottomans, returning all Austria's gains. The Russians now redoubled their efforts to force the Turks to submit. The Russian Black Sea fleet, under Admiral Ushakov, defeated a Turkish squadron off Tendra, and before the end of 1790 Russian forces under Suvorov stormed Ismail, the last major Turkish fortress on the lower Danube. The Turks now entered peace negotiations, but their procrastination provoked further Russian attacks in the summer of 1791. Ushakov won a further naval success, while a Russian army crossed the Danube and defeated the Ottomans at Manchin. A truce was then agreed and peace was finally achieved by the treaty of Jassy in January 1792. The Ottomans accepted the Russian annexation of the Crimea, gave up Ochakov, and brought their frontier back to the river Dniester.

The wars of 1768–74 and 1787–92 had given the Russians control of the northern shores of the Black Sea. The Ukrainian steppes were excellent agricultural country, and the Russians soon brought in colonists to develop them. One of the motives for the Russian wars against the Ottomans was to obtain harbours on the Black Sea to provide outlets for the new agricultural region. As early as 1793 a fifth of Russia's cereal exports went through the Bosphorus and the Dardanelles. Turkish control of these straits would remain a major vexation for the Russians, but for the moment peace returned to the Ottoman frontiers in Europe as even the Russians became concerned about the activities of revolutionary France.

FRIEND AND ENEMY OF FRANCE

Religious Muslims might seem to have little in common with 'godless' French revolutionaries, but the old alliance with France was not forgotten in the Ottoman empire and the Turks shared the same enemies, such as Austria and Russia, with the French revolutionaries. In addition, Selim III, sultan from 1789, was a keen francophile. After the conclusion of the war with Russia in 1792, Selim sought to build a new, modern army, separate from the old janissaries and *sipahis*, and he hoped for French assistance in this task. However, the new army grew only slowly and for effective military forces Selim had increasingly to rely on those maintained by the provincial notables or *ayans*. Most of the Ottoman sultans during the eighteenth century were weak characters and the distant provinces of the empire became increasingly independent under the rule of local families. Although none of these *ayans* wished to break up the empire, some of them carried on their own foreign and trade policies. In Egypt, for example, the Mamluks had regained control and in 1785 opened the country to French traders, who already dominated most of the external trade of the Ottoman empire.

It was against this background of growing local autonomy and increased French economic penetration that Napoleon Bonaparte made his decision to launch a seaborne attack on Egypt in 1798. He seems to have expected Sultan Selim to raise no objection to French occupation of part of his empire. However, the sultan's sympathy for France did not extend that far. Although Napoleon was a godless revolutionary who played at being a Muslim sympathizer once he reached Egypt, the appearance of his army in the Middle East could only be viewed in one way by most Muslims. For the first time since the fall of the crusader states in 1291, western Christians were making a direct attack on the heartland of Islamic civilization.

Napoleon had already disposed of two old enemies of the Ottoman empire, abolishing the Venetian republic in 1797 and ending the rule of the Hospitallers on Malta in 1798. Once in Egypt he defeated the Mamluks at the battle of the Pyramids and occupied Cairo, one of the greatest cities of the Islamic world. Then Admiral Nelson destroyed the French fleet at the battle of the Nile, and a British naval blockade cut Napoleon off from France. Undaunted, the French general now put forward wild schemes for either marching across the Middle East to expel the British from India or marching to Vienna via Constantinople. Either way, he seemed ready to break up the Ottoman empire.

Reluctantly, Selim III went to war with the French and enlisted British support. In 1799 Napoleon invaded Palestine and marched on Acre, the base of one of the most formidable of the *ayans*, Ahmed Jezzar Pasha. Using his own forces, reinforced by troops from Selim and British sailors under Sir Sydney Smith, Ahmed Jezzar Pasha repulsed all Napoleon's attacks on the walls of Acre. Eventually Napoleon gave in and withdrew to Egypt. An Ottoman army then attempted a seaborne invasion, but the invaders were destroyed by Napoleon soon after they came ashore at Aboukir Bay. Despite this success, Napoleon no longer felt his destiny was in the east. He managed to slip through the British naval blockade and returned to France, leaving most of his army behind. Eventually in 1801 the British invaded Egypt and forced the French to surrender, thus restoring the country to Ottoman rule.

When the Napoleonic war broke out in 1803, the French avoided provoking the Ottomans and did their best to win Selim over to their side. Finally in 1806 the Ottomans declared war on France's enemy Russia, and this also led to conflict with the British. In 1807 Admiral Duckworth forced his way through the Dardanelles and anchored his fleet off Constantinople, but the Turks were unimpressed and Duckworth was lucky to get his fleet back safely to the Mediterranean. Similarly, a British invasion of Egypt was a failure, being successfully opposed by the new Ottoman viceroy, Muhammad Ali. The Turks achieved less success against the Russians, who soon overran Moldavia and Wallachia. More damaging for Selim was his failure to prevent Wahhabi Islamic fundamentalists, led by the Saud family, from sweeping out of Arabia and seizing the holy cities of Mecca and Medina. Muslim religious leaders in Constantinople turned against Selim and supported the janissaries when they revolted in protest at the continued growth of the sultan's new army. Selim was deposed and a truce arranged with Russia. In 1808 a new sultan, Mahmud II, narrowly survived another janissary revolt. Further French encouragement led the Ottomans to renew the war with Russia in 1809, but two years later a successful campaign by General Kutuzov exposed the continuing Ottoman military weakness. Finally, in 1812 Britain was able to arrange peace between the Turks and Russians, although the Ottomans had to give up Bessarabia as part of the deal.

Revolutionary and Napoleonic France had distracted most of the main enemies of the Ottoman empire for several decades. Apart from the French intervention in Egypt in the years 1798–1801, the Ottomans had generally been favourable to their old ally. By 1815, however, they had paid a price for this, losing more territory to Russia, and the czar's armies emerged from the French wars apparently stronger than ever. French predominance in Europe could no longer be taken for granted and new forces were at work on the international stage.

BARBARY AND THE CREATION OF THE UNITED STATES NAVY

One new power was the United States of America, and the creation of its navy was to be closely linked with the Barbary states of North Africa. For much of the seventeenth century the Barbary pirates had gone from strength to strength. In the first decades of the century Christian renegades such as the English pirate John Ward had introduced them to the merits of the square-rigged sailing ship, and this had allowed the corsairs to visit more distant waters. Galleys were still useful in the Mediterranean, but square-rigged sailing ships could raid far into the Atlantic. Before 1650 the Barbary corsairs had carried out raids for slaves on the southern coasts of both England and Ireland, and had even gone as far as Iceland and the Newfoundland fisheries in their quest for captives and booty. The growth of British, French and Dutch sea power did something to curb their activities, but the Barbary pirates were never completely halted. Even the great Christian naval powers were ready to make some payments to the pirates. In return the pirates promised not to molest merchant ships of those nations if they were carrying the appropriate Mediterranean pass. The smaller maritime powers had to pay regular tribute to the Barbary states in the hope of obtaining immunity. The Spanish, however, remained the constant enemy for the Muslim corsairs. Only in the 1790s did Algiers make its first treaty with Spain, 300 years after the fall of Granada.

Before the American revolution, American ships on trading voyages to the Mediterranean were protected by the world's greatest naval power, Britain. After the United States achieved its independence, such ships had no protection at all since its Continental Navy had been abolished at the end of the revolutionary war. The Barbary states were not slow to exploit American weakness and many ships were lost to the corsairs. Finally, in 1794 Congress laid the basis for a United States navy by ordering the construction of a number of frigates suitable for fighting the Barbary pirates. Between 1795 and 1797, treaties were agreed between the United States and Algiers, Tripoli and Tunis, with the Americans agreeing to pay tribute in return for immunity for their ships. These diplomatic agreements did not, however, stop the construction of the frigates, and by 1800 the United States had a strong naval force ready to oppose the Barbary corsairs if required.

Attacks by Muslim corsairs on American ships in 1800 brought an American naval squadron to the Mediterranean in the following year. Tripoli was the worst offender, but US operations had little impact on the Libyan port. Then in 1803 an American frigate ran aground off Tripoli and was captured along with its crew. A daring American operation in 1804 destroyed the captured frigate, but the crew remained prisoners. A scheme was then hatched to support a pretender to the throne of Tripoli, and in 1805 his supporters captured Derna in eastern Libya with American assistance. With a strengthened us squadron blockading his port and a pretender on the march, the ruler of Tripoli came to terms and released his American prisoners.

American warships returned to the Barbary states in 1815 to inflict punishment on Algiers for attacking American merchantmen. After this action the United States did not encounter militant Islam again until the American occupation of the Philippines from 1898 led to conflict with the Muslim (Moro) inhabitants of the group's southern islands. A British and Dutch squadron bombarded Algiers in 1816, but such punitive acts never had much lasting impact. The piracy of the Barbary states would end only when they were actually occupied by Christian powers, which in the case of Algiers and Tunis meant France. The physical occupation of Muslim countries by the imperialist Christian powers of Europe was to be one of the major developments in the Christian–Muslim conflict during the nineteenth century.

9

TRIUMPH OF THE WEST, 1815–1918

A CHRISTIAN TRIUMPH?

The nineteenth century saw European civilization triumph on a world-wide scale. Its economic and military power seemed irresistible, and the roots of this success lay in the scientific, commercial and industrial revolutions that had been going on in Europe since the seventeenth century. To some commentators, European power represented the triumph of secular materialism, but most nineteenth-century Europeans (and their American offspring) would have rejected any idea that worldly success could be separated from divine favour. Just as the Arabs had seen their spectacular conquests after the death of the Prophet as a sign of God's approval of Islam, so Europeans in the nineteenth century saw their economic and military dominance as proof of God's support of Christianity.

As European imperialism spread across the globe, Muslims were among its principal victims. They could never accept that European success had anything to do with the superiority of the Christian religion. Yet Christianity benefited enormously from the spread of European power and influence. The nineteenth century saw an expansion of Christianity on a scale not seen since apostolic times, with Christian missionary work spreading around the world. For centuries Islam had been slowly moving southwards in Africa making converts. Now it was challenged by a wave of Christian missionaries, whose spiritual message was reinforced by European traders and European gunboats.

International diplomacy seemed to have moved away from ideological conflict to careful adjustments of a secular balance of power. In this practice Christian states had no qualms about supporting Muslim Ottomans against other Christian powers. However, the centuries-old Christian–Muslim conflict was never far below the surface of events. When the Ottomans oppressed Greeks in the 1820s, Maronites around 1860, Bulgarians in the 1870s and Armenians in the 1890s, European diplomats had to come to the defence of these Christians because of feelings of Christian solidarity in their own countries. It was only in the twentieth century that Christian concerns began to disappear from international diplomacy.

European success was due not only to their own power but also to the failure of other civilizations to adapt to the challenge of modernity. Outside Europe and North America, only one country, Japan, was capable of welding old traditions with new techniques and so matching Western economic and military power. Muslim societies seemed incapable of making such a change. Christians believed that one reason for this was the rigid, conservative nature of Islam, which seemed opposed to all modern innovations. Yet when Muslim states did attempt to modernize, all too often the process only opened them up to even more European interference and control. Muslims struggled to find a way of reconciling Islam with modernity, a struggle that continues to this day. In the nineteenth century Europeans took it for granted that material progress and Christianity marched together and would triumph together. It was only in the twentieth century that it became clear that the success of scientific materialism did not require any religious accompaniment.

European success in the nineteenth century was also a triumph of sea power. When the Portuguese reached India at the end of the fifteenth century, they began an age of oceanic exploration and trade that took European vessels to every sea in the following centuries. The Europeans were no longer confined to a western peninsula of the Eurasian land mass, hemmed in by Muslim power. They had effectively outflanked the Muslims and staked their claim to the wider world. Of the three great Muslim states of the sixteenth century, Safavid Persia and Mughal India had no significant naval power with which to resist the Europeans. Only the Ottoman empire had an effective navy, but that was largely restricted to the Mediterranean, a sea that the Iberian expansion across the oceans soon turned into a maritime backwater.

Not until the opening of the Suez Canal in 1869 was the Mediterranean restored to world importance as a sea route. Even before the canal was built, the Christian powers of Europe were taking a greater interest in the eastern Mediterranean because the Ottoman empire was showing further signs of breaking up, a trend encouraged by both Christian and Muslim forces within it.

BREAKING AWAY

A Serb rebellion in 1804 showed that Christian subjects of the Ottomans were becoming increasingly discontented, but more important separatist tendencies had already been shown by Muslim provincial leaders or *ayans*. Since the 1770s Ali Pasha of Janina had been building up his own territory in Albania and northern Greece, while Muhammad Ali in Egypt was increasingly independent from 1811 onwards. In that year he crushed the old military power in Egypt, the Mamluks, and began to modernize his government and his military forces. The Ottoman sultan, Mahmud II, longed to treat his janissaries in the way that Muhammad Ali treated the Mamluks, but for the moment he was unable to do so. Instead he asked for Muhammad Ali's assistance in crushing the Wahhabi revolt in Arabia. Between 1813 and 1818 Egyptian forces liberated Mecca and Medina and crushed the last Wahhabi resistance. Mahmud II had been unable to act in Arabia, but he did make efforts to curtail the power of the *ayans* in areas near to Constantinople. In a prolonged campaign between 1820 and 1822 his forces finally destroyed the power of Ali Pasha of Janina.

Unfortunately, while Ottoman forces were distracted fighting Ali Pasha, revolts broke out among Greek Christians. A force of Greek nationalists based in Russia invaded Moldavia but were soon defeated. More dangerous was a Christian rising in southern Greece. The Ottomans lost control of the Morea, with many Turks being massacred, while Greek naval forces led by Andrea Miaoulis achieved successes against the Ottoman fleet in the Aegean Sea. On land Greek military leaders like Theodoros Kolokotronis achieved further successes and Ottoman forces proved largely unable to contain the rebellion. This discredited the janissaries and finally gave Mahmud a chance to move against them. By 1826 there were 135,000 janissaries receiving pay and provisions from the Ottoman government, but most had other jobs as well and were militarily useless. Their arrogant ways had finally alienated most sections of Ottoman society, including the religious leaders. In the summer of 1826 Mahmud used his small cadre of modern troops to crush the janissaries in Constantinople, and his example was followed in most major provincial cities with janissary garrisons. The sultan followed up this success by discharging the remaining *sipahis*, whose remaining land grants or *timars* were taken back by the government in 1831. The old Ottoman army was gone, but the new army was barely in existence and would take a long time to organize and train. In the twenty years after 1826 Ottoman military power slumped to its lowest level for centuries. Mahmud was free of the janissaries, but how was he to crush the Greek revolt?

As in the case of the Wahhabis, the sultan turned to Muhammad Ali in Egypt and asked for his military assistance. Muhammad Ali sent a fleet and army under his son Ibrahim to Greek waters in 1825, and by the end of the following year the Egyptians had taken Crete, over-run the Morea, and were attacking towns such as Messolonghi on the mainland. The Greek revolt seemed on the verge of collapse. How-ever, the Greek insurgents had powerful friends among the Christian powers, where public opinion was stirred by the examples of pro-Greek volunteers such as the poet Lord Byron, who died at the siege of Messolonghi. In 1827 a combined British-French-Russian fleet appeared in Greek waters and destroyed Ibrahim's Ottoman-Egyptian fleet at the battle of Navarino. Just as the Christian–Muslim naval battle of Lepanto in 1571 was the last great battle between galley fleets, so Navarino turned out to be the last great battle between fleets of sailing warships.

Ibrahim began to withdraw his forces from Greece, leaving the Ottoman sultan with few military forces to oppose a Russian attack in the Balkans in 1828. The Turks were driven back almost to the gates of Constantinople before they came to terms in 1829. With the other great powers watching them carefully, the Russians could no longer take sig-nificant territory for themselves from the Ottoman possessions in Europe. Instead, they sought to weaken the Ottomans by encouraging Christian separatism within the borders of the empire. The Ottomans were compelled to give autonomy to both the Serbs and the Greeks. In 1832 the Christian powers forced the sultan to make even more conces-sions to the Greeks by agreeing to the establishment of a small, but sovereign, Greek kingdom. For the first time an independent state, and a Christian one at that, had been carved out of the Ottoman empire. Such an event could only encourage the national aspirations of those Balkan Christians still under Ottoman rule.

However, the next threat to the integrity of the Ottoman empire did not come from Christians. Claiming the sultan had failed to reward him adequately for his assistance during the Greek war, Muhammad Ali allowed his son Ibrahim to invade and conquer Palestine and Syria in 1831–2. Ibrahim then led his troops towards Constantinople, and in des-peration the sultan asked for Russian help. The arrival of Russian forces at the capital forced Ibrahim to leave Anatolia, but he still retained Syria and Palestine. In 1839 the sultan tried to recapture Syria, but his forces were easily defeated by Ibrahim and the Ottoman fleet went over to the Egyptians. Once again in fear of an advance on the capital, the Ottoman government called for action by the Christian powers, and even offered reforms within the empire to win that assistance. Muhammad Ali had close links with France and hoped this might deflect Christian actions against him.

The British, however, were deeply concerned about the rise of a modernizing, militarily competent Muslim state in Egypt, since it straddled one of the main routes to India. In 1839 they seized Aden so they could exercise greater control over the Red Sea. The British were determined to humble Muhammad Ali, and the French did little to stop them. In 1840 British, Austrian and Ottoman warships bombarded Beirut and Acre, and Ibrahim was forced to leave Syria and Palestine. Muhammad Ali was compelled to restrict his power to Egypt, with his army and fleet much reduced. He had to renew his obedience to the Ottoman sultan, but his family were confirmed as hereditary rulers of Egypt. If Muslims were not to be allowed to break up the Ottoman empire, this prohibition did not apply to the Christian powers themselves. By the middle of the nineteenth century they had already taken large territories from the Ottomans and other Muslim states, and would continue the process throughout the rest of the century.

EMPIRES

The Dutch had long ruled diverse Muslim populations in the East Indies (now Indonesia), but much of this rule had been indirect, through compliant local sultans. During the Napoleonic wars the British captured Java from the Dutch in 1811 and seriously weakened their hold on the East Indies. Java was returned at the peace, but the Dutch felt the need to reassert their power in the area, especially as Muslim revivalist leaders were encouraging local resistance. From 1821 to 1838 the Padri movement in Sumatra led to a long war with the Dutch, in which the latter finally prevailed. A more serious threat to the main Dutch base of Java was the rebellion inspired by the pious Muslim prince Diponegoro, which began in 1825 and was not suppressed until 1830. The province of Aceh in northern Sumatra had been a major area of Muslim resistance to Christian advances since the sixteenth century. In 1873 the Dutch embarked on what was to prove a very long struggle to subdue the area, not finally being completed until 1908.

Whatever the struggles of the Dutch in the East Indies, their efforts were largely concerned with ending Muslim resistance in areas they already claimed to control. The significant feature of European imperialism in the nineteenth century was its success in bringing new Muslim populations under Christian control. The French began the process in 1830 by seizing Algiers, still tenuously linked to the Ottomans. The invaders alleged they wished to curb the actions of the Barbary pirates, but that threat had declined greatly since 1815. Their real intention was to extend French control along the southern shores of the Mediterranean, but it was to prove no easy task.

Even by 1835 the French hold on Algeria was still restricted to Algiers, Oran and four other coastal towns. Particularly strong resistance was encountered in western Algeria. It was led by Abd el-Kader, the emir of Mascara, who defeated a French force at the Macta Marshes in 1835. In the following year the French managed to capture Mascara and General Bugeaud defeated Abd el-Kader at the Sikkak River. Even so, in 1837 the emir still managed to persuade Bugeaud to agree to the treaty of Tafna, which actually increased the area under Abd el-Kader's control. Both a pious Muslim and an admirer of Muhammad Ali's reforms in Egypt, Abd el-Kader was determined to drive out the French, so in 1839 he renewed the war. In the following year, General Bugeaud returned as governor of Algeria and ordered new offensive tactics to hunt down the elusive emir. Creating mobile columns, stripped of baggage, Bugeaud sent them into Abd el-Kader's country to destroy his supply bases. Harried by the French flying columns, the emir eventually fled to Morocco in 1843. He convinced its ruler to declare war on France, but Bugeaud's victory at Isly in 1844 brought the conflict to a swift end. Undaunted, Abd el-Kader moved back into Algeria and inflicted a defeat on the French at Sidi Brahim in 1845. Nevertheless, internal divisions among Muslims were weakening the emir's power. He retreated once again to Morocco, only to be expelled by the ruler. Finally, in December 1847 Abd el-Kader surrendered to the French and went into exile.

The prolonged struggle of Abd el-Kader had been strengthened by the Sufi brotherhoods, and they were to play an important role in many Muslim resistance movements. Sufism is the mystical branch of Islam and Sufi orders are usually made up of followers who subordinate themselves to a spiritual leader. The Sufi brotherhoods could provide both the motivation and the organization to sustain Muslim resistance activities over long periods. After Abd el-Kader in Algeria, Sufi brotherhoods supported Shamil's resistance in the Caucasus, the Mahdi's uprising in Sudan and the struggle of Senussi tribesmen in Libya.

The French decided on a policy of Christian settlement in Algeria, the first such policy in a Muslim land since the days of Outremer. Bugeaud took a particular interest in such activities, and under his regime the number of French colonists in Algeria was said to have increased from 17,000 to 100,000. France went on to take Tunisia in 1881 and to impose a protectorate on Morocco (never part of the Ottoman empire) in 1912, the same year Italy seized Libya. Muslim North Africa was now entirely under European control. The French also expanded their empire in Muslim West Africa, despite prolonged resistance by local leaders such as Samori Touré.

Russian victories over the Ottomans had brought them control of the northern shores of the Black Sea by the mid-1780s. This success led to greater Russian interest in the Caucasus region that lay between the Black Sea and the long-established Russian possessions on the Caspian Sea. Beyond the Caucasus mountains were Christian Georgians and Armenians who might welcome Russian protection, but most of the local peoples were Muslims, under the largely nominal authority of the Ottoman sultan in the west and the Persian shah in the east. Victory in the Russo-Persian wars of 1811–13 and 1826–7 and the Russo-Turkish war of 1828–9 allowed the Russians to expel these powers from most of the region, but the Muslim tribesmen in and around the Caucasus mountains remained largely unsubdued.

These peoples had first risen against the advancing Russians as early as 1785. Their leader, Sheikh Mansour, however, was captured by the Russians when they took the Ottoman-held port of Anapa in 1791 and died in captivity. In 1818 the Russian general Yermolov set up the fortress of Grozny ('the terrible') in the northern Caucasus in an attempt to control raiding, but with only limited success. In 1829 Imam Ghazi Muhammed roused the Chechens and Daghestanis of the eastern Caucasus against the Christian invader. His declaration of jihad against the Russians began the conflict known as the Murid wars, which would last for the next thirty years. In 1832 Ghazi Muhammed was killed when the Russians stormed his base at Ghimri, but his pupil Shamil escaped and in 1834 he was recognized as imam of Daghestan. Imam Shamil was to be the principal Murid leader for the next quarter of a century.

The Russians struggled to cope with guerrilla attacks from Shamil's followers, but in 1839 General Grabbe finally stormed Akhulgo, Shamil's main stronghold. However, the Muslim leader escaped. He continued his raids, and Russian expeditions against him became almost annual events during the 1840s. Usually the Russian columns wandered through forest and mountain destroying empty villages, but were savaged by guerrilla attacks when they began their long journey back to base. In 1845 General Vorontsov's column reached Shamil's new headquarters at Dargo, only to find it had already been destroyed by the insurgents themselves. When Vorontsov withdrew, his force was so severely harried that it covered only 30 miles in one week and suffered nearly 3,500 casualties.

By 1847 Shamil had an army of about 20,000. He had taken some artillery pieces from the Russians, but these proved more a hindrance than a help, slowing down the movements of his forces. In 1851 a young officer (and later novelist), Leo Tolstoy, joined the Russian forces in the Caucasus and used his military experiences as a basis for later literary output. During the Crimean war Shamil made contact with the Ottomans, but was wary of their British and French allies. The allies sent some arms and money to Shamil's forces, but the imam made no major efforts against the Russians. After the Crimean war was over, the Russians were determined to crush the Caucasian rebel. General Baryatinsky led a large army against Shamil and drove him out of his stronghold at Dargo in early 1859. Shamil moved from place to place, but popular support for his struggle was waning and later in the year he surrendered to the Russians. Muslim resistance now shifted to the Circassians in the western Caucasus, and they were not finally beaten until 1864. Much of the Circassian population then emigrated to the Ottoman empire rather than live under infidel rule.

Once Muslim resistance in the Caucasus had finally been overcome, the Russians increased their expansionist pressure on the Muslim states of Central Asia, aiming particularly at the emirate of Bukhara, the khanate of Khiva and the khanate of Kokand. In 1865 General Cherniaev took Tashkent and in 1868 von Kaufman seized Samarkand. In 1873 the conquest of Khiva was completed, and by 1876 Kokand had been subjugated. Bukhara accepted the status of a Russian protectorate. Turkmenistan was the only Muslim state in the area that had avoided Russian rule, even defeating a Russian invasion in 1879. In 1881, however, General Skobelev stormed the Turkmen fortress of Gok-Tepe and local resistance soon collapsed. Once in control of Muslim Central Asia, the Russians began to encourage Christian Slav settlement, a policy they had already followed in the Crimea and the Caucasus. By 1885 the Russians had advanced to the borders of Afghanistan, and the British rulers of

India became alarmed at the supposed Russian threat, a threat they had been anticipating for the previous fifty years.

By 1830 the British had completed the collapse of the Mughal empire in India and imposed their control over nearly all the sub-continent. It was Afghanistan that was to be the main Muslim challenge for the British in the area. Fearful of possible Russian advances in Central Asia, the British attempted to impose direct control on Afghanistan. In 1839 a British army marched to Kabul and set up a pro-British ruler. He was overthrown a few years later, and when in 1842 the British tried to withdraw from Kabul to India, their army was destroyed by the Afghans before it could reach the Khyber Pass. This disaster would remain the worst British defeat in Asia until the fall of Singapore in 1942. A new British army went into Afghanistan to exact punishment, but did not remain. Instead the British compromised with the new Afghan ruler, accepting his promise not to admit the Russians. A similar scenario of intervention, resistance, punishment and final compromise was played out in the second Anglo-Afghan war in 1878–80. From then on, and despite alarm about Russian advances in the mid-1880s, the British were content to leave Afghanistan as a buffer state over which they had only indirect control.

Concern about the security of communications with India led the British to take a renewed interest in Egypt after the opening of the Suez Canal in 1869. Attempts at indirect control, with French assistance, broke down in 1882 when a nationalist revolt led by an army officer, Ahmad Muhammad Urabi (Arabi Pasha), took place. After bombarding Alexandria, the British invaded Egypt and defeated Urabi's forces at Tel el Kebir. The British permitted an Egyptian government, still nominally under the Ottoman sultan, to continue, but the British themselves were to retain the real power for the next 70 years.

The occupation of Egypt led to British involvement in the Sudan, where Muhammad Ahmad ibn Abdullah, the self-proclaimed Mahdi (the expected deliverer of the Muslims), organized local resistance to both Egyptians and British. Attempts to suppress the Mahdi in 1884–5 were unsuccessful and General Gordon was killed at Khartoum. The Mahdi died soon afterwards, but his successor, the Khalifa Abdullah, held the new state together. Only in 1896 did General Kitchener begin the conquest of the Sudan, finally destroying the Mahdist army at the battle of Omdurman in 1898. A more protracted Muslim resistance was sustained in Somalia under the leadership of Muhammad Abdallah Hasan from 1899 to 1920. Known to the British as the 'Mad Mullah', the

Somali leader forced them to recognize his authority in certain areas in 1904. Hostilities were soon resumed, and it was not until 1920 that Somali resistance was finally crushed.

For Dutch, French, Russian and British imperialists, Muslims were always their most persistent opponents. Usually the Christian powers were victorious in the end, but some Muslim states, chiefly Persia and Afghanistan, retained a measure of independence by becoming buffer states between competing imperialisms. Nevertheless, the main theatre of Christian–Muslim conflict still remained the Ottoman empire, because its fate would have a direct influence on the European balance of power.

THE EASTERN QUESTION

Since the early eighteenth century Russia had emerged as the chief European threat to the continued existence of the Ottoman empire. By the 1850s Czar Nicholas I was calling the Ottoman state the 'Sick Man of Europe' and putting forward suggestions for its partition as the best solution to the 'Eastern Question'. However, Russia's plans were soon to be brought to a halt. Growing tension between Russia and the Ottomans, which worried the British, came at a time when Russia and France were in dispute about the rights of Orthodox and Catholic Christians to look after the holy sites in Palestine. In 1852 Czar Nicholas demanded that the Ottomans reverse their decision to recognize France as the protector of the Christian holy places. In April 1853 the Russian demand became an ultimatum, but the sultan refused to back down; in retaliation, Russian forces occupied Moldavia and Wallachia. Diplomatic efforts were made to persuade the Russians to withdraw, but finally in October 1853 the Ottomans declared war on Russia.

Omar Pasha led an Ottoman force across the Danube and actually inflicted a small defeat on the Russians in early November, a sign that the Ottoman army had recovered some of its military skill. At the end of November 1853, however, a Russian fleet under Admiral Nakhimov attacked a Turkish squadron in the port of Sinope on the southern shores of the Black Sea. Firing explosive shells, the Russians swiftly destroyed the Turkish force. This event outraged public opinion in Britain and France, and warships from those two nations moved into the Black Sea at the start of 1854. In March Britain and France made an alliance with the Ottoman empire and joined the war against Russia.

British and French troops at first landed at Varna to assist Ottoman forces facing the Russians along the Danube. They helped the Turks thwart a Russian attempt to capture Silistria. Then Austria threatened to enter the war on the allied side unless Russian forces withdrew from the Balkans. Reluctantly, the Russians left Moldavia and Wallachia in August 1854, and the allies accepted a temporary Austrian presence in those territories to separate the warring parties. With peace restored to the Balkans, the allies decided in September 1854 to invade the Crimea and capture Sevastopol, the principal Russian naval base on the Black Sea. With their base and fleet gone, the Russians would not be able to repeat the battle of Sinope. The allies soon found the siege of Sevastopol to be a prolonged undertaking and fought several battles to prevent Russian forces from relieving the fortress. Only in June 1855 did Sevastopol finally fall, but by then the Russians were increasingly ready to bring the war to a close.

The Russians made peace by the treaty of Paris in 1856. The Black Sea was to be demilitarized, which was more a blow to the Russians than the Turks. Russia had to give up her Black Sea fleet, but the Turks merely moved their ships through the Straits to the Mediterranean, from where the fleet could easily return. Nevertheless, even when on the winning side, the Ottomans still had to give up territory in the peace settlement. The autonomy of Moldavia and Wallachia was recognized and soon those provinces would unite as the Christian kingdom of Romania, although still nominally subject to the sultan. In return for their assistance, Britain and France insisted that the Ottomans open the Black Sea and the River Danube to the merchant ships of all nations. Russia ceased to be a threat to the Ottomans for a while, but when the Franco-Prussian war of 1870–71 distracted the other powers, the czar denounced the demilitarization of the Black Sea.

The treaty of Paris also admitted the Ottoman empire 'to the public law and system of Europe'; in other words, it became the equal of the great Christian powers of Europe. One consequence of this new status was that the Ottomans could now have access to large financial loans, chiefly from British and French bankers. Such money was in large part used to buy armaments, both to improve external security and to increase the centralized control exercised by the Ottoman government within the empire. In 1867 Sultan Abdul Aziz made an official visit to Britain and France, becoming the first Ottoman sultan to visit Christian countries other than as leader of an invading Muslim army. However, European acceptance of the Ottomans had its limits. The massacre of

Maronite Christians in the Lebanon in 1860 led to French intervention, and when the inhabitants of Crete revolted against the Turks in 1866 the Christian powers almost intervened once again in the internal affairs of the empire.

In the mid-1870s Balkan Christians still under Ottoman rule revolted and were supported by Serbia and Montenegro, which were already autonomous states. The Turks moved to suppress the risings and carried out savage reprisals, which became known as the 'Bulgarian horrors'. Christian Europe was outraged, and in 1877 the czar sent his armies into the remaining Ottoman territory in the Balkans. The new sultan, Abdul Hamid II, sent troops to resist the invaders, and also tried a new weapon. Caliph had been among the titles of the Ottoman sultan since the sixteenth century, but this claim to be the religious leader of all Muslims had not been greatly stressed in the past. Now Abdul Hamid used his authority as caliph to call on all Muslims to resist the Russians, including the Muslims within the Russian empire. The response to this call was not great, but with large Muslim populations in their empires, the British, French and Russians were bound to be concerned about this precedent.

Since the end of the Crimean war the Ottoman government had raised large financial loans in western Europe. Much of the money was spent on armaments, including a fleet of ironclad battleships that for a time made the Ottoman empire the third greatest naval power in Europe after Britain and France. When war broke out with Russia in 1877, the Ottomans had fifteen ironclads in the Black Sea while the Russians had none. Yet by a daring use of torpedo boats and mines the Russians gained ascendancy over their much more powerful rival. The early loss of one ironclad to Russian artillery fire did little to raise the low morale of the Ottoman navy. Its nominal commander, Hobart Pasha, a former British naval officer, made suggestions for offensive operations, but was ignored by the Ottoman government, and most of the Turkish ironclads stayed in port for the duration of the conflict.

If the Russians had been initially worried about the imbalance of forces at sea, they had been much more confident of a swift victory on land. Certainly the Russians advanced quickly through Romania, crossed the Danube, and advanced to the Balkan mountains with little trouble. Then a Turkish army under Osman Pasha threatened the Russian right flank and took up well-entrenched positions at Plevna. Equipped with modern Krupp field guns and the latest American breech-loading rifles, the Turks mowed down the attacking Russian infantry. Finally realizing that the Plevna positions could not be taken by assault, the Russians brought in General Todleben, the famous defender of Sevastopol during the Crimean war, to direct siege operations. Osman Pasha finally surrendered in December 1877, having delayed the whole Russian advance for five months and inflicted more than 40,000 casualties on the Russians and their Romanian allies.

Once Plevna had fallen, the Russian advance picked up speed. In January 1878 they broke through the Shipka pass in the Balkan mountains, took Adrianople and reached the outskirts of Constantinople. The Ottomans made peace at San Stefano, conceding the creation of a large Bulgarian state under Russian influence. The other European powers were unhappy about this expansion of Russian influence, and the treaty was revised by the Congress of Berlin. Only a small Bulgarian kingdom was carved out of Ottoman territory, and it remained nominally subject to the sultan. The Turks, however, were required to recognize Serbia and Romania as fully independent states. The 'defenders' of the Ottoman empire against the Russians also took their shares: Austria began a military occupation of Bosnia-Herzegovina; Britain received Cyprus; and France (in 1881) took Tunisia. It was hard to tell who posed the greater danger to the territorial integrity of the Ottoman empire, the aggressive Russians or the Christian 'defenders' of the Turks.

The events of 1875–8 had been a great blow to the Ottomans. The empire had lost a third of its territory and more than 20 per cent of its population, while 800,000 Muslims fled as refugees to the remaining Ottoman territory. Almost as important, the recognition as a 'European power' that the Ottomans had won at Paris in 1856 was tacitly taken away at Berlin in 1878. Burdened with foreign loans, the Ottoman government had stopped interest payments in 1875. Now much of the country's finances were taken under European control, with the setting up of an Ottoman debt authority in 1881. European diplomats and consuls, aided by local Christians, were ready to intervene in Ottoman internal affairs in many parts of the empire. Understandably, the Muslims increasingly resented the control that the Christian powers exercised over their country.

France, the oldest Christian ally of the Ottomans, fell from favour at Constantinople during the last decades of the nineteenth century, especially after her alliance with Russia in 1894. Britain had done much to defend the Ottomans against the Russian threat during the century, but after seizing Egypt in 1882 the British were more interested in safeguarding the Suez Canal route to India than in bolstering the authority of the sultan. With old supporters drifting away, the Ottomans looked for new allies and found an important one in Germany. Already the leading military and industrial power in Europe, Germany had relatively few Muslims in her overseas empire and had no predatory designs on any Ottoman territory. When German emperor Wilhelm II paid a state visit to the Ottoman empire in 1898 he declared himself 'the friend of the world's 300 million Muslims', and Ottoman-German economic and military links were to grow after 1900.

Yet in the short term the German link could not halt the steady decline of the Ottoman empire. During the 1890s the position of Armenian Christians in the empire became a focus of international attention, and Muslim attacks on them in the years 1894–6 almost led to intervention by the Christian powers. In 1897 open support by Greece for a revolt in Crete led to war with the Ottomans. When there seemed a danger that the Turks might beat the Greeks, the Christian powers intervened to impose a peace, with Crete being given autonomy under international administration in 1898.

The 1890s also saw the beginnings of the political movement that became known as the Young Turks. A modernizing faction who were particularly strong in the Ottoman army, the Young Turks were encouraged by Japan's victory over Russia in their war of 1904–5. For the first time an Asian state had defeated a European imperialist power. If the Ottoman empire could adapt to modern civilization as Japan had done, perhaps it too could revive its power and shake off European domination. An army mutiny at Thessalonica in 1908 led to a political revolution in the capital. The Ottoman constitution of 1876 had been suspended by Sultan Abdul Hamid in 1878; now it was put back in operation. Reactionaries attempted a counter-coup in 1909 and were defeated, with Abdul Hamid deposed and a new sultan installed. If the Young Turks believed the political revolution would halt the Ottoman empire's decline, they were soon to be disappointed.

The Ottoman political upheavals of 1908–9 were quickly exploited by the empire's Christian enemies. Crete passed to Greece; Austria formally annexed Bosnia; and an expanded Bulgaria renounced its last ties to the Ottoman government. In 1911 Italy invaded Libya, the last part of North Africa not under European control. The Ottoman garrisons of the coastal cities were soon overwhelmed, but inland the Senussi tribesmen began a resistance to the Italian invaders that would last for twenty years before they finally succumbed. In Libya the Italians made the first use of aircraft in warfare, carrying out both reconnaissance and bombing missions, but this innovation had little impact. The Ottomans were reluctant to come to terms, so the Italians used their naval superiority over the Turkish fleet to extend operations to the Aegean Sea. The Dardanelles were blockaded for a time, while Rhodes and the rest of the Dodecanese islands were captured by Italian forces. The Ottomans tried to fight on, but attacks by new enemies in the Balkans compelled them to make peace with the Italians in October 1912, letting them retain their conquests.

The poor Ottoman military performance against the Italians had encouraged the small Christian states of the Balkans to seize the chance of expelling the Turks completely from Europe. In October 1912 Montenegro, Serbia, Bulgaria and Greece launched a concerted attack on the Turks, whose military resistance rapidly collapsed. This first Balkan war came to an end early in 1913, with the Ottomans having been driven back almost to Constantinople. Then Bulgaria fell out with her allies, and in the second Balkan war later in 1913 she fought Serbia, Greece, Romania and the Turks, who managed to recapture Adrianople. The great powers then halted the war and the Ottomans preserved a foothold in Europe, while an Albanian state was created at Austrian insistence to prevent the Serbs reaching the sea.

Russia, humiliated by her defeat by Japan in 1905, took no major part in these Balkan upheavals, but they all served her long-term goal of breaking up the Ottoman empire. The most important Ottoman territory that Russia wished to take for herself was the city of Constantinople and the Straits. The grain export trade from the Ukraine was booming, and Russian control of the exit from the Black Sea was vital. For the Turks the defeats of 1912–13 meant the loss of almost all their European territories, including areas such as Macedonia and Thrace that had been part of the Ottoman empire for more than five centuries. In 1908 Thessalonica had been the cradle of the Young Turk revolution; in 1913 the city was in Greece. Almost all the European Christians under Ottoman rule had been liberated by 1914, but it seemed the Christian great powers were still determined to undermine the Ottoman empire, the last bulwark of Muslim power in the world.

FINAL VICTORY

The assassination of the Austrian archduke Franz Ferdinand in Sarajevo in Bosnia in July 1914 began the train of events that led to the First World War. Having been almost completely driven out of the Balkans, the Turks might have avoided any involvement in the war, but the close links of the Ottoman government with Germany made it difficult for them to remain neutral. Britain antagonized the Turks by seizing two battleships being built in British shipyards for the Ottoman navy. Then two German warships, fleeing the British Mediterranean fleet, reached Turkish waters. The German government gave them to the Turks, complete with German crews, and soon the ships were bombarding Russian ports in the Black Sea. By mid-November 1914 the Ottoman empire was at war with Britain, France and Russia.

Once the Ottomans had entered the war on the German side, the sultan exercised his power as caliph by calling on all Muslims in the British, French and Russian empires to rise up against their oppressors. The response to this call was negligible. There would be serious Muslim revolts in Algeria and in Central Asian areas of Russia during the war, but these were caused by French and Russian efforts to force local men into military service rather than as a response to the caliph's call. Nevertheless, the allied powers were conscious of the importance of Muslim troops to their war effort. More than 200,000 North African troops served in Europe for France during the war and most were Muslims. Similarly, Muslims made up a significant part of the army of British India and many would fight against the Turks in the Middle East. The British retaliated against the caliph's call by stirring up revolt among Muslims in the Ottoman empire. They intrigued with the Hashemite ruler of Hejaz, which contained the Muslim holy cities of Mecca and Medina, to launch an Arab revolt against the Turks, although it did not take place until 1916.

The allied powers did not expect the Ottoman army to be a major threat, given its poor record during the wars of 1911–13, and its early performance in the world war seemed to confirm that view. A Turkish offensive against the Russians in the Caucasus region ended in disaster at Sarikamish in January 1915. When the Russians began to advance into eastern Anatolia, the Ottomans alleged that local Armenian Christians were assisting the invaders. The decision was taken to move much of the Armenian population out of the war zone and southwards into Syria and Iraq. In the course of this exodus in 1915–16 the Armenians suffered greatly, with perhaps one million of them dying from ill-treatment, starvation or disease. Removing the Armenians did nothing to halt the Russian advance, and in early 1916 they took the major cities of Erzerum and Trabzon from the Turks.

When the British and French made their amphibious attack on the Gallipoli peninsula in the spring of 1915, they expected a swift breakthrough to Constantinople that might knock the Turks out of the war. Such hopes were quickly dashed. The Ottoman army put up a fierce resistance, and although German officers helped organize the defence, it was the grim tenacity of the Turkish troops, led by officers such as Mustafa Kemal, that brought the victory. In early 1916 the last allied forces were evacuated from the peninsula. The successful defence cost the Turks more than 300,000 casualties, but the losses of the defeated British and French were only a little smaller at 250,000 casualties.

The Turkish victory at Gallipoli came as a shock to the allied powers. Further shocks were administered when a British army advancing in Iraq during 1916 was captured at Kut, and the first British attempts to invade Palestine from Egypt were repulsed at Gaza in early 1917. The British now decided to take their Turkish enemy more seriously. Careful preparations were made and large forces assembled for new attacks in Iraq and Palestine during 1917. General Maude took Baghdad in March 1917, and after turning the Gaza position at the battle of Beersheba in September 1917 General Allenby's army went on to take Jerusalem before Christmas.

East of the River Jordan, Allenby's efforts were assisted by Arab forces that had come north from Hejaz and captured Aqaba on the way. With the Arabs were a number of British army officers, including T. E. Lawrence, better known as 'Lawrence of Arabia'. However, the Arab leaders were angered when details of a secret Anglo-French plan to divide up the Middle East between those powers was made public. The Arabs were similarly antagonized by the Balfour Declaration of November 1917, which favoured the creation of a national home for the Jews in Palestine, but they still continued to assist the British in the war against the Turks.

If Ottoman forces were being driven back in Palestine and Iraq by the end of 1917, their fortunes were improving on the Russian front. The Bolshevik revolution in November 1917 led to the withdrawal of Russian forces from eastern Anatolia, and the Turks followed up by advancing into the Caucasus during 1918, eventually reaching Baku on the Caspian Sea. However, this advance meant that there were no reinforcements available to bolster the fronts facing the British. In the autumn of 1918 Ottoman resistance began to collapse, with the British taking Damascus and Aleppo in Syria and capturing Mosul in northern Iraq. An armistice was agreed at Mudros and allied forces took possession of Constantinople and the Straits. The remains of the Ottoman army withdrew to Anatolia.

The Ottoman Turks were soon reconciled to the fact that they had lost the Arab lands of the empire, but allied plans also called for the partition of Anatolia between the victors. French troops from Syria began to move in from the south; a Greek army landed at Smyrna in the west in May 1919; and the Armenians started to take control of territory in the east of Anatolia. For the Greeks this was an opportunity to carry out the final completion of the so-called Great Idea. This was the belief that all Greeks, including those of Anatolia, should be gathered into one state, a sort of reborn Byzantine empire, with its capital at Constantinople. Since the borders of the Greek state had steadily expanded in the decades after 1832, it seemed only right that places such as Smyrna, which in 1919 had a larger Greek population than most cities in Greece, should be brought under Greek control.

A Turkish national revival, however, eventually led by Mustafa Kemal (Ataturk), began in the middle of 1919, with its main base at Ankara in central Anatolia. Kemal ignored the peace treaty of Sèvres imposed by the allies in 1920 and began to push back enemy forces. A treaty with the new Soviet Union aided the Turks in crushing Armenian resistance in eastern Anatolia, while the French eventually agreed to withdraw to Syria. The Greek forces in western Anatolia made several attempts to reach Ankara, but were repulsed. In 1922 the Turks counter-attacked and drove the Greeks back to Smyrna, much of which was destroyed by fire. The army was then evacuated to Greece, along with thousands of Greeks whose families had lived in Anatolia for centuries. The 'Great Idea' had ended in tragedy.

Kemal then moved towards Constantinople and the Straits, which were still held by allied forces. There was a serious confrontation with the British at Chanak, but war was avoided. The allies now had little choice but to accept Kemal's victory. In 1923 the new peace treaty of Lausanne was more acceptable to Kemal's government, which was committed to secularism and modernization. The Republic of Turkey was proclaimed, with the sultanate abolished in 1922 and the caliphate in 1924. The Ottoman empire was at an end.

So too, it seemed, was the Christian–Muslim conflict that had lasted for more than 1,300 years. In the 1920s only a handful of Muslim states retained any sort of independence from the European Christian empires. In the mountains of Afghanistan and Yemen Muslim freedom lived on, as it did in the deserts of what would soon become the kingdom of Saudi Arabia. Turkey and Persia (soon to be renamed Iran) also had independence, but were Muslim states being reformed by secularist, pro-Western governments. After serious disturbances in 1919, Britain had given 'independence' to Egypt in 1922, but the British retained the crucial levers of power.

Most Muslims were under the control of the Christian empires of France and Britain, while those in the East Indies were ruled by the Dutch and those in the Philippines by the Americans. The old Russian empire had now become the anti-religious Soviet Union, with little improvement in the treatment of Muslims. In Central Asia Muslim resisters, known as *basmachi*, fought the Soviets from 1918 to 1929 but were eventually subdued. Islam seemed beaten, but during the next 50 years it was both to survive and break free from its imperialist oppressors.

10

BREAKING FREE,
1918–1979

Since Napoleon Bonaparte landed in Egypt in 1798 a new Christian invasion of the Muslim heartlands had been growing in strength. At the end of the First World War Britain and France dominated the Middle East, and it seemed that Christianity had achieved final victory over Islam. Despite General Gouraud's words at Saladin's tomb, however, the French and the British were not new Christian crusaders. There might be some pro-Christian actions, such as the French favouritism towards Maronite Christians in Lebanon, but in general the dominant European powers took a more balanced view of their responsibilities. The British occupation of Jerusalem from 1917 to 1948 was not a Christian occupation in the sense of a regime that oppressed members of other religions such as Jews and Muslims. Indeed, Britain's first High Commissioner for Palestine, Sir Herbert Samuel, was a Jew and made every effort to be impartial between the various religious communities. This eventually earned him the hostility of the Zionist Jews, who were determined to set up their own state in Palestine.

One reason that there was no Christian triumphalism was that secular attitudes were now increasingly common in what was once Christendom. Even by the end of the seventeenth century, commentators were noting that many Europeans visiting Jerusalem acted more like tourists looking at historic sites than Christian pilgrims visiting the holiest city of their religion. This trend towards a more sceptical, secular outlook had greatly increased by the early twentieth century. Although the Christian churches were still strong in the West and would not go into serious decline until after the Second World War, the idea of imposing a Christian regime on foreign countries was already repugnant. Another reason for limitations on the consequences of Christian victory was the fact that the Arab lands had not been taken as colonies, but as mandates supervised by the new League of Nations.

These were territories where the occupying power was to act as a trustee, helping the inhabitants to achieve eventual self-rule and independence. The French mandates were Syria and Lebanon, while the British presided over Iraq, Palestine and Transjordan.

If the Christian triumph was not as complete as some had hoped and was governed by many limitations, the Muslim defeat was not complete either, but it did require greater readjustments within the Islamic world. Whatever its shortcomings, the Ottoman empire had been the last great Muslim power in the world, while its sultan's role as caliph provided a religious figurehead for all Muslims. With the disappearance of the Ottomans, many Muslims felt disoriented. In India during the early 1920s the 'Khilafat' movement among Muslims attempted to save the universal caliphate; yet such concern was seen as foreign interference by the new Turkish republic, and only made the abolition of the caliphate in 1924 more certain. The 'Khilafat' movement was one of the causes of the Moplah revolt in Malabar, India, in 1921, but the British soon suppressed the Muslim rebels. In the 1920s there was no hope of any Muslim state resurrecting the military power of the Ottoman empire, but some Muslims still hoped for a revived caliphate.

Sharif Hussein, the Hashemite ruler of Hejaz, which included the holy cities of Mecca and Medina, made a short-lived attempt to claim the title of caliph, but few Muslims accepted him. Hussein's sons Feisal and Abdullah had become the British-backed rulers of Iraq and Transjordan respectively, but their father had fallen out with the British. The Wahhabi warriors of Abdul Aziz ibn Saud (known in the West as Ibn Saud), ruler of Nejd in central Arabia, were angered by Hussein's claim to be caliph and invaded Hejaz. The British ignored Hussein's appeals for help, and by the end of 1924 Ibn Saud had control of Hejaz. He promised that all Muslims would continue to have access to the holy cities for the *hajj* (annual pilgrimage), and he specifically renounced any idea of declaring himself caliph. Britain and other states recognized the new Saudi regime, and in 1932 Ibn Saud officially united his various possessions into the kingdom of Saudi Arabia. Although it was one of the few independent Muslim states, the new kingdom attracted little international attention since it was militarily weak and economically impoverished. The economy of Saudi Arabia, however, like that of other Muslim states in the Middle East, would eventually be revolutionized by the growth of the oil industry, and a new factor would be introduced into the relationship between the West and the Islamic world.

Oil had first been found in the Middle East in Persia before the First World War, and the British government had been quick to realize its importance, taking a controlling interest in the Anglo-Persian Oil Company. By 1920 Britain saw Persian oil as the major strategic and economic interest in the region alongside the Suez Canal. Since oil deposits seemed likely in other areas near the Persian Gulf, the British were determined to take control of them as well, but soon encountered objections from other countries, especially the United States of America. The American government took little interest in the Middle East during the interwar period, but one thing it did insist upon was access for American companies, particularly those in the oil industry. Thus when the British set up a company to extract oil in Iraq, they had to give shares in it to the Americans as well as the French. Then Ibn Saud of Saudi Arabia took the daring step of granting an oil concession exclusively to an American company, Standard Oil of California, in 1933. The British were furious, but the deal went through and started a close relationship between the USA and Saudi Arabia that would endure for decades. The great boom in the Middle East oil industry would not come until after the Second World War, but the world's growing demand for oil could only enhance the importance of the Muslim states of the area.

AIR POWER AND MUSLIM REVOLTS

Being one of the few independent Muslim states in the interwar period, Saudi Arabia could defy Britain and agree an oil deal with the USA, a country with no imperialist record in the Muslim heartlands. Most Muslims did not have this luxury, being directly oppressed by European imperialists. However, they did not let their oppressors go completely unchallenged in the interwar period. First came the last of the tribal, religious revolts; then came the less directly militant but ultimately more effective rise of secular nationalism, which stressed Western ideologies in the fight against the West rather than just relying on Islam. The European imperialists were to find it increasingly difficult to counter the second of these challenges, but the British thought they had found a new method to curb tribal revolts. Emerging from the First World War with the world's largest air force, the British government thought it had found in air power a new method of imperial policing that was both effective and cheap.

The first test was carried out in British Somaliland, where Mohammad Abdallah Hassan, known to the British as the 'Mad Mullah', had been leading the local Muslim resistance since 1899. Six RAF bombers were delivered to Berbera at the end of 1919 and in January 1920 they dropped leaflets on the Mad Mullah's strongholds calling on the inhabitants to overthrow him or face the consequences. The first bombing missions soon followed and had a severe impact on the morale of local people. The Mad Mullah fled and died in hiding, while follow-up operations by camel-mounted levies led to the occupation of his former possessions. In a campaign lasting just three weeks and costing only £70,000, air power seemed to have been largely responsible for ending Muslim resistance that had dragged on for nearly two decades. That this might be the best method of imperial policing in the future was underlined by the costs and casualties of the revolt in Iraq, which also took place in 1920.

The British had created what would become the kingdom of Iraq by linking three provinces of the Ottoman empire. In the south was Basra, dominated by Shiite Muslims; in the centre was Baghdad, with a mix of Sunni and Shiite Muslims; and in the north was Mosul, a province where the Kurds were dominant and hostile to both Sunni and Shiite Arabs. Iraq contained the holy cities of the Shiites, Najaf and Karbala, and Shiites made up a majority of the population. The Sunni Arabs, however, had been given preference during the rule of the Sunni Ottoman Turks, and the British continued to perpetuate this tradition, installing the Sunni Arab prince Feisal as king of Iraq.

Resentment at the continued British presence in Iraq after the Turks had gone led to a major revolt in July 1920. The revolt began among Shiite tribes in the middle Euphrates area, but soon spread to other Shiite populations in southern Iraq and around Baghdad. The Kurds then seized the opportunity to revolt in the north, but their activities had no direct link with the Shiite revolt. After initial setbacks the British forces, under General Haldane, began to counter-attack, but large reinforcements had to be rushed in from India and elsewhere. The crisis had passed by the end of September, but mopping-up operations continued for months. In December 1920 there was still a large garrison in Iraq: 17,000 British and 85,000 Indian troops. By early 1921 the revolt had been suppressed, but the costs had been high. British and Indian dead numbered around 500, while at least 6,000 Iraqis had been killed. Suppressing the revolt cost the British around £40 million, three times the money they had spent on subsidizing the Arab revolt during the Great War, and many times more than the cost of the successful air campaign against the Mad Mullah.

The important part that aircraft had played in crushing the Iraq revolt was a further encouragement to the idea of air policing. In 1921 the British government decided that in future the principal military assistance to local police in maintaining order in Iraq, Palestine and Aden would come not from the British army but from the Royal Air Force. Air squadrons would be available to bomb any local rebels, while RAF armoured car units would follow up on the ground. In Iraq later air operations against Kurdish tribesmen seemed to show the system worked, as did similar operations on the North-West Frontier of British India. British army officers, however, continued to express doubts about the effectiveness of air power alone against a large-scale Muslim rebellion, and their reservations seemed to be borne out by the vast army the French and Spanish had to assemble to crush a Muslim revolt in the first half of the 1920s.

This was the largest Muslim revolt against European imperialism in the interwar period. Led by Abd el-Krim, it took place in northern Morocco in the first half of the 1920s. In the years immediately before the First World War the French had steadily taken control of Morocco, and in 1912 they had concluded an agreement with the Spanish about their respective zones in the country. The Spanish claimed to rule an area in the north of Morocco from their bases at Ceuta, Tetuan and Melilla, but their hold on the interior, including the Berber tribes in the Rif mountains, was tenuous. Abd el-Krim was the son of an influential member of one of the leading Berber tribes, and, unusually, he received both a Muslim and a Spanish education. He worked for the Spanish in Melilla and became a Muslim judge in their administration. By the end of the First World War, however, Abd el-Krim had become disillusioned with Spanish rule and rejoined his tribe to prepare a revolt.

In July 1921 Abd el-Krim's forces crushed a Spanish army under General Silvestre at Anual, with the death of the general and perhaps 10,000 of his men. It was one of the worst defeats a Christian army had suffered at the hands of the Muslims for centuries. The Spanish were driven back to Melilla, and for a time it seemed that port might be lost to the rebels. Abd el-Krim now set up a 'Republic of the Rif' and made himself its president. Nevertheless, this use of Western political terms could not obscure the fact that the revolt was basically a tribal uprising, with a strong emphasis on Muslim struggle against the infidel. Despite Abd el-Krim's sensitivity to the new political currents at work in the world after the Great War, as far as most of his followers were concerned the revolt was in the old tradition of Muslim resisters such as

Abd el-Kader and Shamil. Spanish reinforcements were rushed to Melilla and some territory was recovered, but Abd el-Krim's forces remained a major threat.

In 1923 General Primo de Rivera seized power in Spain with the approval of the Spanish monarch. Personally he was opposed to continuing the struggle in Spanish Morocco, but considerations of national prestige compelled him to continue with the war. In 1924 Primo de Rivera personally supervised the defence of Tetuan against the rebels, but he was also carrying on negotiations with Abd el-Krim in the hope of reaching a political settlement. The Muslim leader might have achieved autonomy under some sort of Spanish suzerainty, but he was determined to achieve total independence for the Rif, something to which the Spanish would not agree.

By the start of 1925 Abd el-Krim had an army of 20,000 men, with plenty of machine guns and artillery captured from the Spanish. European soldiers of fortune and deserters from the Foreign Legion provided training in modern warfare for his forces. The rebel supply route to Tangier, then under international administration, remained open, and foreign mining companies gave money to Abd el-Krim in return for mineral rights in his Rif republic. The years of success had, however, made the Muslim leader overconfident, and in the spring of 1925 he made the fatal mistake of invading the French zone of Morocco.

The French and Spanish had been on bad terms, and General Lyautey, the French commander in Morocco, had done little to assist his neighbours in their struggle against Abd el-Krim. News of an expected attack by the rebels was depressing for Lyautey, since his forces in Morocco had been reduced by his political masters in Paris. In April 1925 Abd el-Krim's army, assisted by thousands of tribesmen, assaulted the French line of outposts between Fez and Taza, overrunning most of them. Only with difficulty did the French establish a new defence line further to the south. After this attack, former enmities were forgotten and the French and Spanish began to work out joint plans aimed at crushing the Muslim rebels.

The new allies now assembled forces of a size rarely seen in colonial operations. France prepared an army of 160,000 men under Marshal Philippe Petain, the hero of Verdun. Spain collected forces of more than 75,000 men. In all, nearly a quarter of a million troops were to be sent against Abd el-Krim. In September 1925 a Spanish force, covered by the guns of French and Spanish warships, landed in the Bay of Alhucemas on the north coast of Morocco near the heart of Abd el-Krim's territory.

At the same time, Petain launched an overland French invasion of the Rif mountains from the south. The early onset of winter weather finally halted the Spanish and French attacks, but they had made substantial gains. The allies had made use of air power against the Muslim rebels, and although Abd el-Krim was said to have several aircraft of his own, they do not seem to have taken to the air.

When the allied campaign was renewed in 1926, Abd el-Krim soon found himself in a difficult position. Trapped in his capital of Targuist, he decided to surrender in May 1926, wisely choosing to do so to the French rather than the Spanish. The French sent him into exile, but Abd el-Krim would live long enough to see Morocco freed from both French and Spanish rule in the 1950s.

Many of the Spanish army officers who fought against Abd el-Krim would later lead the nationalist side in the Spanish civil war of 1936–9, most notably Francisco Franco. To these officers the war against Abd el-Krim was just another round of the centuries-old struggle of Spain against Islam, and they saw their role almost as modern crusaders. Their hostility to Islam had its limits, however, and they had no hesitation in using large numbers of Muslim troops from Spanish Morocco against the 'godless' socialists, communists and anarchists on the republican side during the civil war.

North Africa was to see another war against Muslim tribal rebels during the 1920s, this time in Libya. The Italians had made the first military use of aircraft there in the war against the Turks in 1911–12, and air power was to play an important role in the later conflict. The tribesmen of the Libyan interior, who were followers of the Senussi sect of Islam, never accepted the peace of 1912 and continued a guerrilla war against the Italians. In 1917 the Italians were forced to grant semi-independence as emir of Cyrenaica to the Senussi leader Idris al-Senussi in return for peace. However, when Mussolini and his Fascists came to power in Italy in 1922, they decided to complete the conquest of Libya. In 1923 the Italians launched new attacks into the interior, Idris fled into exile and Umar al-Mukhtar became the principal leader of Senussi resistance. A long and bitter war of attrition ensued, with Italian tactics including air attacks on oases and nomad encampments. General Graziani ravaged Cyrenaica and built a fortified line along the open frontier with Egypt. Senussi resistance finally collapsed in 1931, when Umar al-Mukhtar was captured and executed. In the conflict between 1923 and 1931 some 230,000 Arabs were said to have died, including three-quarters of the Libyan nomad population.

The Abd el-Krim revolt clearly showed that in face of a major Muslim revolt large military forces would have to be assembled to suppress it. The British, however, still clung to the idea that imperial policing by air power could do the job cheaply and effectively. They were to be taught otherwise by the Arab revolt in Palestine between 1936 and 1939, the most enduring Muslim revolt in the British empire during the inter-war period. Palestine was always the most potentially volatile of the British mandates in the Middle East – a result of the contradictory promises the British had given to the native Arab population and the fast-growing Jewish immigrant population who had been promised a 'national home' there by the Balfour Declaration of 1917. Arab resentment at the growing Jewish presence had led to communal violence in 1920 and 1929, the latter outbreak being particularly severe. Although the RAF was said to be in charge of security, bombing Jerusalem or Hebron was hardly a realistic proposition because of the holy sites, so troops were brought in to end the riots in 1929.

In the first half of the 1930s there was a sharp rise in Jewish immigration to Palestine, from only 4,000 in 1930 to more than 60,000 in 1935. This increase was due partly to fears generated by Hitler's rise to power in Germany, but also by growing confidence in the future of the Jewish settlements in Palestine. The Arabs were alarmed and demanded that the British curb Jewish immigration, stop land sales to Jews and establish democratic institutions in which the Arab majority in Palestine would be reflected. The British offered minor concessions that pleased neither Arabs nor Jews, and in April 1936 the Arab political parties formed a joint committee under Hajj Amin al-Husaini, the Grand Mufti (principal Muslim religious leader) of Jerusalem, which called a general strike. This in turn led to violent incidents and the start of what proved to be a three-year Arab rebellion in Palestine.

Arab guerrilla bands began to form in the hills of Palestine, but at first they carried out only limited attacks. Security was in the hands of the Palestine police and the RAF, but initially their efforts were limited by the colonial government's reluctance to take severe measures. The Peel commission was set up to find a political solution to the crisis. Its final report suggested for the first time that Palestine might be divided into separate Arab and Jewish states, a proposal that was unacceptable to both sides. From November 1937 Arab guerrilla attacks on the British and Jews increased and by the summer of 1938 a large part of Palestine was under rebel control.

Finally the British government began to take the Muslim revolt in Palestine seriously. After the Munich agreement of September 1938 postponed the likelihood of war in Europe, troop reinforcements poured into Palestine. In October 1938 the British army was at last made responsible for public order in the country, and by the end of the year two infantry divisions had been deployed in Palestine. The British also had the unofficial assistance of armed Jewish groups. By the spring of 1939 military measures had broken the back of the revolt, while British political concessions, such as promising to reduce Jewish immigration, had reduced some of the resentment which caused it. During the revolt some 200 British personnel, 400 Jews and more than 5,000 Arabs were killed.

Despite anti-imperialist slogans and political programmes, the Palestine revolt was largely an old-style tribal, religious rising against foreigners. Wide-ranging hit-and-run attacks exaggerated its dimensions, while lack of overall strategy and coordination reduced its long-term impact. Nevertheless, the Palestine revolt did show that leaving imperial policing to air power did not work in populous territories, and large-scale troop deployments were required in the end to stamp out the revolt.

By the 1930s it was becoming clear that if Muslims wanted to have any success in undermining European imperialist domination, they would have to forget the methods of Abd el-Krim and follow the secular, nationalist policies that Ataturk had used so successfully in modernizing Turkey. To do this, Arab states had to regain at least some degree of independence allowing them to build up their own institutions, such as a national army. In Egypt, the British still retained a large degree of control over both the government and armed forces, and also kept a large garrison in the country, ostensibly to protect the Suez Canal. After a new Anglo-Egyptian treaty in 1936, however, British control of the Egyptian army was weakened, while the social origins of its officer corps was widened so that young nationalists such as Gamal Abdul Nasser and Anwar Sadat could gain admission.

In 1932 the British had given an 'independence' to Iraq that was as limited as that given to Egypt ten years earlier. The British retained many military and other rights in the country, with the RAF presence being concentrated at two main bases, Habbaniyah near Baghdad and Shaibah near Basra. Both bases were on the main air route from Britain to India and the Far East. Nevertheless, as in Egypt, a native political class and officer corps began to form, with many nationalists in their ranks. In 1936 an Iraqi general seized power in the country, only to be overthrown ten months later. But the coup was an event of greater long-term significance, since it established a precedent for military coups in the Arab world. The Iraqi army gained a new self-assurance and a taste for interfering in politics. For the moment, however, the army returned to being a power behind the scenes and allowed a pro-British politician, Nuri al-Said, to come to power in 1938.

As the enemies of Britain and France, both Fascist Italy and Nazi Germany were viewed favourably by secular – and even religious – nationalists in the Muslim world. The great military successes of Germany in 1940, defeating France and driving the British back to their home island, greatly enhanced the prestige of the Axis powers in the Middle East. In March 1941 an anti-British nationalist group of civilians and military officers seized power in Iraq and Rashid Ali al-Gailani became prime minister in a pro-Axis government. Rashid Ali played for time while the first Axis aircraft began to reach Iraq via Syria, which was controlled by Vichy French collaborators. Meanwhile, the British sent troops from India to Basra, and the Iraqis began besieging the British air base at Habbaniyah.

Although British forces in the Middle East were desperately over-stretched at this time, there could be no question of allowing the oilfields of Iraq to fall into Axis hands. Troops were flown from Basra to Habbaniyah to reinforce the garrison, while aircraft from Habbaniyah flew bombing sorties against the Iraqis surrounding their base. A British relief force from Transjordan entered Iraq from the west and, despite Axis air attacks, reached Habbaniyah in mid-May. At the end of the month the British force was poised to attack Baghdad, but Rashid Ali fled to Iran and the Iraqis agreed to an armistice. The Axis danger in this area was finally removed in the following months when the British overran Syria and Lebanon, despite fierce resistance from the Vichy French.

In June 1941 Nazi Germany invaded the Soviet Union, and Britain decided to send supplies to her new ally. One potential supply route was via Iran, where the British were already concerned that the activities of Axis agents posed a threat to the oilfields. In August British forces invaded Iran from Iraq and Soviet forces moved into the country from the north. Iranian resistance was overcome, the capital Tehran occupied, and Reza Shah was replaced on the throne by his son Mohammad Reza Pahlavi. The Iranians naturally resented occupation by their old enemies the Russians and the British, but the supply route to the Soviet Union also brought many Americans into the country; the latter received a warmer welcome from the inhabitants, since they had no past history as imperial predators in the region.

Although almost all the Middle East was under allied control by 1942, this did not necessarily promise success against the Axis enemy. General Rommel's German and Italian army was driving back the British once again to the borders of Egypt and many Egyptians regarded Rommel as a potential liberator rather than a conqueror. Early in 1942 the British compelled King Farouk of Egypt, almost literally at gunpoint, to appoint a pro-allied government, and later in the year some Egyptian army officers, including Anwar Sadat, were arrested for plotting with Axis agents. Only the British victory at El Alamein in October 1942 finally ended the Axis threat to the Middle East and extinguished the hopes of Muslim nationalists that they might find aid for their cause in that quarter.

Nevertheless, since the allies made much of their commitment to freedom and democracy, it was becoming increasingly difficult for countries such as Britain to justify their imperial domination of other peoples around the world. The British had promised to end their military occupation of countries such as Iran, Iraq and Egypt after the war, while Libya, liberated from the Italians in 1943, was promised eventual independence. As Lebanon and Syria were also under British military control, the British insisted that General Charles de Gaulle's Free French government should honour past French commitments to give independence to those countries. When the French tried to curb local nationalists, the British opposed the French and forced them to give way, providing General de Gaulle with yet another example of British perfidy. At one time disputes between Britain and France would have been of major importance, but by the end of the Second World War their great power status was eclipsed by the rise of the two superpowers, the Soviet Union and the United States of America. Both these states, for very different reasons, were opposed to the continued existence of European overseas empires. The post-war world would witness the end of those empires, and most of the Muslim world would finally break free of their domination.

END OF EMPIRE

The Axis powers failed to liberate any Muslim population from European imperialist rule, but the same was not true of their Japanese ally. During the Second World War the Dutch East Indies were occupied by the Japanese, who encouraged the growth of Indonesian nationalism, which had both Islamic and secular elements. The secular nationalists were led by Ahmed Sukarno, and when Japan surrendered at the end of the war, he declared an independent republic in Indonesia. In September 1945 British forces landed at Batavia, the Dutch colonial capital on the island of Java. Their first task was to round up surrendered Japanese forces, but they were also to prepare for the return of Dutch rule. Indonesian nationalists were to make violent opposition to such a restoration.

The British had also taken possession of Sumatra and were planning to put further troops ashore on Java at Semarang and at Surabaya, the principal naval base. Local resistance was encountered at both places and the battle of Surabaya in November 1945 quickly escalated into a major action, with air attacks and naval gunfire being called in to assist the troops, who eventually took control. From early in 1946 Dutch forces began to arrive in strength and take over from the embattled troops. The last British forces left in November 1946, at a time when the Dutch and the Indonesian nationalists seemed to have reached a political settlement.

Under the terms of this settlement, the Indonesian republic was to be restricted to Java and Sumatra, while the other islands of the archipelago formed states that would be joined to the republic in a federation that would retain links with the Netherlands. However, this agreement did not prove lasting. In July 1947 the Dutch launched a 'police action' against the republic, overrunning Sumatra and most of Java. The nationalists were left in control of a region around Yogyakarta in central Java. In 1948 the rump nationalist state was threatened by internal divisions. A breakaway Islamic state was set up in one part of Java, while there was a leftist rising in another area. Both threats were dealt with, but in December 1948 the Dutch launched their second 'police action'. Yogyakarta was captured and most members of the republican government taken into custody. Nationalist resistance was now reduced to guerrilla attacks.

However, if the military battle seemed to be won, the Dutch were losing the political struggle for international support. At the start of 1949 international pressure, particularly from the United Nations and the United States of America, compelled the Dutch to begin negotiations with the nationalists, and a timetable for Dutch withdrawal was finally agreed. The Dutch transferred sovereignty to the Republic of Indonesia in December 1949. Most outlying island states were soon absorbed by the republic, but in April 1950 the Republic of South Molucca was set up at Ambon. The people of these islands were Christian and had long served the Dutch, particularly in the colonial army. The new republic was suppressed in November 1950, however, and many Ambonese and their families were allowed to go to the Netherlands.

If the Dutch did not give up their greatest colony without a struggle, the British took a different course with India, the 'jewel in the crown' of their empire. Accepting the inevitable, Britain gave up India in 1947 without a fight, but the decision to partition the country into Muslim Pakistan and a strongly Hindu India led to communal violence and massacres during the transfer of populations.

Partition was also to be the intended solution of Britain's intractable problems with Palestine. In 1947 the United Nations proposed a division of the country between Arabs and Jews. When the British finally left Palestine in May 1948 the forces of neighbouring Arab states poured in, aiming to destroy the new Jewish state of Israel at birth. By 1949 the Israelis had defeated the invaders and most of what remained of the proposed Arab state in Palestine had been absorbed by the kingdom of Jordan (formerly Transjordan). Thousands of Palestinian Arabs had fled Israel and were housed in refugee camps in neighbouring countries.

For centuries Jews and Muslims had often found themselves on the same side in the struggle against the Christians. Now Jewish–Muslim enmity was to become fundamental in international relations. In its original form the religious elements of this hostility were not dominant. Few of the founders of Israel would have considered themselves religious Jews, and the structures of the new state owed as much to secular east European socialism as to Judaism. Similarly, Israel's principal enemy, Gamal Abdul Nasser, President of Egypt, was a secular nationalist who, after using them for his own purposes, actively suppressed the Muslim Brotherhood, a powerful Islamic fundamentalist group set up in Egypt in 1928.

Many Muslims saw Israel as a new Western colony in the heartland of Islam. The very idea that a Jewish state could be seen as one showed how much the old Christian–Muslim conflict was changing. Supporters of Israel did not repudiate the idea that it represented Western values, but these were secular political values rather than religious ones. Israel claimed to be the only true democracy in the Middle East, an example and a reproach to the mostly authoritarian governments of the Arab states. Arabs preferred to see Israel as a new version of the Christian crusader states of the medieval period, an artificial creation that would eventually be overwhelmed by the forces of Islam.

Indian independence in 1947 undermined the reasons for British control in many countries that had been taken over to protect the route to India. By the end of 1947 British forces in Egypt had all been concentrated in the Suez Canal zone, but the need to protect that waterway could no longer be linked to India. Instead, the zone was seen as Britain's strategic base in the Middle East from which the region could be protected from the growing Soviet threat in the Cold War. However, the Egyptians did not feel threatened and continued their efforts to remove British troops from their country. After negotiations broke down, the Egyptian government did nothing to prevent terrorist attacks on the canal zone from 1951 onwards. Egyptian police were implicated in these attacks, so in January 1952 British troops stormed the police barracks in Ismailia, leading to anti-British riots in Cairo.

The old Egyptian political class seemed unable to control the situation, so in July 1952 army officers under General Neguib overthrew King Farouk and established a republic. In April 1954 Neguib was replaced as leader by Colonel Gamal Abdul Nasser, who signed a treaty with the British later in the year that promised the removal of British forces from Egypt. The last British troops left in March 1956, by which time Nasser had established himself as the leader of pan-Arab nationalism in the Middle East. Israel regarded him as the major threat to its security; the French blamed him (incorrectly) for being an instigator of the revolt in Algeria; and the British prime minister, Sir Anthony Eden, saw him as the 'new Hitler', threatening Western interests throughout the Middle East. Nasser's refusal to take sides in the Cold War aroused American suspicion, and his decision to buy arms from Czechoslovakia in 1955 seemed to confirm where his true loyalties lay. Nevertheless, Nasser still looked to the West for money to finance his project to build the Aswan High Dam. The Americans made sure he did not get the required loans. Nasser then looked elsewhere for finance, and in July 1956 he found a new source of money by nationalizing the Suez Canal Company. Henceforth canal tolls would be paid to the Egyptian government rather than an Anglo-French consortium based in Paris.

Britain and France immediately began to talk of taking military action to secure the canal, but both the superpowers cautioned against such old-fashioned gunboat diplomacy. The Soviet Union threatened a violent response if an Anglo-French invasion took place, but the Soviets were soon distracted by a revolt in their client state of Hungary. Mindful of the anti-colonial mood in the post-war world, President Eisenhower saw diplomacy as the best way forward for the aggrieved parties and immersed himself in his re-election campaign. The British and French chose to ignore both threats and advice, being convinced that only direct action could stop the 'new Hitler'.

Initially the British wanted to land at Alexandria and march on Cairo, but they had insufficient forces for such an operation and no idea who to put in Nasser's place. A more limited operation to seize the Suez Canal was then proposed, and this was linked with Franco-Israeli plans for an attack on Egypt. Finally, it was decided that Israel would invade Sinai and tie down the bulk of the Egyptian army; the British and French would then ask both sides to remain 10 miles away from the Suez Canal on either bank. This would obviously inconvenience Egypt more than Israel, and Egypt would reject the request. After that, British and French forces would seize the canal, cutting off the Egyptians in Sinai and leaving them to be crushed by the Israelis.

While misleading the Americans about their true intentions, Britain and France assembled large forces in the eastern Mediterranean. The British had 45,000 men, 300 aircraft and 100 warships, including five air-craft carriers; the French provided 34,000 men, 200 aircraft and 30 warships, including two aircraft carriers. The overall commander was to be General Keightley from Britain, with Admiral Barjot, commander of the French Mediterranean fleet, as his deputy. On 29 October 1956 Israel attacked the Egyptians in Sinai, and soon afterwards the Anglo-French ultimatum was delivered to both parties. After the expected Egyptian refusal, Britain and France began air attacks on Egypt, and within a few days the Egyptian air force had been largely destroyed. On 5 November British and French paratroops landed in the Port Said area at the northern end of the Suez Canal, and on the following day tanks and further troops came ashore. Losses were light and the invaders pushed south along the canal, only to be halted by a sudden ceasefire.

Both the United States and the Soviet Union were outraged by the Anglo-French attack on Egypt, as were most other members of the United Nations. There was a run on the pound sterling and Britain faced financial collapse. Only a loan from the International Monetary Fund could stabilize the situation, but this required approval from the United States. The price for American compliance was an immediate ceasefire, followed by a rapid withdrawal, and Britain had no option but to give in. France could not go on alone. Nasser had been beaten militarily, but the humiliating Anglo-French retreat gave him a major propaganda victory which boosted his prestige in the Muslim world to new heights. Britain and France lost what little credibility they had left with Arabs and the Muslim world in general.

France granted independence to most of her Muslim territories with comparatively little trouble, but one possession was to prove a terrible exception to that rule. The greatest Christian–Muslim conflict of the post-1945 period took place in Algeria between 1954 and 1962. Yet both the French government and the Algerian rebels would have been unhappy with the Christian–Muslim label. The Algerian side was led by the FLN (National Liberation Front), a secular nationalist group. As the title suggests, its members saw themselves as waging a war of national liberation, not a Muslim holy war against infidels. Similarly, the French would say they were merely defending their country against leftist rebels. Algeria, unlike the neighbouring countries of Morocco and Tunisia, was officially part of metropolitan France and not a colony; its population included more than one million settlers of European origin (known as *colons*); and nearly half the French forces fighting against the rebels were made up of Muslim Algerians. Nevertheless, the old religious divide still existed behind the secular façade and helped to poison an already bitter struggle that devastated Algeria and led to the collapse of the Fourth Republic in France.

In 1954 the French finally had to admit defeat in their long-running war with communist insurgents in Indochina. This defeat was one factor encouraging the FLN to launch their guerrilla war against the French in Algeria on 1 November 1954. Attacks on military, government and communications targets took place across the country and continued into the following year. The nature of the conflict changed for the worse in August 1955 when FLN guerrillas raided a suburb of Philippeville and killed more than 100 French civilians. The 'Philippeville massacre' led to an even more brutal French response which killed thousands of Algerians. All-out war between the two sides was now unavoidable.

In 1956 France gave independence to Morocco and Tunisia, allowing more French troops to be concentrated in Algeria. However, the newly independent states became bases for the FLN, with Tunisia being particularly important. The Suez operation in November 1956 took away some French troops for a time, but in all some 400,000 troops were to be deployed by France in Algeria. More than 150,000 of these troops were Muslim Algerians, while the principal French strike force was made up of 40–50,000 paratroopers and Foreign Legionnaires. At any one time the FLN probably had no more than 40,000 guerrillas active in

Algeria. From September 1956 the FLN stepped up terrorist attacks in the city of Algiers and casualties among French civilians began to mount. From January 1957 General Massu's paratroopers were given a free hand to win the 'battle of Algiers', and by ruthless methods they largely destroyed the terrorist network within six months.

In 1957 the new French commander in Algeria, General Raoul Salan, divided the country into sectors, each with a garrison of troops responsible for curbing local rebels. This strategy cut down the number of FLN attacks but tied down a large number of troops in static defence. Salan also built barbed-wire frontier fences, with minefields and artillery support, to stop FLN infiltration from Morocco and Tunisia. As in other guerrilla wars of this period, a major effort was made to resettle the rural population so that they could not have contact with the rebels. Between 1957 and 1960 two million Algerians, a fifth of the total population, were moved from mountain villages to camps in lowland areas.

By 1958 many people in France were weary of the Algerian conflict, but the *colons* still had powerful supporters in Paris and the French army was reluctant to contemplate another defeat like that in Indochina. In May 1958 *colons* led a rising in Algiers that had some support from the military. They demanded an end to political weakness in Paris and the installation of a strong leader, specifically General Charles de Gaulle. The Fourth Republic collapsed and de Gaulle became president of the new Fifth Republic. At first it seemed the general would continue the war, and in 1958–9 offensives organized by General Maurice Challe reduced FLN resistance in Algeria to its lowest ebb. However, de Gaulle soon had to adapt to the political realities in France and the wider world, where international pressure for the granting of Algerian independence steadily increased.

By 1960 it was clear that de Gaulle was looking for a political deal with the FLN, and this infuriated the *colons* and many officers in the French army. In January 1960 and April 1961 there were insurrections in Algeria by elements in the army, but each time de Gaulle suppressed the malcontents and retained the loyalty of most soldiers. The general's opponents then set up their own terrorist force, the OAS (Secret Army Organization), and began to kill all those opposed to the continued existence of a French Algeria. Despite the continued bloodshed, the French government finally agreed a settlement with the FLN at Evian in March 1962, and in the following July Algeria attained its independence.

The long and bitter war had led to the death of 17,500 men in the French forces, 3,000 French civilians, and hundreds of thousands of

Algerians. The French claimed that 350,000 Algerians had died in the struggle; the new Algerian government alleged that the figure was at least one million. Even if the true figure is somewhere between the two estimates, the Algerian war of independence may have been the bloodiest war in the long history of Christian–Muslim conflict. After years of violence, forgiveness was in short supply. Almost the entire European population of Algeria, more than one million people, left the country soon after the end of the war, most going to France. Relatively few of the Muslim Algerians who had been in the French forces managed to leave, and thousands were massacred by the victorious FLN.

The granting of independence to Algeria in 1962 ended direct French military involvement in the Muslim world, and by the end of the 1960s improved relations with the Arabs encouraged France to end her formerly close links with Israel. Britain still retained a residual military role in the Muslim, chiefly Arab, world, but it steadily declined during the 1960s. The pro-British monarchy in Iraq had been overthrown in 1958, and even Jordan sought to play down its British links. Secular nationalists started an anti-British revolt in South Arabia, and in 1967 Britain finally withdrew from Aden. The small sheikdoms along the southern coast of the Persian Gulf remained Britain's last defence responsibility in the area. Kuwait had become independent from Britain in 1961, but the other little states preferred continued British protection. Due to financial problems at home, however, the British government announced in 1968 that it would withdraw its military forces from the Gulf by 1971. This marked the end of the old European imperialism for the Muslim states of the Middle East.

NEW PLAYERS

One of the crucial changes in the post-1945 period was the ever-increasing involvement of the United States of America in the Muslim world in general, and the Middle East in particular. In the interwar period American business interests were drawn to the Middle East by the growing importance of the oil industry. After the Second World War oil from the Middle East became increasingly important, but as the major oil companies (most of which were American) had economic domination over the producing countries the American government could avoid direct involvement in oil politics. Only after the foundation of the Organization of Petroleum Exporting Countries (OPEC) in 1960 did the oil producers begin to exert significant power, and the oil companies turned to the US government for support.

Another reason for US interest in the Middle East was the need to protect the state of Israel, which had been established in 1948. Since the Muslim states possessed the oil resources, American policy had to aim at a balance between Israeli and Arab interests. Indeed, although the Zionist lobby was an important influence in US domestic politics, American support for Israel was not always consistent before 1967. This was one reason that the chief suppliers of arms to Israel in this period were France and Britain rather than the USA.

The third reason for increased American involvement in the Middle East, and the wider Muslim world, was the Cold War between the West, led by the USA, and the communist bloc, led by the Soviet Union. In the 1950s US interest was strongest in the so-called northern tier, the states of Turkey and Iran, which bordered directly onto the Soviet Union. Both were largely secular nationalist states, following policies of Westernization, and playing down the continued Muslim loyalties of most of their populations. Their American links were strengthened when Turkey joined the North Atlantic Treaty Organization (NATO) in 1952 and Iran ratified a treaty with the USA in 1955. Unlike Turkey and Iran, the Arab countries did not face a direct threat from the Soviet Union, and the new secular nationalist rulers in many of them attempted to remain uncommitted in the Cold War. However, the anti-Western rhetoric of many Arab nationalists eventually encouraged links with the communist bloc. Egypt, for example, had close relations with the USSR from 1955 to 1972. More conservative and religious Arab states, such as Saudi Arabia, were implacably opposed to any link with 'godless' communism.

Israel's great victory over Egypt, Jordan and Syria in the Six Day War of June 1967 was to have consequences that undermined secularism on both sides. In Israel the religious right grew in power, determined to retain and settle the land taken from the Arabs. On the Arab side, the secular nationalism of men like Nasser, who died in 1970, seemed to have brought nothing but failure. Stressing the importance of Islam, Saudi Arabia tried to take over leadership of the Arab states from Egypt. When the Arab League had been set up in Egypt in 1945 it largely supported secular nationalism; when Saudi Arabia took the lead in creating the Organization of the Islamic Conference in 1969 it was perhaps the largest religious interstate body in the world. While deeply Muslim, however, the Saudis were politically conservative and retained their close links with the USA. The revolutionary element in the Islamic revival was to come from a totally unexpected direction.

The war of 1967 encouraged the rise of Muslim fundamentalism; another consequence was to generate a separate Palestinian nationalism, although this still tended to be expressed in secular nationalist terms rather than religious ones. The regular armies of the Arab states had failed to liberate Palestine, so the Palestine Liberation Organization (founded in 1964), under Yasser Arafat, set up its own military forces. Guerrilla raids were launched across Israel's borders and there were terrorist attacks in the wider world on Israelis and their supporters. The military impact of these operations was negligible, but they helped to draw attention to the Palestine issue in international politics. The PLO, however, was based in Arab countries bordering Israel, and while some kept it under close control, others allowed it to form 'a state within a state'. The Jordanians eventually used military means to drive out the PLO in September 1970 ('Black September'), and the organization now made Lebanon its chief base.

The political structure of Lebanon had always been fragile, and the principal posts in government were divided between the Maronite Christian minority, the Muslims and other groups, most notably the Druze, a sect related to the Shiites, but considered heretics by most Muslims. In 1975 the right-wing Christian militia clashed with leftist forces led by the Druze. It was the beginning of a civil war that would last on and off for the next fifteen years. At first the PLO tried to stay out of the conflict, but by the start of 1976 the organization was assisting the leftists, and soon their side controlled 80 per cent of Lebanon.

Back in 1860 when the Muslims had been attacking the Maronite Christians, France had rushed troops to their aid, but such feelings of Christian solidarity hardly existed in the secularized West of the 1970s. The Lebanese Christians found help this time from the Syrians, who did not want a Muslim state being created in Lebanon that would be outside their control. In 1976 the Syrian army entered Beirut and imposed a temporary ceasefire. Within a year, however, the Christians were as hostile to the Syrians as were the Lebanese Muslim factions, and it was Israel that soon became the principal ally of the Lebanese Christians.

The civil war in Lebanon was a conflict that did not as yet excite the interest of the two superpowers. Of more significance to them was the Yom Kippur War of October 1973, which for the USA brought together its three principal reasons for being active in the Middle East: Israel, oil and Cold War strategy. After her 1967 victory, Israel had grown complacent about the Arab threat, while the two superpowers had lost interest in the Middle East peace process. Nasser's successor, Anwar Sadat, sought to stimulate renewed interest in the region by launching a surprise attack on Israel. In October 1973 the Egyptians and Syrians had considerable initial success, but the USA poured military assistance into Israel and the Jewish state soon reasserted its old military superiority. For a brief moment a superpower military clash between the USA and the Soviet Union seemed possible, but was avoided. During the war the Arab oil producers attempted to exploit Western dependence on their oil by imposing an embargo on supplies to friends of Israel and raising the general price level of oil. Hints of a possible Western military occupation of the Arab oilfields soon ended the embargo, but by the end of 1974 the price of oil had quadrupled, damaging Western economies.

America was now determined to reduce Soviet influence in the Middle East and to achieve some sort of peace between Israel and her principal enemy, Egypt. Between 1977 and 1979 the two protagonists settled their differences, with US assistance, and Egypt was rewarded with American financial aid. The other Arab nations launched a boycott of Egypt, and in 1981 Sadat was assassinated by Islamic extremists in the Egyptian army. Nevertheless, at the start of 1978 the USA could be well satisfied with its position in the Middle East. Israel and Egypt were making peace; the Arab oil producers had been brought to heel after their use of the oil weapon in 1973–4; and Soviet influence in the region was in decline. Then the American position suddenly began to collapse when revolution broke out in Iran, which had replaced Britain as the West's policeman in the Gulf during the 1970s.

Since he came to the throne in 1941, the Shah of Iran had favoured modernization and Westernization and had become a close ally of the USA. Internal opposition to his rule had come from leftists and from Islamic religious leaders, but both the Shah and the Americans had only really paid attention to the threat from the left because of its links with the Soviet Union. However, the discontented mass of the population looked more to the Muslim clerics than to the communists, so when major rioting broke out in 1978 it was the religious opposition that derived most benefit. Eventually, in January 1979, the Shah fled from Iran, and Ayatollah Ruhollah Khomeini returned from exile to set up an Islamic republic run as a theocracy by Shiite clerics.

After decades of conflict with secular nationalists in Muslim countries, the West had been taken by surprise. The unimaginable had happened. A popular revolution had led to the creation of an Islamic fundamentalist state, and a Muslim country that had been in the fore-front of modernization and Westernization had turned against the West, and particularly against its closest ally, the USA. In future, the conflict between the West and Islam would take on a very different form.

11

CHALLENGING AMERICA, 1979–2005

IRAN AND LEBANON

Between the end of the First World War and the 1970s the Christian–Muslim struggle had changed its character. On one side the Christian West had become increasingly secularized, while on the other the most successful Muslim forces opposing Western domination were those that accepted modern secular ideologies like nationalism and socialism. Because of its all-embracing nature, Islam was harder to put aside than Christianity, so even secular Arab nationalists like Nasser had to make at least token gestures of acceptance towards it. From 1967 onwards the failure of the secular nationalists to defeat Israel and the Western enemies of Muslim states encouraged those who believed that such failure was due not to insufficient Westernization among Muslims but rather was caused by renunciation of the eternal truths of Islam. In 1979 the Iranian revolution was the first great political triumph for Islamic fundamentalism, and it re-injected religion into at least one side of the old Christian–Muslim conflict.

Khomeini and his fellow ayatollahs (Shiite religious leaders) were bitterly hostile to 'godless' communism, but they were equally hostile to the West, and above all its leader, and former supporter of the Shah, the United States of America. Khomeini called America the 'Great Satan' less because it had evil designs on the Muslim world than because it represented in the highest form the Western materialism that could tempt Muslims from the religious path. After the American government allowed the former Shah to enter the USA for medical treatment, Iranian students seized the US embassy in Tehran in November 1979 and took 50 staff hostage. President Jimmy Carter at first attempted to obtain the release of the hostages by diplomacy, but negotiations made slow progress. In April 1980 Carter decided on a daring military operation to rescue the hostages, but it had to be aborted at an early stage due to technical problems and a crash in the Iranian desert. This highly embarrassing failure meant a return to negotiations, and the hostages affair was one of the reasons Carter was defeated by Ronald Reagan in the presidential election of November 1980. Eventually the Iranians agreed to free the hostages, but did not do so until after Carter had left the White House in January 1981.

Any Iranian pleasure at their humiliation of the USA must have been tempered by growing concern about the war with Iraq that had broken out in September 1980. The revolution had left the Iranian armed forces in a state of confusion, with many officers killed or purged, and the leader of Iraq, Saddam Hussein, undoubtedly intended to exploit this situation when he invaded Iran. To add to Iran's problems, most military equipment in the country came from the USA or other Western suppliers, who were unlikely now to provide spares or replacements. At first the Iraqi invaders made advances, but once Iranian Revolutionary Guards tied them down in street fighting in towns near the border, their progress came to a halt.

Saddam Hussein had become President of Iraq in 1979, but had in fact been a major figure in the secular nationalist government of the Baath ('renaissance') party for the previous ten years. His ostensible reason for attacking Iran was to obtain a revision of the borders forced on Iraq by the Shah in 1975. However, the Iraqi dictator probably hoped to seize the Iranian province of Khuzistan, which had both oil reserves and a large Arab population that might welcome the invaders. Saddam was to be disappointed in the latter hope, just as the Iranian ayatollahs were to be disappointed when they called on Iraq's majority Shiite population to support their Iranian co-religionists, and met with little response. Saudi Arabia and the other Arab states along the shores of the Gulf were not unhappy about the Iraqi attack on Iran, since the resulting war would distract the ayatollahs from fomenting revolution in other Muslim countries. Iraq's principal arms suppliers were the Soviet Union and France, but the USA and other countries were ready to supply military equipment and intelligence to Iraq in its struggle against the ayatollahs, just as the Gulf Arabs gave Saddam Hussein considerable financial support.

The USA and the Arab Gulf states were not the only countries that found the Iran–Iraq war a useful conflict. Israel was initially more worried about the growing military potential of Iraq than the religious revolution in Iran. Israeli aircraft had bombed a nuclear reactor under construction in Iraq in 1981, but now it seemed that Iraq's military efforts would be concentrated on Iran. The Iran–Iraq war was a useful distraction that would permit Israel to carry out its own plans. Having made peace with Egypt, the Israeli prime minister Menachem Begin wanted to achieve peace on his northern border by exploiting the continuing civil war in Lebanon. The PLO and the Syrians were to be driven out of Lebanon, and a pro-Israel, Christian-dominated government set up there. Using a Palestinian assassination attempt on the Israeli ambassador in London as an excuse for war, an Israeli army of 90,000 men was sent into Lebanon in June 1982. Lebanese and PLO resistance was easily overcome, while more serious action by Syrian ground and air forces was heavily defeated.

Soon the Israelis were besieging the PLO in Beirut, with the assistance of Lebanese Christian forces. International diplomatic pressure forced Israel to permit the PLO fighters to leave Beirut for foreign countries. Then in September 1982 many Palestinian civilians were massacred in the Sabra and Chatilla refugee camps in Beirut. The killers were Lebanese Christian militia, but the area had been under Israeli military control. This atrocity led to the dispatch of an international force of American, French, Italian and British troops to Beirut to keep the peace between the contending parties.

A significant Shiite Muslim population existed in Lebanon, and the Iranian ayatollahs were keen to exploit that group's hostility to foreign invaders, whether Israeli or Western. The Israelis had removed the secular PLO guerrillas from Lebanon, but now had to face Islamic fundamentalist terrorist groups, above all the Iranian-backed Hizbollah ('party of God'). However, the first attacks of the new groups were directed at Western peacekeepers rather than the Israelis, who had withdrawn from Beirut itself. The suicide car or truck bomb now made its appearance in the terrorist arsenal, and showed itself to be a highly effective weapon. In 1983 the US embassy in Beirut was destroyed, as were the barracks of French paratroopers (58 killed) and US Marines (241 killed). In the face of such effective terrorist attacks, the Western governments did not wish to continue their commitment in Beirut and soon withdrew their forces. The suicide bombers then moved on to the Israeli-occupied zone in southern Lebanon and destroyed an Israeli headquarters at Tyre later in 1983. The Israelis withdrew from most of Lebanon in 1985, but retained a security zone just north of its southern border.

Delighted by the success of their terrorist surrogates against the Americans and other Western forces in Lebanon, the Iranians then introduced Hizbollah and similar groups to the hostages game. Between

1984 and 1992 approximately 100 Westerners were kidnapped in Lebanon. Some, such as William F. Buckley, the CIA station chief in Beirut, never returned alive, but others were ransomed by Western governments who made payments or other concessions to the kidnappers. Aware of the part the Tehran hostages affair played in the downfall of his predecessor, President Reagan was very sensitive to the fate of American hostages in Lebanon. This concern led him into one of the most embarrassing incidents of his presidency. Reagan secretly agreed to supply several thousand anti-tank missiles to Iran for use in its war with Iraq, in return for which the ayatollahs would use their influence with the Lebanese kidnappers to secure the release of American hostages. Officially, the Reagan administration refused to negotiate with terrorists, but between 1985 and 1986 it did just that, using Iran as an intermediary. Three hostages were released, but others were then seized. In November 1986 the whole affair became public; President Reagan had difficulty explaining his policy, and several members of his staff faced legal proceedings. The Iranians could now claim to have humiliated two American presidents in hostage cases and to have driven the American military out of Lebanon.

Nevertheless, the ayatollahs were still struggling under one great burden: the Iran–Iraq war. Although Iran was a larger and theoretically more powerful country than Iraq, it was virtually isolated in the world. The war was costing Iraq dearly in men and money, but it still retained considerable international support, which brought it ample funding, modern weapons and accurate intelligence. The Iraqi air force was superior to that of Iran and launched attacks on Iranian oil facilities and tankers, thus threatening to cut off Iran's main source of income. Iran's superior numbers of troops did begin to wear down the Iraqis, however, and by 1986 the Iranians had entered Iraq and seized positions near Basra. In early 1987 the Iranians advanced to within seven miles of Basra and called on the Arab Gulf states to stop supporting Saddam Hussein.

When the Arabs ignored the Iranian call, Iran made efforts to attack Kuwaiti tankers with either mines or missiles. Kuwait accepted an American offer to protect the tankers if they were transferred to the American flag. Ironically, the first US escort vessel to suffer attack was mistakenly hit by an Iraqi missile and not an Iranian one. Iran ignored United Nations calls for a ceasefire in the war and US/Iranian relations became even more strained than usual. Between October 1987 and April 1988 there were a number of clashes between Iranian forces and the much expanded US naval forces in the Gulf, with the Iranians suffering significant losses. During 1988 the Iraqis began to push the Iranians out of their territory, and in August Iran finally agreed to accept a ceasefire after almost eight years of war. The increased US naval presence in the Gulf had been an important factor in forcing Iran to make peace and showed that ultimately the ayatollahs were not ready to go to war with the USA.

By the end of the 1980s most of the worst fears about the impact of the Iranian Islamic revolution had proved unfounded. It had failed to spark a series of similar Islamic fundamentalist revolts across the Muslim world because it could not cross several crucial divides. Iran was the most powerful Shiite country, but most Muslims were Sunnis and regarded the Shiites as heretics. Similarly, the Arabs were always suspicious of the Iranians, whose racial origins were Indo-European not Semitic, and the Shiites of Iraq largely put Arab national feeling before religious loyalties. Although the Iranians had inflicted humiliation on two American presidents in hostage crises and their terrorist surrogates had driven US forces out of Lebanon, the West and the Arabs had sustained Iraqi resistance during the long war that crippled Iran's economy, and US naval intervention in 1987–8 had forced Iran to make peace. The 'Great Satan' had thus finally got the better of the ayatollahs.

AFGHANISTAN AND THE GULF

The Islamic revolution in Iran at the start of 1979 was a blow to American strategy, yet the Soviet invasion of Afghanistan in December 1979 proved an even greater challenge. It was feared that a successful Soviet occupation of Afghanistan would pose a threat to the oilfields of the Gulf upon which the West was still dangerously dependent for fuel supplies. Suddenly Afghanistan was plucked from obscurity and became the central focus of the intensifying Cold War. With regard to Iran, the USA was a bitter opponent of Islamic fundamentalism, but in Afghanistan the Americans were to support and supply Islamic resistance fighters in their jihad against the Soviet invaders.

In April 1978 left-wing members of the Afghan army seized control of the government and began to impose a communist regime upon the country. This policy soon provoked Muslim tribal risings, and by 1979 the resisters were receiving support from neighbouring Pakistan, where General Zia al-Haq had seized power in 1977 and favoured

Islamic and anti-communist policies. In February the US ambassador in Kabul was killed, and in the following month a major anti-communist rising took place in the city of Herat. Soviet advisers were among those killed by the rebels and the USSR thought for the first time of invading Afghanistan. However, the Afghan communists recaptured Herat and killed more than 20,000 people in the process. The summer of 1979 saw further tribal revolts and the Soviets sent attack helicopters to Kabul for use against the insurgents.

The Afghan communists had always been divided into factions, and in September 1979 the group supporting Hafizullah Amin overthrew and killed the Afghan leader Mohamed Taraki. Amin soon faced problems as the Islamic insurgents gained successes and the Afghan army became depleted by desertions. He began to make friendly overtures towards Pakistan and the USA, thus arousing the suspicions of Moscow. In late December 1979 the Soviets invaded Afghanistan, killed Amin and installed a new Afghan leader, Babrak Karmal. The foreign invasion caused even more Afghans to rally to the side of the insurgents, who were known as the *mujahideen* ('practitioners of jihad'). The Soviet forces in Afghanistan soon rose to more than 100,000 men. With air superiority and armoured vehicles, the Soviets easily took control of the main towns, but guerrilla leaders such as Ahmed Shah Massoud in the Panjshir valley kept resistance alive in the rugged terrain of the countryside.

The various factions of the Afghan resistance were given increasing support from abroad. Although the initial American reaction to the Soviet invasion of Afghanistan had not been very impressive, once President Ronald Reagan took office in 1981 American support for the mujahideen increased dramatically. Between 1981 and 1985 annual US military aid to the mujahideen grew from $30 million to $280 million, making it the largest covert operation in the world for America's Central Intelligence Agency (CIA). Over the whole course of the war, the USA and Saudi Arabia each spent around $4 billion funding arms supplies and other support for the Afghan resistance. Countries as far apart as Britain and China also sent aid to the anti-Soviet forces, but the Islamic world made perhaps the biggest effort to rally behind the mujahideen. Most aid was channelled through the Inter-Services Intelligence (ISI) agency of the Pakistan military, and ISI also sought to encourage unity between the seven main mujahideen groups that used Pakistan as a base for their operations in Afghanistan.

The mujahideen made excellent guerrilla fighters, but their methods were essentially those of tribal fighting. Their attacks were localized and pursued for immediate tangible gains, such as loot (arms, food, etc.), or for the prestige of their commander, with no higher strategic objective. Many guerrillas took their families to safety in Pakistan before embarking on the jihad, and they would often suspend operations so they could make visits to family in the refugee camps. By 1983 Pakistan had 2.7 million Afghan refugees on its soil. These safe havens in Pakistan were of immense help to the mujahideen, providing a place to rest, rearm, train and plan new operations.

Although the USA at one time feared a Soviet advance into Pakistan, it soon became clear that the Soviet strategy in Afghanistan was essentially defensive. Most Soviet forces were concentrated around Kabul and on the lines of communications leading north to the Soviet border. The main Soviet aim was to rebuild Afghan government forces so that they alone would be capable of dealing with the mujahideen, but it was a slow process. Soviet forces did undertake sweeps and raids into guerrilla-held territory, but they could never establish permanent control of those regions. Instead, the Soviets carried out a 'scorched earth' campaign, laying waste to areas before withdrawing to their main bases. This policy ruined large areas of the country and forced more and more Afghan refugees to flee to Pakistan or Iran. Soviet pressure on the mujahideen reached a peak around 1984–5, but the resistance continued in existence.

Nevertheless, although the mujahideen could be kept in action, they lacked sophisticated weapons, above all weapons that could challenge Soviet air superiority. In April 1986 President Reagan decided to supply the mujahideen with hand-held Stinger anti-aircraft missiles and this was to prove one of the turning points of the Soviet–Afghan war. The Stingers were first used in late September 1986, when the mujahideen shot down three Soviet attack helicopters near Jalalabad, not far from the Khyber Pass. Suddenly Soviet helicopters and low-flying aircraft became vulnerable to mujahideen attack and the balance of the war began to shift towards the Islamic resistance. In all, the USA supplied about 900 Stingers to the mujahideen, but after the Soviet withdrawal in 1989 more than 200 unused Stingers were not recovered by the Americans and may have reached Islamic terrorist groups.

Also in 1986 the CIA decided to give active support to the policy ISI had begun in 1982, of recruiting radical Muslim volunteers from around the world to join the Afghan resistance. Between 1982 and 1992 some 35,000 Muslim volunteers from 43 countries fought alongside the mujahideen. The recruitment policy had apparent advantages for the leading players on the anti-Soviet side. General Zia aimed to cement Islamic unity and make Pakistan a leader of the Muslim world; the USA wanted to show that the whole Muslim world was fighting the USSR beside the Afghans and their American benefactors; and Saudi Arabia saw a chance to promote Wahhabism, its own Islamic fundamentalist ideology, to a wider audience. Unfortunately, in time it became obvious that many of the volunteers had their own agendas. Their hostility to the Soviets would one day be turned against the USA and the Muslim governments that were its allies.

While the Stinger missiles and the growing band of foreign Muslim volunteers gave the mujahideen an increasing military advantage, political changes on the Soviet side were already weakening the resolve of the communist forces in Afghanistan. Since coming to power in 1985, Mikhail Gorbachev had become increasingly keen to end a war that was unpopular with the Soviet public and seemed unlikely to end in victory. In 1986 President Mohammad Najibullah became the new Afghan leader. In the following year he made efforts to reach some sort of political settlement with the mujahideen. Najibullah's overtures were rebuffed, but Gorbachev could wait no longer. In February 1988 he announced the phased withdrawal of Soviet forces from Afghanistan, and this was completed a year later.

To the surprise of many observers, the Najibullah regime did not collapse immediately, but struggled on until 1992, when Kabul was finally captured by the mujahideen. More than 15,000 Soviet troops had died in Afghanistan, which many people saw as the Soviet Union's Vietnam; yet the losses among the Afghan people had been much greater, with more than one million people losing their lives as a result of the war.

By 1990 it seemed that the USA had surmounted its main problems in the Muslim world. Revolutionary Iran had been contained and weakened by its long war with Iraq, while the Islamic resistance movement in Afghanistan had forced the Soviets to admit defeat and withdraw. Then, in August 1990, the whole Middle East situation was thrown into turmoil once more when Saddam Hussein's Iraqi army invaded Kuwait. The Iraqi leader had been driven to this action because of the dire financial condition his country was in after its long struggle with Iran ended in 1988. Feeling that he had been fighting on behalf of all Arabs, Saddam Hussein resented the refusal of other Arab governments to waive the debts Iraq had built up during the war. Taking control of oil-rich Kuwait seemed one way of solving Iraq's financial problems. The USA and other Western states had been friendly to Saddam during the Iran–Iraq war, but such naked aggression that would put an even bigger share of world oil reserves under the control of the Iraqi dictator was bound to produce a different response.

Claiming that the conquest of one country by another could not be allowed to stand and that Saddam Hussein now posed a threat to Saudi Arabia, the USA set about assembling an international coalition that was intended to stop the Iraqi dictator in his tracks. The ruler of Saudi Arabia, the custodian of the holy mosques of Mecca and Medina, reluctantly agreed to invite American, British, French and other 'infidel' forces into the heartland of Islam. Most Muslim governments around the world condemned Saddam and large numbers of Muslim troops, chiefly from Saudi Arabia, Egypt and Syria, were to join the coalition army sent to oppose him. However, many ordinary Muslims around the world saw Saddam Hussein as a hero, a new Saladin opposing Western imperialists.

American plans for such an intervention had been in preparation for almost a decade, so the United States was able to move forces to the Gulf quickly. After the Soviet invasion of Afghanistan President Carter had set up a rapid reaction force ready to move into Iran or Pakistan if the Soviets attacked those countries. In 1983 President Reagan replaced Carter's force with US Central Command (CENTCOM), which was to plan for possible American military intervention in an area stretching from Sudan to Pakistan and including all of the Middle East. By the second half of the 1980s the potential trigger for American action in this area was no longer Soviet military invasion, but rather aggression by a regional power, in particular a possible Iranian threat to the Arab states of the Gulf. American attempts to obtain military bases in those Arab states were largely rebuffed, however, and when General Norman Schwarzkopf became commander of CENTCOM in 1989 advance preparations for intervention were largely restricted to pre-positioning of stores in the area. Nevertheless, the plans for intervention were ready, and the growing collapse of the communist bloc gave the United States both more freedom to act and more forces to send.

By the end of 1990 diplomatic efforts to persuade the Iraqis to leave Kuwait had largely failed and military action seemed unavoidable. On paper, Saddam Hussein's armed forces seemed to be among the most formidable in the world, but as events were soon to reveal, warfare had moved into a new age in which few countries could match the technological superiority of the USA, especially in air power. Of the 38 nations in the anti-Iraq coalition, only a dozen sent significant military forces to Saudi Arabia and the Gulf, where the American general Norman Schwarzkopf was the overall commander. The American contingent was the largest, with more than 500,000 men and women, and it included over 100 naval vessels, 2,000 tanks, 1,800 fixed-wing aircraft and 1,700 helicopters. Other nations contributed more than 200,000 troops with further tanks and aircraft. Approximately 500,000 Iraqi troops took up defensive positions in Kuwait and southern Iraq. They could match the coalition in such areas as tank numbers, but they were much inferior in air power.

The war opened in mid-January 1991 with a sustained air campaign by coalition aircraft. The United States led the way with stealth aircraft, precision-guided bombs and cruise missiles. The Iraqi air defence system was soon destroyed with the surviving Iraqi air force planes fleeing to Iran. With total air superiority so quickly gained, bombing sorties were now concentrated on Iraqi ground defences around Kuwait. In retaliation, Saddam Hussein ordered the firing of a number of Scud missiles at Saudi Arabia and Israel, but they had only limited impact. In particular, the missile attacks failed to provoke a violent response from Israel that might have caused Muslim nations to leave the coalition.

In the second half of February 1991 General Schwarzkopf launched the coalition ground offensive aimed at liberating Kuwait. Distracting Iraqi forces in Kuwait by threatening an amphibious landing and launching some direct attacks on their positions, Schwarzkopf made his main effort many miles inland through the desert. This left hook around the flank of the Iraqis achieved swift success and only narrowly failed to trap the Iraqi forces trying to escape from Kuwait. In only 100 hours of ground combat dozens of Iraqi divisions were destroyed, along with all their tanks and other equipment that had not already been knocked out by air attacks. The declared object of the war, to free Kuwait, had been achieved, but coalition forces were now deep in southern Iraq, and many people hoped they would go on to Baghdad and overthrow Saddam Hussein. President George H. W. Bush decided otherwise, and a ceasefire was agreed with the Iraqis.

The disproportion in losses between the two sides was astonishing. The coalition destroyed 4,000 Iraqi tanks, more than 1,000 other armoured vehicles and 3,000 artillery weapons. The coalition lost four tanks, nine other armoured vehicles and one artillery weapon. The Iraqi air force was largely destroyed, but in flying almost 110,000 sorties the coalition lost only 38 aircraft, the lowest loss rate of any air combat in history up to that date. Estimates of Iraqi dead have gone as high as

100,000, and were certainly in the tens of thousands; coalition fatalities in battle did not even reach 200. The overwhelming coalition victory was largely due to superior technology allied to dominant air power, and it was a success that particularly bolstered the American armed forces. Nearly two decades after the American defeat in Vietnam and almost one decade after the humiliating withdrawal from Lebanon, the reputation of the us armed forces had been decisively restored.

For a time it seemed that even though the coalition had not brought down Saddam Hussein, his own people were going to overthrow him. A Shiite revolt broke out in southern Iraq, and in the north Kurdish insurgents began to expand the area under their control. However, Saddam Hussein still had sufficient of his elite Republican Guard units left to send against the rebels. The Shiite uprising was crushed, but when attacks were made on the Kurds the usa and Britain created 'safe haven' areas for those people and threatened to launch air attacks on the Iraqis if they continued their offensive. Saddam Hussein gave way and seemed content just to have survived in power.

One reason President Bush allowed the Iraqi dictator to survive was because of fears of what sort of regime would succeed him. The majority Shiite population in Iraq would probably have taken power in Baghdad. Although Iraqi Shiites had shown little solidarity with the Iranian Shiites during the Iran–Iraq war, there was still a worry that a Shiite Iraq would be drawn into the orbit of Iran. For all his many sins, Saddam Hussein, an old-style, secular Arab nationalist, seemed for the moment to be preferable in Baghdad to a possible Islamic fundamentalist regime.

In any case, the Gulf war of 1991 had crippled the Iraqi military machine and brought more us forces into the region than ever before. Many of them would remain, even in Saudi Arabia, after peace was made, thus completing a process that had begun in the latter years of the Iran–Iraq war. In 1987–8 the United States Navy increased its presence in the Gulf during the clashes with Iran and remained after the peace. The Gulf War added large American ground and air forces to the us presence, giving CENTCOM the local bases it had long desired. For the first time, the United States was ready to maintain a large and permanent military presence in the heartland of the Muslim world.

THE END OF THE SOVIET EMPIRE

The conclusion of the Cold War and the break-up of the Soviet Union in the period 1989–91 had major implications for the Muslim world. The

USSR had been a secular version of the Christian Russian empire of the czars, and its demise gave Muslim peoples a chance to regain their independence. In Central Asia the Russians did not resist the creation of five new Muslim states: Kazakhstan, Uzbekistan, Kyrgyzstan, Tadjikistan and Turkmenistan. Russian approval was due to a number of factors: the new states largely retained links with Moscow; their new rulers were generally the old communist bosses; and the new governments were vigorously opposed to the spread of Islamic fundamentalism. Russian intervention occurred only in the case of Tadjikistan. Islamic guerrillas, supported by groups in Afghanistan, precipitated a civil war that lasted from 1992 to 1997, and Russian troops intervened to ensure the victory of the Tadjik government.

If the Russians were largely unworried by events in Central Asia, they took a different view of Muslim independence movements in the Caucasus region and were prepared to take military action. While still part of the USSR, the constituent republics of Armenia (mostly Christian) and Azerbaijan (mostly Shiite Muslim) had come to blows in 1988 over the status of Nagorno-Karabakh, an Armenian enclave within Azerbaijan. The Soviet government had calmed things down, but when in 1990 it seemed Azerbaijan might fall under the control of Islamic groups seeking union with Iran, the Soviet response was swift and brutal. Soviet forces attacked the Azeri capital, Baku, and there were heavy casualties on both sides. The reassertion of Soviet control was, however, only temporary. As the decline of the USSR continued, both Azerbaijan and Armenia declared independence in 1991.

After independence the two states renewed their conflict over Nagorno-Karabakh, and in 1992–3 the fighting intensified. The Russians supported the Armenians, who could also call on aid from the Armenian diaspora in western Europe, particularly France, and the USA. In a number of battles Russian tanks and troops openly assisted the Armenian forces. The Armenians preserved their hold on Nagorno-Karabakh, and also seized Azeri territory, so that the enclave could be linked with Armenia. Although receiving support from both Turkey and Iran, the Azeri government finally gave in to Russian pressure and agreed a ceasefire in 1994, leaving the Armenians with their conquests. Negotiations still continue to find a political solution to the dispute, but for the moment Armenia retains the disputed territory.

Russia may have retained a measure of dominance over Azerbaijan, but its greatest Muslim challenge in the Caucasus area is Chechnya, which is within the Russian Federation. Chechnya declared its independence in

November 1991, shortly before the disappearance of the USSR, and chose General Dzhokhar Dudayev as its leader. Russia refused to recognize Chechen independence, but took no military action to suppress it for several years. Then in December 1994 President Boris Yeltsin launched an invasion aimed at defeating the rebels and keeping Chechnya within the Russian Federation. Russian hopes of a swift victory soon proved false and a siege of the Chechen capital, Grozny, was begun. Much of the city was destroyed and more than 20,000 people were killed before the Russians finally took possession of Grozny in February 1995. As inheritors of the traditions of Shamil, the Chechens refused to surrender and fought on in a determined guerrilla war that inflicted many casualties on the Russian invaders.

In April 1996 the Russians pinpointed the location of the Chechen leader Dudayev when he used his satellite phone and killed him with a missile attack. This success did not, however, bring a Russian victory any nearer. The Chechen war was increasingly unpopular with the Russian people, and Boris Yeltsin was facing a presidential re-election campaign. Negotiations made little progress, but then in August 1996 the Chechen military leader Shamil Basayev recaptured Grozny from the Russians. The Moscow government now hastened to make peace with the Chechens, who achieved a form of independence.

Chechnya remained an unstable region, however, and in August and September 1999 Chechens made a number of raids into neighbouring Dagestan, leading to clashes with Russian forces. A spate of apartment bombings in Russian cities in September was blamed on Chechen separatists, and this led to Russian air attacks on targets in Chechnya. In October the Russian leader Vladimir Putin ordered ground troops into Chechnya, and the intensive bombing of Grozny began in November. In February 2000, after much heavy fighting, the Russians took possession of Grozny, which by now was largely a city of ruins from which most of the population had fled. The Chechen rebels once again reverted to guerrilla warfare, and an increasing number of Muslim volunteers from other countries came to join them in their fight.

In June 2000 the Russians installed a pro-Russian Chechen government which was condemned by the elected Chechen leader, Aslan Maskhadov, and the military commander, Shamil Basayev. The latter claimed responsibility for the assassination of the pro-Russian Chechen president in 2004, while Maskhadov was killed during a Russian search operation in 2005. Basayev died in 2006 and by 2009 the Russians felt confident enough to declare that the ten-year second

Chechen war was over. However, some Islamist insurgents remain active in the Caucasus area.

THE FALL OF YUGOSLAVIA

While the break-up of the Soviet Union gave independence to many Muslim peoples, the dissolution of Yugoslavia after 1991 brought both freedom and suffering for its Muslim populations. These were the Muslim remnants left behind as the Ottoman empire diminished during the nineteenth and early twentieth centuries. The chief groups in Yugoslavia in 1991 were the Muslims of Bosnia, sometimes known as Bosniaks, and the Albanian Muslims who dominated Kosovo, a province of Serbia, and had a large minority in Macedonia. The Serbs had dominated the old Yugoslavia and they were determined that even if that state was broken up, one of its successors would be a 'greater Serbia' which included the Serb populations in Croatia and Bosnia. In 1991 Slovenia and Croatia declared independence from Yugoslavia. Slovenia broke away with little trouble, while after some heavy fighting a UN-backed ceasefire was achieved in Croatia in 1992, leaving only a few Serb areas outside the control of the new government in Zagreb. The worst violence in the fall of Yugoslavia was to occur in Bosnia, where the Muslim population found itself under threat from both groups of Christian inhabitants, the Orthodox Serbs and the Catholic Croats.

In 1991 the main ethnic divisions of the population of Bosnia and Herzegovina were 44 per cent Muslim, 31 per cent Serb and 17 per cent Croat. There were hopes that a unitary, multi-cultural state could be established when Bosnian independence was declared in March 1992 with Alija Izetbegovic, a Muslim, as president of the new country. Unfortunately, most Bosnian Serbs were opposed to independence and a civil war soon broke out. As the remains of the federal Yugoslav army withdrew from Bosnia, they handed over most of their weapons, including artillery, to the Bosnian Serbs. This military advantage allowed the Bosnian Serbs to overrun most of the country and begin a siege of the Bosnian capital, Sarajevo, which would continue intermittently for the next three years. Although comprising only one-third of the population, the Bosnian Serbs took control of 70 per cent of the country, and their political leader, Radovan Karadic, set up his 'capital' at Pale, near Sarajevo. Slobodan Milosevic, president of what remained of Yugoslavia, continued to give military and other assistance to the Serbs in Bosnia.

The Bosnian Serb advances in 1992 saw much brutal 'ethnic cleansing', with non-Serbs (usually Muslims) being massacred or forced to flee as refugees. This policy outraged Western countries, and led the United Nations to impose sanctions on Yugoslavia for aiding the Bosnian Serbs and to maintain its international embargo on the supply of arms to all the combatants in the region. Unfortunately, this latter restriction did much to hamper the Bosnian government's efforts to build up its defences, and these were further undermined in July 1992 when the Bosnian Croats broke with the Bosnian government. Although not helping the Serbs, the Croats began to expel Muslims from their own areas of Bosnia, and a particularly bitter Croat–Muslim struggle took place around Mostar, the capital of Herzegovina. Now Bosnia was being torn apart by a three-way fight between Serbs, Croats and Muslims.

Despite many resolutions, sanctions and embargos, the United Nations remained unwilling to intervene directly in the Bosnian conflict. Only in June 1993 did the UN declare six towns in Bosnia – Sarajevo, Bihac, Tuzla, Zepa, Gorazde and Srebrenica – to be 'safe areas' for Muslims, where they would be protected by UN troops. Some 25,000 UN peacekeeping troops went to Bosnia, but they had only limited success in setting up and protecting the 'safe areas'. The United States showed a marked reluctance to become involved in any ground commitment in Bosnia that might lead to military losses. The American preference was for a policy of 'lift and strike', that is, lift the arms embargo so that anti-Serb forces could obtain better weapons and then support their operations with selective air strikes. For many months, however, the Americans did little to carry out even this policy, and the winter of 1993–4 was one of the darkest periods for the people of Bosnia and Herzegovina.

Although reluctant to act itself, the United States was prepared to turn a blind eye to the military assistance that Bosnian Muslims were receiving from the Islamic world in defiance of the UN arms embargo. Thus arms shipments to Bosnia from Iran, supposedly America's great enemy, enjoyed tacit US approval, and such shipments were often financed by Saudi Arabia, a major American ally and usually hostile to Shiite Iran. The Saudis also mobilized the Organization of the Islamic Conference to send other forms of aid to the Bosnian Muslims, and to pressure the West for direct intervention in the conflict. As in Afghanistan in the 1980s, Muslim volunteers from around the world came to Bosnia to assist their co-religionists, and their total number probably exceeded 4,000. Some had fought in the earlier Afghan war, while others were from the Iranian Revolutionary Guard. The European allies of the United States were uneasy about this increased Islamic activity in the Balkans, but since neither they nor the Americans were ready to undertake a decisive military intervention in Bosnia, there was little they could do to curb it. By the second half of 1994, Islamic military support had helped the Bosnian government army to become a much more effective fighting force.

Early in 1994 increased Bosnian Serb attacks on Sarajevo brought threats that the UN would authorize air strikes against the besiegers. More importantly, in March the Bosnian Muslims and the Bosnian Croats made peace and agreed to cooperate in the struggle against the Bosnian Serbs. By the end of 1994 the USA had declared it would no longer observe the UN arms embargo and gave substantial military assistance to Croatia; lesser military aid went to the Bosnian government. Diplomatic efforts to find a way to peace also continued, and during 1994 the five-nation Contact Group (USA, Russia, France, Britain, Germany) put forward a plan for settling the Bosnian war. A Muslim-Croat federation would have 51 per cent of the country, a Serb republic would have 49 per cent, and they would be linked in a joint Bosnian government. Since they still controlled more than two-thirds of Bosnia, the Serbs rejected the plan, but it would eventually form the basis of the final peace agreement in 1995.

In March 1995 an alliance was agreed between President Franjo Tudjman of Croatia and President Izetbegovic of Bosnia, aimed at the final defeat of the Serb insurgents in both their countries. Occasional NATO air strikes on the Bosnian Serbs now started, and in June the Bosnian government felt its forces were strong enough to launch offensives against its enemies around Sarajevo and at Bihac in western Bosnia. The Bosnian Serb reaction was to launch attacks on the UN 'safe areas' for Muslims. In July General Ratko Mladic's forces took Srebrenica and massacred 8,000 Muslim men and boys in the worst single atrocity of the Bosnian war. Mladic went on to take Zepa and then threaten Gorazde, but overall the Bosnian Serb position was beginning to collapse. NATO air attacks on the Bosnian Serbs became more numerous and effective during August, and the Serb forces in western Bosnia were steadily driven back by the Croats and Muslims. The Bosnian Serbs began to withdraw their heavy weapons from around besieged Sarajevo in September, and soon afterwards they agreed to a ceasefire.

Perhaps the most important reason for the collapse of the Bosnian Serbs was the decision of President Milosevic of Yugoslavia to cut off assistance to them. In November 1995 Milosevic met the presidents of

Croatia and Bosnia at Dayton, Ohio, in the United States to bring an end to what has been called the 'third Balkan war'. Milosevic forced the Bosnian Serbs to accept a settlement in Bosnia that largely followed the proposals made by the Contact Group in 1994, and American, British and French troops were sent into Bosnia to implement the Dayton Peace Agreement. In all, perhaps 250,000 people were killed during the Bosnian war and several million became refugees. It was the worst conflict in Europe since the Second World War, and even after the Dayton Accords relations among Serbs, Croats and Muslims in Bosnia remained strained.

If President Milosevic looked like a peacemaker at Dayton, this did not imply any slackening in his commitment to Serb nationalism. The province of Kosovo in southern Serbia was almost holy ground to Serbs because they believed that it was there that the Ottoman Turks had destroyed the independence of Serbia in battle in 1389. The problem for the Serbs was that, by 1991, 90 per cent of the population of the province was made up of Muslim Albanians, usually known as Kosovars, and only 10 per cent were Serbs. With other areas of the former Yugoslavia breaking away from Serb control, it was hardly surprising that the Kosovars would want to do the same, or that Milosevic would seek to prevent them.

In 1996 the so-called Kosovo Liberation Army (KLA) began terrorist attacks on Serbs in the province. The KLA's stated aim was independence for Kosovo, but this might only be a prelude to union with Albania in a 'greater Albania' that could also include Muslim Albanians in Macedonia. In 1998 Serbian forces stepped up their operations against the KLA, and the international community became concerned that 'ethnic cleansing' activities similar to those in Bosnia might take place in Kosovo. International pressure forced the rival parties to attend a conference in Paris in March 1999 and attempt to find a peaceful settlement. The KLA agreed to accept autonomy rather than independence for the province, but Milosevic refused to allow a NATO force to enter Kosovo to implement the agreement. This defiance led to eleven weeks of NATO air attacks on Yugoslavia. The intention was said to be to discourage the Serbs from driving out the Kosovars; the result was just the opposite. Within weeks the Serbs had forced more than half a million Kosovars to flee as refugees to neighbouring countries.

NATO had originally declared that it would not launch a land attack on Yugoslavia, hoping that the KLA would exploit the air attacks to advance on the ground. The Yugoslav (Serb) military in Kosovo largely survived the bombing, however, and prevented a KLA advance. By the summer of 1999 it became clear that some NATO land intervention might be needed. This possibility, added to the increasing wider impact of the air attacks, led Milosevic to give in to international demands in June 1999. Serb forces were withdrawn from Kosovo, NATO forces replaced them, and the province came under UN administration while its future was determined. Nevertheless, the peace settlements achieved in Bosnia and Kosovo remain fragile, and the activities of Muslim Albanians in Macedonia have begun to destabilize that country as well. In the context of the break-up of Yugoslavia, the Western powers liked to see themselves as defenders of the Muslims, whether in Bosnia or Kosovo, against the Serbs. In the Bosnian war, however, the most important outside assistance to the Muslims came from the wider Islamic world, a fact that has not been forgotten.

THE WAR ON TERROR

After the Israeli victory in the Six Day War in 1967, the Palestinians became disenchanted with the efforts of Arab states on their behalf. Instead, they expanded their own forces and the following decades saw a major growth in Palestinian terrorism against Israel and its supporters. Similarly, after the US victory in the Gulf war of 1991, some Islamic militants came to regard the USA, despite its support of Muslims in Afghanistan and the Balkans, as imposing a new Western tyranny on the Middle East, a tyranny that existing Arab governments were unwilling to oppose. The Islamic militants were to launch a new and deadly wave of terrorism against the USA and its allies, both Western and Muslim.

The 1980s had been a transitional period for terrorism, with the old secular nationalist groups steadily giving way to the new Islamic groups. The PLO was driven out of Beirut, and in the occupied territories (Gaza and the West Bank) it was increasingly replaced by overtly Islamic terror groups like Hamas. Muammar al-Qaddafi had led one of the last secular nationalist revolutions in the Arab world when he seized power in Libya in 1969, and he went on to support a variety of terrorist groups, including some that were unrelated to the Arab–Israeli struggle. His terrorist operations eventually provoked the USA to launch an air attack on Tripoli in 1986, which convinced the Libyan leader that he should be more cautious for a time. By his own admission, Qaddafi was involved in the destruction of Pan Am Flight 103 over Lockerbie, Scotland, in

1988, but after 1990 he became less involved in terrorism against the West, partly because he was as hostile to the growth of Islamic fundamentalism as any Western state. Duing the 1990s the PLO and Qaddafi would be replaced by a new age of Islamic terrorism.

To the embarrassment of the USA, the roots of this growth in Islamic terrorism lay not so much in Iran as in the Islamic resistance movement in Afghanistan, which the Americans had done so much to support. For the Americans, victory over the Soviet Union in Afghanistan was the victory of the free world over communism. For the Islamic fighters – particularly the foreign Muslim volunteers – it was the victory of Islam over godless infidels. One superpower had been humbled; now it would be the turn of the other superpower, the USA. The Soviet–Afghan war left behind a wide coalition of Islamic organizations intent on promoting Islam against all non-Muslim forces. They had thousands of experienced fighters, training camps, links across the Islamic world, large quantities of arms and explosives, and, most importantly, the confidence that victory in Afghanistan had given them.

One individual who had been active in supporting the Afghan resistance during the 1980s was the Saudi businessman Osama bin Laden. Although he had visited the battlefront, his principal role was in financial and other support operations in Pakistan, operations that brought him into contact with ISI and Saudi intelligence. After the Soviet withdrawal in 1989, bin Laden helped found al-Qaeda ('the base'), a loose grouping of Islamic organizations and individuals ready to continue the holy struggle against the enemies of Islam. Returning to his native Saudi Arabia, bin Laden expressed his opposition to the American military presence in that country during and after the Gulf War of 1991. Eventually the Saudi authorities forced bin Laden to leave the country, and he was later stripped of Saudi citizenship. Bin Laden went to Sudan, where an Islamic revolution inspired by Hassan Turabi had in 1985 overthrown the secular nationalist Nimeiry government, and he set up a training camp for Islamic fighters near Khartoum.

In 1993 US forces were among the international force sent by the United Nations to Somalia, a country torn apart by civil war between various Muslim tribal factions. In confused fighting in the Somali capital Mogadishu, the US forces lost several dozen dead, mostly in the 'Black Hawk down' incident, and the American government soon withdrew them. Bin Laden later claimed that he had some role in supporting the Muslim resistance in Mogadishu, but the evidence is not entirely convincing. What bin Laden and other Islamic terrorists took from events in Somalia in 1993 was a belief that, as in Beirut a decade earlier, the USA would quickly give up military adventures if they looked like inflicting significant casualties. It seemed the world's remaining super-power might be forced out of the Islamic world without the need for major military operations. Yet Somalia was a minor intervention, and the Gulf War of 1991 had shown clearly that the USA was ready to unleash massive military power if it felt its core interests were at stake.

Islamic terrorists who had been trained in the Afghan war were also active in the Algerian civil war from 1992 onwards. This was largely a struggle between a Westernized Muslim government and Islamic mili-tants, but it also included attacks on Westerners in Algeria and bomb attacks in Paris – a response to French support for the Algerian regime. In 1993 more Afghan-linked terrorists, inspired by an Egyptian religious leader, launched the first bomb attack on the World Trade Center in New York City, killing six people and injuring hundreds. This attack was a great shock to the Americans, but Osama bin Laden did not fig-ure greatly in their investigations, even though at least one of the attackers had links to al-Qaeda. Bin Laden's position in Sudan was to be undermined by more local events. Islamic terrorists were active in Egypt, killing local Coptic Christians and visiting Western tourists, but their main target was the pro-American government of President Hosni Mubarak. After a failed attempt to kill Mubarak during a visit to Ethiopia, the Sudanese government came under increasing pressure to expel bin Laden. The terrorist leader went before action was taken, moving his operation to Afghanistan in May 1996.

By this time the situation in Afghanistan was ideal for Osama bin Laden's intention of setting up more training camps for Islamic fight-ers. The Afghan communist government had been overthrown in 1992, but the different mujahideen factions then started a civil war among themselves. By 1994 the long-suffering Afghan people were desperate for peace and order, conditions that a new movement promised to bring about. The Taliban ('students of Islam') took control of Kandahar in southern Afghanistan in 1994 and restored peace and order, though at the price of imposing a particularly severe brand of fundamentalist Islam. Backed by ISI and Saudi Arabia, the Taliban went on to capture Herat in 1995 and Kabul in 1996. By 1997 it seemed that all Afghanistan might come under the control of the Taliban and their leader, Mullah Mohammad Omar. Osama bin Laden soon established a close relation-ship with the Taliban leader and was allowed to set up several training camps for foreign Muslim fighters.

Osama bin Laden had issued his first declaration of jihad against the Americans in 1996. He made further threats in his February 1998 manifesto for the so-called International Islamic Front for Jihad against Jews and Crusaders. However, bin Laden only achieved major international notice in August 1998, when suicide bombers linked to al-Qaeda attacked the US embassies in Nairobi, Kenya, and Dar-es-Salaam, Tanzania, killing more than 200 people, mostly Africans. In retaliation, President Bill Clinton ordered cruise missile attacks on bin Laden's bases in Afghanistan and on a supposed base in Sudan. The Afghan training camps at Khost and Jalalabad were hit, with more than 30 fatalities, but bin Laden was untouched. By the end of 1998 Osama bin Laden had gone from comparative obscurity to being demonized by the Clinton administration and blamed for almost every anti-US attack in Muslim countries during the 1990s.

American pressure on the Taliban to hand over bin Laden got nowhere, and while Saudi Arabia cut links with the protectors of its former citizen, Pakistan still continued to aid the Taliban. Al-Qaeda was not deflected from its terrorist activities and in 2000 it launched a suicide boat attack on the American warship USS *Cole* in Aden harbour, killing seventeen sailors. The al-Qaeda terrorist attacks culminated in the atrocities of 11 September 2001. Hijacked airliners were crashed into the World Trade Center in New York City and the Pentagon in Washington, DC, killing almost 3,000 people.

President George W. Bush reacted to these attacks by declaring a relentless 'war on terror', Islamic or otherwise. After the Taliban regime refused to hand over Osama bin Laden, the USA prepared to attack Afghanistan. At first a conventional invasion on the lines of the Gulf War of 1991 was planned, but then a lighter and swifter approach was proposed. This involved large-scale air attacks linked with ground advances by local forces. The CIA had existing links with the principal anti-Taliban group in Afghanistan, the Northern Alliance. Now some 500 CIA operatives and US special forces entered the country and organized the Northern Alliance for an attack on Taliban positions. US air attacks began in October 2001 and in the following month the Taliban were driven out of Kabul and other Afghan cities. In December Osama bin Laden, apparently trapped at Tora Bora, managed to escape to Pakistan, while Mullah Omar fled from Kandahar to the same destination. The Americans had driven the Taliban and al-Qaeda out of Afghanistan in only a few months, and not a single American had been killed in combat.

Despite events in Afghanistan, Islamic terrorist attacks continued after 2001, with the bombing of a Bali nightclub in 2002 that killed more than

200 people, mostly Australian tourists, being a prime example. Fears grew that al-Qaeda might find new countries in which to establish bases and might acquire new and more terrible weapons. Although Saddam Hussein's political roots were in secular Arab nationalism, it was feared by the USA that he might be ready to provide weapons of mass destruction to Islamic terrorists. This was one of the reasons that the Americans, with some British assistance, invaded Iraq in March 2003 to overthrow Saddam Hussein's regime.

With his military machine barely recovered from its crushing defeat in 1991, Saddam had no hope of survival. As in the previous war against Iraq, CENTCOM, now led by General Tommy Franks, organized the attack. Originally the plan was for a double invasion of Iraq from Turkey in the north and Kuwait in the south, but the Turkish government refused to allow US troops to attack from its soil. Instead local Kurdish forces, with some US assistance, drove back Saddam's forces in northern Iraq. The air attack on Iraq began on 19 March 2003 and the ground invasion came the following day. Over 120,000 US soldiers and marines, along with 20,000 British troops, crossed from Kuwait into Iraq. Although a much smaller force than the army used against the Iraqis in 1991, the invaders enjoyed total air superiority and crushed Saddam's forces within three weeks. Baghdad fell on 9 April and Saddam went into hiding. Only 139 American and 33 British military personnel were killed in the invasion, but thousands of Iraqis died. On 1 May the Americans announced that major combat operations in Iraq had ended and President Bush declared: 'Mission accomplished.' All too soon he would come to regret those words.

12

THE 9/11 WARS

(TO 2015)

The swift victory of the United States and its allies in Afghanistan in 2001 and in Iraq in 2003 seemed to promise an early return to normality on the international scene. Instead these successes were merely the opening battles of what have been termed the 9/11 wars. Over the following decade the conflict between Islamist militants and Western powers and their local allies would spread around the globe: from terrorist attacks in Europe and North America to open warfare in Nigeria and Somalia; from kidnappings in the Philippines to drone strikes in Yemen. The intensity of the conflict would ebb and flow, and at some points it seemed the war was winding down, only to flare up anew on an old battlefield or break out in an area previously considered peaceful.

One consequence of the 9/11 wars has been that the Israel–Palestine conflict, which dominated relations between the West and Muslim countries in the Middle East for most of the second half of the twentieth century, has begun to seem of secondary importance. Israel's war with Hizbollah in Lebanon in 2006 and its repeated attacks on the Palestinians in Gaza certainly stoked the fires of Muslim hatred, but with Western armies now present in Muslim countries, they became the main enemy.

Afghanistan and Iraq remained the principal theatres of the 9/11 wars, but by 2011 it seemed that warfare in both countries was at last beginning to wane. Then came the so-called 'Arab Spring' of that year, when popular revolts spread across the Arab world. Hopes of secular, democratic change were soon dashed as jihadist groups took control of most opposition groups. A civil war in Libya was short-lived, but left the country in chaos. The civil war in Syria seemed never-ending and began to encourage a revival of jihadist activity in neighbouring Iraq. By 2014 large areas of Syria and Iraq were under the control of the world's first jihadi state since Mahdist Sudan in the late nineteenth century. This new state was ruled by ISIS (Islamic State in Iraq and Syria), also known as ISIL (Islamic State in Iraq and the Levant) – or simply IS, Islamic State. This group had its origins in the al-Qaeda movement, but by 2014 had become a greater threat to international security than Osama bin Laden's organization had ever been.

IRAQ

After the removal of the Taliban and al-Qaeda from Afghanistan in late 2001, that country was to enjoy some years of comparative peace. This was not to be the case in Iraq, however, after the successful Anglo-American invasion overthrew Saddam Hussein in March–April 2003. The continuing sporadic attacks were blamed on disgruntled Saddam loyalists, but in August suicide bombings indicated the arrival of jihadist terror groups. The capture of Saddam Hussein in December 2003 gave some hope that the insurgency might die down, but in fact the situation was to become far worse in the following year. (Saddam Hussein was executed by the Iraqis in 2006.)

The Americans and their allies were to find themselves between a rock and a hard place. On one side was the Sunni Muslim minority in Iraq, who had dominated the country for centuries and resented their loss of power. On the other side was the Shiite Muslim majority, who would inevitably get to rule Iraq once democratic elections were held. Sunnis feared Shiite retaliation for years of Sunni oppression, but even some Shiites were hostile to their Western 'liberators'. Unlike Afghanistan, where an Afghan interim government was established soon after the fighting ended, the Americans initially installed their own provisional government in Iraq, causing Shiites to fear a prolonged foreign occupa-tion that would keep them out of power. Sunni fears were encouraged by jihadi terrorists, who spearheaded attacks on Americans and Shiites. Shiite fears led to the rise of militias such as the Mahdi army led by Muqtada al-Sadr which, encouraged by neighbouring Shiite Iran, were ready to attack both Americans and Sunnis.

In 2004 the most brutal of Iraq's Sunni jihadist terror groups, known as al-Qaeda in Iraq (AQI), was led by the Jordanian militant Abu Musab al-Zarqawi. Despite its name, the group was not under the direct con-trol of Osama bin Laden and its leaders often ignored directives from him and other al-Qaeda leaders who were hiding in Pakistan. Although suicide bombers and improvised explosive devices (IEDs) by the road-side would soon be the principal weapons of Iraqi insurgents, in 2004 they dared to confront United States forces in open battle. During the spring US troops attempted to retake Fallujah from Sunni insurgents. At the same time Sadr's militia launched uprisings in Shiite cities, notably Najaf. For several weeks the Americans were battling both Sunnis and Shiites, but then Iraqi political and religious leaders brought about ceasefires in both Fallujah and Najaf. This was only a temporary halt, with battles renewed in both places later in the year. Shiite religious leaders eventually forced Sadr to withdraw his militia, but Fallujah required a full-scale military assault by the Americans – their most bloody urban battle since the recapture of Hue City in South Vietnam in 1968. The city was taken, but many of the jihadist insurgents had already slipped away. The Fallujah battles, in which 83 Americans were killed and over 500 were wounded, had confirmed that guerrilla forces could never defeat the US military in a conventional battle, so the insurgents returned to their suicide attacks and IEDs.

Despite the intensity of the battles at Fallujah and Najaf in the central area of Iraq, much of the country remained largely unaffected by military operations. In the north the Kurdish areas were peaceful under an increasingly autonomous local government. In the south of the country, where the population was mostly Shiite, there was similarly little violence, with the British force in the city of Basra initially facing few problems there. The principal battlegrounds were in and around the capital city, Baghdad, and in the Sunni-majority province of Anbar to the west of that city. Further to the north the city of Mosul also witnessed unrest, as did areas near to the Syrian border. Arms supplies and foreign Sunni Muslim fighters coming to join AQI mostly entered Iraq from Syria, while explosives and advisers arrived from across the border with Iran to support Iraqi Shiite militias.

One of the aims of counter-insurgency operations was to win the support of the local population, but in this the United States initially had only limited success. The scandal in 2004 concerning the ill-treatment of Muslim prisoners in the Abu Ghraib prison by their American captors seemed to show them as being little better than Saddam Hussein's torturers. Similarly, inaccurate air strikes, whether by aircraft, attack helicopters or the increasingly ubiquitous unmanned aerial vehicles (UAVs, better known as drones), killed many innocent civilians, further antagonizing the local population.

By 2005 there was a democratically elected national government in place in Iraq, and a new Iraqi army and police force were being assembled. However, both the political administration and the security forces were largely dominated by Shiites, thus alienating the Sunni minority in the country. At this time the US strategy within Iraq was to clear out insurgent areas and then hand them over to the Iraqi security forces, but it soon became clear that most Iraqi units were incompetent, corrupt and riddled with sectarian bias. As US casualties increased, with a total of around 1,700 fatalities in the years 2004 and 2005, the military began to retreat to big, fortified bases outside urban areas, only sallying forth for specific patrols and raids. It was even a struggle just to keep open the main supply routes to these bases.

One of the aims of Zarqawi's AQI was to create a civil war between Sunnis and Shiites in Iraq, in order for the Sunni minority to be forced to turn to the jihadist armed groups for protection. Initially they had not been too successful in this aim, but after the February 2006 Sunni jihadist bombing of the Shiite al-Askari mosque at Samarra, the Shiite retaliation spread across the central belt of the country and religious civil war became a reality. The sectarian clashes were particularly severe in Baghdad, where there were a number of mixed Sunni/Shiite districts. Sadr's militia and other Shiite gangs drove the Sunnis out of most of these districts and forced others out of the city altogether. Apart from a few Sunni areas in the west of the city, Baghdad soon became a largely Shiite city, while the Iraqi government, American commanders, foreign embassies and international aid organizations remained separate from the tide of violence in their massively fortified 'Green Zone' in the centre of the city.

Zarqawi himself did not live to see all the mayhem, as he was tracked down to a hideout near Baquba by American special forces in June 2006 and killed by an American air attack. Nevertheless once it had started, the sectarian civil war proved difficult to stop, and casualties rose rapidly. By late 2006 it seemed that violence in the central zone of Iraq was out of control. In December 2006 over 3,000 Iraqis were killed, two-thirds in sectarian violence. Pessimists foretold that the United States would be forced to withdraw from the country in the same way it had been forced to pull out of Somalia in 1993. However, there were already signs of hope that the chaotic situation might yet be mastered.

Within Iraq, significant numbers of Sunnis were beginning to turn against AQI. Just as Islamist insurgents in the Algerian civil war of the 1990s had alienated their supporters by their extreme violence and brutality, so AQI had angered many Iraqi Sunnis in similar fashion, especially among the tribes of Anbar province. In Algeria the government created and armed a local militia to protect people from the jihadi extremists, who became isolated and were eventually defeated. In Anbar US officers were ready to do something similar once local Sunni tribal leaders turned against AQI. The process began in late 2006, but with one important difference from the Algerian case. In Algeria the national government set up the militia; in Iraq it was the US military, fully aware that most of the Sunni militia were hostile to Iraq's Shiite-dominated national government. The Americans ignored protests from Baghdad, paying and arming the militia themselves. If the Sunnis were ready to stop attacking American troops and to drive out AQI, the Americans were not complaining.

However, this changing of sides by the Sunni tribes, known as 'the Awakening', could only prosper if the United States showed clearly that it was committed to increased military force in Iraq, that it was 'the strongest tribe' in the country. The previous US counter-insurgency strategy in Iraq had been built on the premise that suppressing the insurgency and handing over security to the Baghdad government would lead to a steady reduction of US forces in Iraq. However, Iraqi Sunnis were unlikely to reject AQI and back the Americans if the American presence in the country was declining. The US war in Iraq, apparently headed for defeat in 2006, was turned around in 2007 by doing exactly the opposite: the number of US forces in the country massively increased.

By the end of 2006 the Iraq war was deeply unpopular with most of the American public and President George W. Bush was desperately looking for a new strategy. It came in the form of 'the surge'. Some 30,000 extra US troops would be poured into Iraq in 2007, particularly in and around Baghdad, and they would be spread among outposts in local districts rather than isolated in big bases. They were to protect the local population from sectarian killers and from jihadi insurgents. Local defence forces would be set up, armed and paid by the Americans. General David Petraeus was sent to Iraq to command the new offensive. The US force in Iraq increased to over 160,000 personnel, but it would always be a temporary surge, with the military expected to achieve measureable results in a finite period. After violence had been reduced, the additional surge units would be withdrawn.

Initially casualties increased (some 904 Americans were killed in 2007, the highest ever annual total) but by September 2007, when General Petraeus gave his first report to the US Congress, violence was beginning to fall, and by the end of that year there were clear signs of success. The surge forces were not finally removed until mid-2008, but by then AQI had been largely driven out of the central region of Iraq, pulling back to Mosul in the north, while the Shiite militias had been curbed, with Sadr's men being forced to accept another ceasefire. Clearly the troop surge of 2007 was a short-term, tactical success, but did it mean long-term peace for Iraq? This would only come if the Shiite-dominated Baghdad government was ready to achieve reconciliation with Iraq's Sunni minority and the USA was ready for a lengthy commitment to Iraq. Neither would happen.

In January 2009 Barack H. Obama became the president of the USA and was determined to carry out his election campaign promise to end US combat operations in Iraq within sixteen months of taking office. Although violence continued in Iraq, it was at a lower level and less directed at US troops. In December 2009 no US troops were killed in combat in Iraq for the first time since the invasion in 2003. In the summer of 2009 US forces withdrew from Iraqi cities, except Mosul and parts of Baghdad, handing over control to Iraqi troops and police. Then, at the end of August 2010, all US combat operations in Iraq ceased and the remaining 50,000 US troops were stationed to assist the Iraqi army and police with training and similar tasks. The last US troops left Iraq in December 2011, after the US refused to accept the terms on which the Iraqi government would allow a token force to remain in the country.

Between 2003 and 2011 almost one million members of the US armed forces served in Iraq. Some 4,485 Americans had been killed in combat in Iraq and over 30,000 were wounded. Around 300 other coalition troops were killed, with 179 British soldiers the largest national group. The number of Iraqis who had died (including insurgents, security forces and civilians) came to at least 150,000. The war had cost the United States over $800 billion.

More than 100,000 Sunnis had been enlisted by the Americans in various local defence militias, but the Baghdad government was willing to enlist only 20,000 into the Iraqi army and police, which remained dominated by Shiites. The Iraqi government made no attempt at national reconciliation and development funds were denied to many war-ravaged Sunni areas. By 2012 Sunni protests at government neglect were becoming much stronger, despite government attempts to suppress them. This situation was soon to lead to dire consequences when the armed Sunnis who had rejected AQI in 2007 rallied to its successor, ISIS, in 2014 and major Iraqi cities began to fall under ISIS control.

AFGHANISTAN

After the expulsion of the Taliban and al-Qaeda from Afghanistan at the end of 2001, one priority was to deal with the 5,000 or so prisoners taken by the Americans and their Afghan allies, the Northern Alliance. President Bush had made clear that enemy combatants captured in his 'war on terror' would not be treated as prisoners of war, thus depriving them of the protection of international law. Most prisoners remained in Afghanistan, held in places such as Bagram, but 800 others, both Afghans and foreign Muslim fighters, were shipped to the US base at Guantanamo Bay in Cuba. Whether in Afghanistan or Cuba, many prisoners were ill-treated; when the abuses were later exposed, the United States' claim to be morally superior to its Islamist enemies was seriously eroded.

An interim Afghan government had been established in Kabul, with Hamid Karzai, a Pashtun, as president. However, this government was largely dominated by members of the Northern Alliance, who came from non-Pashtun ethnic groups within the country. Pashtuns were the largest ethnic group in Afghanistan and had traditionally provided the country's rulers. They felt excluded from the new government in Kabul and this resentment could easily be channelled into armed resistance to the government and its foreign, infidel supporters. In Iraq, losing political power drove the Sunni minority into revolt; in Afghanistan, losing power motivated the largest ethnic group to take up arms.

With preparations for the 2003 invasion of Iraq under way, the United States was reluctant to keep any large military force in Afghanistan, particularly as local violence was at a low level. Only a force of 8,000 troops, mostly special forces, was left to continue the hunt for Taliban and al-Qaeda remnants near Afghanistan's border with Pakistan. Nation-building in Afghanistan was to be left to the United Nations and international aid groups, who would be protected by the International Security Assistance Force (ISAF), initially based around Kabul. In 2003 the North Atlantic Treaty Organization (NATO), looking for a new role after the end of the Cold War, had taken control of ISAF, and the NATO force would include a US troop component separate from the US anti-terrorist special forces in the country.

In both Iraq and Afghanistan the United States liked to present itself as the leader of an international coalition ready to fight the threat posed by Islamist terrorism. However, foreign participation in the Iraq war was marginal. Apart from the British, all the other foreign contingents were too small to be of much significance. Iraq was always primarily an American war. The situation would be different in Afghanistan. Having two separate military commands in one country led to friction and confusion, while the much bigger foreign contingents in that country needed careful handling by the Americans. Some contingents, such as the British, the Canadians and the Australians, were willing to take a full part in the war against the Taliban when it revived, but others, such as the Germans, were governed by restrictions that seriously limited their military usefulness. When the fighting in Afghanistan grew increasingly severe from 2006 onwards, dual command quickly proved an obstacle to efficient operations, and eventually a single American commander directed all foreign and Afghan forces fighting the Taliban.

In Iraq and Afghanistan the international coalitions included small contingents from a few Muslim countries, such as Jordan and Azerbaijan, but they were never enough to reduce the overall impression that Iraq and Afghanistan had been occupied by Western armies. In the 1991 war against Iraq, large numbers of Saudi, Egyptian and Syrian troops had joined the coalition army which expelled Saddam Hussein from Kuwait, but the only large Muslim contingent in Iraq or Afghanistan was that sent by Turkey to the latter country as part of its obligation to support NATO. However, the Turkish government refused to allow its troops to be involved in any combat operations against the Taliban.

That the Taliban had the chance to revive its struggle was thanks to the safe haven it, and al-Qaeda, found in Pakistan. Although President Pervez Musharraf, Pakistan's military ruler, promised America that he would crush both organizations, his subordinates had other ideas. Pakistani military intelligence, the ISI, had been a major supporter of the Taliban and saw no reason to withdraw that support. Mullah Omar and other Taliban leaders took up residence in Quetta, not far from the border with Afghanistan. Al-Qaeda was another matter, and a few of its senior figures were picked up in Pakistan, but Osama bin Laden remained elusive.

Only when the war in Afghanistan reached new heights in 2006 did the Pakistanis come under strong pressure from the USA to clamp down on Taliban safe havens in their country. To end the threat of US cross-border raids into Pakistan, the government in Islamabad agreed to allow American drones to carry out missile strikes in Pashtun tribal areas within Pakistan, targeting Taliban and al-Qaeda personnel. However, these attacks, as well as incursions by the Pakistani army, only infuriated the Pashtuns within Pakistan. Soon a Pakistani Taliban arose and it carried out attacks on Pakistan's politicians and military forces, further destabilizing the country.

Just as most of the fighting in the Iraq war was concentrated in one part of that country – the central region – so warfare in Afghanistan would be largely restricted to specific areas. The Pashtun tribes lived mainly in the south and east of Afghanistan, along the border with Pakistan, and these were the principal areas of conflict. In addition, Taliban attacks were also regularly made in the capital, Kabul, largely for their publicity value and to alarm the large foreign community that war and reconstruction had brought there.

After some years of comparative peace, the catalyst for a major revival of fighting in Afghanistan was the steady spread of NATO forces across the country, chiefly to protect civilian provincial reconstruction teams. The Taliban had been increasing its control of southern Afghanistan during 2005 when it was announced that NATO forces would be moving into that region in the following year. American military forces were largely concentrated in eastern Afghanistan, so the southern provinces of Kandahar and Helmand would be given to the Canadians and the British respectively to patrol and police.

The initial forecasts that the arriving NATO forces would face little hostility proved disastrously wrong in 2006. The British were soon engaged in desperate struggles at towns such as Musa Qala and Sangin, while the Canadians, after initial success leading a NATO operation at Panjwei, soon found themselves hemmed into the city of Kandahar. American assistance was soon needed to prevent setbacks turning into disasters. The Taliban might be cleared from one area by coalition troops, but Afghan soldiers and police could rarely hold it for long and the Taliban soon returned. Fighting intensified in the south and east of Afghanistan over the next few years, and although foreign forces grew in numbers, so did their casualties. Local people might resent the deaths of civilians killed by Taliban suicide bombers and IEDs, but they resented even more the civilian deaths caused by errant American air strikes – even the Afghan government was beginning to echo their concerns.

Western forces found themselves fighting the Taliban over and over again for the same territory. A particularly bloody example was the town of Sangin in northern Helmand. A British outpost from 2006 to 2010, some 107 British soldiers were killed there, one-quarter of all British troops killed in the Afghan war. In 2010 Sangin passed to the Americans and in their four-year tenure 115 American troops were killed. During

2006–14 hundreds of Afghans, both insurgents and civilians, died in and around Sangin. In 2014 the Americans handed over the town to Afghan security forces. At the end of 2015 Taliban forces were threatening to overrun Sangin.

Just as the Iraq war seemed to be winding down after the 2007 troop surge, the war in Afghanistan appeared to be getting steadily worse. When Obama became the US president at the start of 2009, he was already committed to ending US combat operations in Iraq, but he saw Afghanistan as the main front for the war against Islamist terrorism. The increasing violence in that country made sending in more US troops inevitable, and between February and August 2009 US forces in the country increased from 37,000 to 68,000. American generals wanted Obama to send even more troops to Afghanistan, creating his own troop surge in the hope that it would have results as beneficial as those achieved in Iraq. Reluctantly the president agreed, but the 30,000 extra troops were only for a limited period. Win or lose, Obama set a deadline after which he would start to reduce American forces in Afghanistan. In hopes he would repeat his earlier success in Iraq, General Petraeus was now sent to Afghanistan to take command and deploy his surge forces. Soon, for the first time, there were more US troops in Afghanistan than in Iraq.

Unfortunately, the surge in Afghanistan, which brought US forces there to more than 100,000, was not to enjoy the same success as in Iraq, largely because circumstances were not so favourable in Afghanistan. Some Pashtun tribes were hostile to the Taliban, but few were ready to turn against them in the way Sunni tribal leaders in Iraq had turned against AQI. In any case there was a strong tradition of resistance to infidel invaders in the Pashtun areas of Afghanistan. Afghans in Helmand were always happy to remind British troops that their Pashtun ancestors had inflicted a crushing defeat on the British army in 1880 at Maiwand, in the neighbouring Kandahar province.

In early 2010 the Americans organized a large US–Afghan joint operation to retake the town of Marjah in Helmand from the Taliban. This operation was successfully carried out, but as usual the Afghan government failed to set up a durable administration in the liberated town or begin aid projects. Within weeks Taliban forces were reported to be returning to the area. Nevertheless, surge troops did drive Taliban insurgents out of many parts of the provinces of Helmand and Kandahar. However, as the Taliban were pushed out of those provinces, they launched attacks in other parts of Afghanistan or retreated to their safe havens in Pakistan to regroup. Time was running out and no decisive success had been achieved before Obama began to reduce US forces in Afghanistan.

Although hostile to having large American armies fighting on the soil of Muslim countries, the Obama administration was still committed to the war against Islamist terrorism, but its war emphasized the rapier rather than the bludgeon, drone strikes and special forces raids rather than huge occupation forces and indiscriminate firepower. This approach was rewarded at the beginning of May 2011 when US Navy SEAL Team Six raided Osama bin Laden's hideout at Abbottabad in Pakistan and killed the world's most famous jihadi. The United States had originally invaded Afghanistan in 2001 to apprehend bin Laden, the man behind the 9/11 atrocities, and war with the Taliban had merely been a means to that end. Now that Osama bin Laden was dead, many Americans felt they had achieved closure and wanted their military forces out of Afghanistan.

Obama was happy to oblige. By the end of 2012 the US force in Afghanistan had declined to 70,000 and in the following year most security operations were handed over to the Afghan army and police. Most American and NATO forces left Afghanistan in 2014, with only 10,000 US troops remaining to continue training Afghan forces and to carry out some counter-terrorist operations. Some 2,271 Americans had been killed in Afghanistan, along with around 1,100 other coalition troops, of whom half were British (453) and Canadian (158). Afghan deaths in the war probably amounted to around 50,000, including insurgents, security forces and civilians. The Afghan war cost the USA around $500 billion.

It seemed the war in Afghanistan was drawing to a close, but then in 2015 it flared up once again. Mullah Omar had died in 2013 and those Taliban commanders seeking to replace him sought to burnish their jihadi credentials with new and daring operations against the Afghan government. Particularly alarming was the Taliban seizure of the city of Kunduz in September 2015. Not only was it the first large Afghan city to fall to the Taliban since 2001, but it was in northern Afghanistan, an area that had not seen much fighting in the past. Supported by US bombers, Afghan government forces soon regained control of the city, but later in 2015 the Taliban seemed to be on the verge of overrunning Helmand province, one of their old battlefields. Again the USA rushed to the assistance of the Afghan government. The 10,000 US troops remaining in Afghanistan will not be reduced in the near future. To add to the Afghan turmoil, ISIS is now beginning to develop a presence in Afghanistan, challenging both the Afghan government and the Taliban.

With the death of Osama bin Laden in 2011, some commentators saw the 9/11 wars coming to an end. The war in Iraq seemed to be largely over and the war in Afghanistan was winding down, while terrorist attacks outside the Muslim world were now rare events. On one calculation, during the first decade of the 9/11 wars (2001–11) some 250,000 people worldwide died in the conflicts. More than 90 per cent of the dead were Muslims, whether insurgents/terrorists, security forces or civilians, and most of them were killed by other Muslims rather than Westerners. Now it seemed that a more peaceful period in world affairs might begin. Such hopes were soon to be brutally crushed.

THE ARAB SPRING AND THE RISE OF ISIS

The suicide of an obscure Tunisian fruit seller in December 2010 as a protest against police oppression was the unlikely event which set off a revolutionary wave that swept across the Arab world in the first half of 2011. This so-called 'Arab Spring' was a protest against government oppression of different kinds in a variety of countries. At first the protesters seemed to be largely secular democrats looking for political progress on the Western model, but soon Islamist groups began to take over the protests and make them yet another front in their war against the West.

Protests in Tunisia led to President Zine El Abidine Ben Ali being overthrown in January 2011. In the following month, unrest in Egypt forced President Hosni Mubarak to resign, and governing authority passed to an army council which promised free elections. Riots in Libya swiftly transformed into a civil war between enemies and supporters of the country's long-time ruler Muammar al-Qaddafi. Similarly, in March 2011, discontent in Syria soon moved from demonstrations to fighting, beginning a civil war against the ruler, Bashar al-Assad. It seemed the revolutionary wave was unstoppable, but not in Bahrain. When the majority Shiite population there rose against the Sunni ruler, Saudi Arabia sent in troops to crush the Shiite protesters.

Muammar al-Qaddafi, who had ruled Libya for more than 40 years, had never been a friend of the West, so the US and its NATO allies were ready to assist in his downfall. When initial anti-Qaddafi opposition seemed to be faltering in March 2011, NATO sent bombers and warships against Qaddafi's forces. This assistance kept the rebels in the field, but it was still not until August that they captured Libya's capital city, Tripoli. Qaddafi still refused to give in, but he was eventually captured and killed by the rebels in October 2011. For some months there were hopes that Libya would become a stable democracy, suitably grateful to its Western friends. However, militant Islamist groups soon became prominent and kept the country in turmoil. One of their most significant blows came in September 2012 when the US ambassador to Libya, J. Christopher Stevens, was killed by jihadis in Benghazi.

Egypt under Mubarak had long been an ally of the USA and Israel, and there was soon concern in the West that the new democracy born there in 2011 might not necessarily bring beneficial results. After further protests, the army council held a presidential election in mid-2012. To the horror of Western observers, the victorious candidate was Mohammed Morsi, a member of the Muslim Brotherhood, one of the oldest Islamist groups in Egypt. Before the year was out, Morsi was said to be planning to give himself unlimited powers so that he could impose his Islamist agenda on Egypt. Protests grew, so in July 2013 Morsi was deposed by the Egyptian military, with General Abdel Fattah al-Sisi becoming head of state. After its brief flirtation with democracy and Islamist rule, Egypt was safely back in the Western camp under its new ruler, the latest in a line of military strongmen who have ruled the country since 1952. The Islamist reaction to this course of events was to carry out terrorist attacks on government forces, particularly in the Sinai region.

The USA and its allies hoped that President Assad would be driven from power in Syria as fast as Qaddafi had been pushed out in Libya, but their hopes for his removal were to be consistently disappointed. The Syrian civil war began with national protests at the authoritarian rule of Assad, but it quickly became a sectarian conflict. Most of the protesters were from Syria's Sunni Muslim majority, but Assad and his associates were Alawites, members of a small sect of Islam sometimes linked to the Shiites. Thus Syria became a new battlefield for the struggle between Sunnis and Shiites that was already being played out in Iraq. Assad was supported by Iran, by the Baghdad government in Iraq and by Hizbollah in Lebanon. His Sunni opponents were backed by Turkey, Saudi Arabia and Gulf states such as Qatar. Assad's longstanding links with Russia brought him support from that country, while the USA and its Western allies favoured his opponents, but they were reluctant to intervene militarily even to the limited extent they had done in Libya's civil war.

Syria quickly descended into chaos and became a patchwork of areas held by the different warring factions. As in Libya, jihadist groups moved in to take over much of the Sunni opposition, and these groups included the remnants of Osama bin Laden's al-Qaeda organization. The official al-Qaeda group in Syria was the al-Nusra Front, but much more important was the transformed AQI moving in from Iraq, now known as ISIS (or ISIL).

After being driven out of central Iraq by the 2007 US troop surge and the 'Awakening' among Sunni tribes, AQI had just managed to survive further north. However, by 2010, the organization seemed to be on its last legs. After its principal leaders were killed in that year, Abu Bakr al-Baghdadi, a religious scholar turned insurgent, took charge of AQI and over the next two years largely rebuilt the movement. It expanded by tapping into Sunni militancy in both Iraq and Syria. In Iraq the Sunnis were increasingly ready to take up arms against an oppressive Shiite government in Baghdad, while in Syria the Sunnis were seeking to overthrow the Alawite ruler Assad. AQI had helped to set up the original al-Qaeda operation in Syria, the al-Nusra Front, and in 2013 it attempted to move into Syria itself and absorb that organization, with the linked group to be called ISIS. Later in the year ISIS helped hundreds of Sunni militants break out of jails in Iraq and it also took control of the city of Raqqa in Syria, the first provincial capital in that country to fall into rebel hands.

The al-Nusra Front had refused to be absorbed in ISIS and at the start of 2014 the clashes between the two groups led the leader of al-Qaeda, Ayman al-Zawahiri, to cut all links with ISIS, but that organization was now sufficiently powerful in both Syria and Iraq to go its own way. In January 2014 ISIS seized control of Fallujah in Iraq, a Sunni city only 40 miles west of the national capital, Baghdad. The Americans had driven AQI out of Fallujah in 2004; now, ten years later, AQI's successor ISIS was back in control. The Iraqi government failed to recapture the lost city and the poor performance of its forces only invited further attacks. In June 2014 ISIS took control of Mosul, Iraq's second largest city, and Tikrit, with the local Iraqi garrisons fleeing after putting up little resistance.

Suddenly ISIS was in control of large areas of both eastern Syria and western Iraq. The land area was said to be larger than Great Britain, while the population of six million was larger than that of a country such as Denmark. For the first time in recent history the jihadis had created their own state, with its capital at Raqqa in Syria. To celebrate this accomplishment, ISIS announced the creation of a caliphate, the first since the end of the Ottoman caliphate in 1924. It claimed authority over the world's 1.6 billion Muslims, almost one-quarter of the global population. Al-Baghdadi took the title of Caliph Ibrahim and declared his movement should in future simply be called Islamic State (IS), although his opponents still preferred to label it ISIS or ISIL.

In reaction to the sudden success of ISIS, the American president, Barack Obama, decided in late June 2014 to send more US military advisers to Iraq, raising the US presence there to 800 troops. During July ISIS had further military successes in Syria, and in August it drove Kurdish forces out of Sinjar in Iraq. As a follow up, ISIS units began to advance on Irbil, the capital of Iraqi Kurdistan. This development finally set alarm bells ringing in Washington, DC. Having defeated the Iraqis, the Syrians and the Kurds, ISIS suddenly seemed invincible. The Kurds were the West's staunchest allies in Iraq and the USA could not allow them to be overrun by ISIS. In August 2014 US aircraft began bombing ISIS targets in Iraq; in September the air attacks were extended to ISIS targets in Syria. In October ISIS attacked Kobani in Syria, a town held by Syrian Kurds. For the rest of the year a bitter struggle took place there, with US air attacks supporting the local Kurdish resistance. Eventually ISIS had to admit defeat and withdraw from the ruined town, but this first defeat did not seem to damage the prestige ISIS now commanded in the Islamic world.

ISIS-affiliated militant groups were active in countries such as Egypt, Libya and Afghanistan, while other militant Islamist organizations around the world were happy to pledge allegiance to ISIS. These included Boko Haram in Nigeria and Abu Sayyaf in the Philippines. Al Shabaab in Somalia suffered a split on the issue, some members wanting to preserve the existing link to al-Qaeda while others wanted to switch allegiance to ISIS. Even the US government was ready to confirm the enhanced status of ISIS when in June 2015 the State Department declared that the organization was now a greater threat than al-Qaeda.

Nevertheless, the repulse of ISIS at Kobani had encouraged the government of Iraq to take action against it in that country. In March/April 2015 Iraqi forces managed to retake Tikrit from ISIS, but in May ISIS hit back by seizing the city of Ramadi, where once again the Iraqi army performed poorly. Tikrit had been largely recaptured by Iraqi Shiite militia, trained and even led by Iranian Revolutionary Guards, much to American annoyance. In a further effort to rebuild the Iraqi army, Obama raised the number of US advisers to 3,000 troops, while increasing air attacks on ISIS targets in both Iraq and Syria.

A new development came in September 2015 when Russia decided to give direct military support to the Assad regime in Syria by starting a bombing campaign against its opponents, including ISIS. In the following month ISIS apparently retaliated by planting a bomb on a Russian airliner in Egypt. It destroyed the plane over Sinai and killed over 200 people. In November the Iraqi Kurds recaptured Sinjar from ISIS, but this success was quickly overshadowed when ISIS claimed responsibility for the killing of 130 people in Paris, France, by jihadi terrorists. Then in December 2015 similar terrorists struck in San Bernardino, California, killing fourteen people, and ISIS once again claimed responsibility. At the end of the year the Iraqi government recaptured Ramadi from ISIS, using its own army for the task rather than Iraqi Shiite militia.

So it goes on. Attack, followed by counter-attack. American generals talk of destroying ISIS through the continued air campaign by the USA and its allies, but that campaign has already been going on for nearly eighteen months with little sign of a decisive breakthrough. Only a land military campaign can be sure of destroying the state ISIS has created straddling Syria and Iraq. At present this is unacceptable to Western countries, but it is, of course, exactly what ISIS leaders want. The return of 'Christian' armies to Iraq and their appearance in Syria would vastly inflame the conflict between the West and the Muslim world. Nevertheless, Western leaders may yet have to risk some form of direct military intervention in Syria and Iraq to destroy ISIS, especially if ISIS continues to launch terrorist attacks in Europe and North America and its affiliates expand their power in Egypt, Libya and Afghanistan.

13

CONCLUSION: A NEW CONFLICT?

It is more than 330 years since the last Muslim invasion of a Christian country, when the Ottoman army tried to take Vienna in 1683. It is only twelve years since the last Christian, or rather Western, invasion of a Muslim country, when the Americans and the British rolled into Iraq in 2003. No wonder it is not hard for jihadists to convince some of their fellow Muslims that the USA and its allies are waging a 'crusader' war against the Islamic world. But is this really just a renewal of the centuries-old Christian–Muslim religious war? Probably not. That religious conflict ended with the fall of the Ottoman empire after the First World War. Most ostensibly Christian states are now in reality secular, leaving their citizens to choose whatever religion they prefer or no religion at all. Indeed, many of the countries which were once in the forefront of the struggle against Islam now have sizeable Muslim populations. In France, for example, nearly 10 per cent of the population are Muslims.

The new conflict between the post-Christian West and Islam is more a clash between secular materialism and a revived religion. Stressing the benefits of liberal democracy and a global free market economy, West-erners claim that their world view has superseded Islam, just as Muslims long ago claimed that their new religion superseded both Christianity and Judaism. Muslims see an essentially 'godless' West tempting their people with material benefits and pleasures, putting individual desires before the wider community and submission to the will of God. Islamic fundamentalist radicals demand a violent reassertion of Islamic values against the Western threat, while even moderate Muslims wish to com-bine the acceptance of many aspects of Western modernity with a continued commitment to basic Islamic values.

What might once have been merely a philosophical debate between the two sides had already become stained with blood even before the events of 11 September 2001. During the period of decolonization the West had largely clashed with secular nationalist movements in the Muslim world. It was the Iranian revolution of 1979 that re-injected religious fervour into one side of the Christian–Muslim struggle and unleashed powerful forces that the West at first struggled to understand. A new variant of the old conflict between the two sides had now begun.

During the overtly religious phase of the Christian–Muslim conflict, from the death of the Prophet Muhammad in 632 to the end of the Ottoman caliphate in 1924, the military contest for the first 1,000 years or so had largely favoured the Muslims. The Arab conquests had largely overrun the Christian heartlands around the Mediterranean Sea, and only the remnants of the Byzantine empire and the backward states of western Europe remained to uphold the Christian cause. The Byzantines beat off Muslim attacks, and in the second half of the tenth century began to win back territory, but they went into decline after their defeat at Manzikert in 1071 by the Seljuk Turks. By the end of the eleventh century the Christians of western Europe had replaced the Byzantines as the principal defenders of Christendom and through the First Crusade had thrust deep into the Muslim heartlands, retaking Jerusalem. By 1300, however, the Muslims had rallied and driven the Christians out of Palestine and Syria once again. This success was of more importance to the wider Islamic world than the loss of most Muslim lands in distant Iberia to the Christian *Reconquista*.

In all these wars the technological gap between the two sides was not great. Innovations such as Byzantine 'Greek Fire' or Turkish horse archers had important short-term impacts, but the opposing side soon adjusted. Muslims mastered Christian siege techniques, while the Christian military orders soon had 'turcopole' light cavalry to complement their own heavy cavalry in the Holy Land. With no major technological advantage on either side, other factors became of more significance in Christian–Muslim warfare, most notably unity, leadership and discipline. The greatest advantage the Muslims gave the Christians was their tendency to dissolve into rival factions. Each of the main Christian advances in Iberia between 1000 and 1250 was preceded by the collapse of al-Andalus into warring *taifa* states. Even during the last stage of the *Reconquista*, the war for Granada, the Muslims were fighting a civil war among themselves as well as trying to fend off Christian attacks. Above all, it was the collapse of the Seljuk Turkish empire in the late eleventh century that gave the Western Christians their chance to invade the Muslim heartlands, capture Jerusalem, and set up the crusader states of Outremer.

To restore unity on the Muslim side and revive the jihad against the Christians required strong leadership. In the Middle East this was provided by Zengi, Nur al-Din and, above all, Saladin. Muslim unity was restored, a united Muslim state was created along the borders of Outremer, and Jerusalem was recaptured in 1187. In contrast, in Iberia the interventions of the Almoravids and later the Almohads could only instil a short-lived unity in al-Andalus, with both these Berber powers always fatally distracted by affairs in North Africa. The Mamluks of Egypt were finally to destroy Outremer, but their strength lay not so much in leadership – although they had great commanders like Baybars – and more in their disciplined military organization. Slave armies had been a feature of the Muslim military world since the ninth century, and when properly controlled they gave the Muslims a significant advantage. After the Byzantine army degenerated into a force of mercenaries, the defenders of Christendom were usually feudal levies raised by Western Christian kings who had no large permanent forces of their own. The Christian military orders of the Templars and the Hospitallers were an attempt to overcome this weakness in the context of garrisoning Outremer. Many Muslim rulers had disciplined bodies of slave troops, which provided a permanent force and a core around which their other military forces could be assembled in wartime. The Mamluks of Egypt carried this process somewhat further. In 1250 they had taken control of the state and their sultans were often no more than the first among equals. Nevertheless, the disciplined Mamluk military machine was capable of both destroying the crusader states and inflicting defeats on the previously invincible Mongols.

The four military factors of leadership, unity, discipline and technology were most successfully brought together in the Muslim world by the Ottoman Turks between 1300 and 1600, producing the greatest threat to Christendom since the Arab conquests. For ten generations almost every Ottoman ruler had significant leadership qualities that were deployed not only to wage jihad against the Christians, but to impose unity throughout the growing Ottoman empire. The Ottomans also brought the disciplined Muslim slave army to its highest peak in their elite household troops, above all the janissaries. The origins of permanent royal armies in Christian Europe are to be found in the late fifteenth century, but the Ottomans laid the foundations of such a force a century earlier and had largely created one by the time they took Constantinople in 1453. The Ottomans also proved willing to adopt the latest military technology, quickly taking up gunpowder weapons, including siege guns, field artillery and handguns.

Although primarily a land power, the Ottomans also built up a navy and by 1500 it was successfully challenging Christian power in the Mediterranean. Naval warfare and maritime endeavour was the one military field in which Christendom had achieved a lasting superiority over the Muslims after the year 1000. The Italian maritime states such as Venice and Genoa, later followed by French and Catalan port cities, achieved ascendancy in the Mediterranean Sea in both naval warfare and maritime trade from the eleventh century onwards. The crusader states of Outremer could not have survived for almost two centuries without the support of Christian shipping. Nor could the later crusaders have pursued 'the way of Egypt' without Christian ships to carry their men, horses and supplies. Outremer eventually fell to the Muslims, but Christian maritime domination of the Mediterranean remained until the Ottomans mounted a major challenge to it during the sixteenth century. Eventually the Christians retained control of the central and western Mediterranean, despite the continued attacks of the Barbary pirates, but the eastern Mediterranean came under Ottoman control.

The Christian–Muslim naval conflict in the Mediterranean during the sixteenth century was important, but already that sea was becoming a comparative backwater in terms of worldwide maritime strategy. The Western Christians had developed the ocean-going sailing ship, and from the late fifteenth century onwards they began to use such ships to venture across the oceans of the world, exploring, trading, fighting and colonizing. The movement was led by Spain and Portugal, the latter nation explicitly aiming to destroy the valuable spice trade routes across the Muslim Middle East by establishing direct sea routes to India and the Far East. Of the three great Muslim empires of the sixteenth century, the Ottoman Turks, the Safavid Persians and the Mughals in India, only the Turks had significant naval forces, and they were largely galley fleets concentrated in the Mediterranean. The Muslim empires were still formidable on land, but they conceded control of the eastern seas to the European maritime powers with comparatively little resistance. Once the Islamic world had hemmed Christendom into a small peninsula of Eurasia; now the Christians had outflanked the Muslims and broken out into the wider world.

Yet the Ottomans, the Safavids and the Mughals were not greatly concerned about their naval weakness. They were primarily land powers, and their large and formidable armies still appeared to have the advantage over Christian forces. All this began to change during the seventeenth century as Christian European armies grew in size, discipline and technological sophistication. Ottoman military decline was marked by a loss of leadership, few sultans after 1600 commanding their armies in the field; by growing disunity within the empire; by the undermining of discipline among the janissaries and other household troops; and by a growing reluctance to adopt the new military methods and equipment of the West. Christian armies became stronger and more efficient, while Muslim military power dwindled. Although Muslim armies were still large and their soldiers often recklessly brave, it was not enough. Increasingly, the Muslims knew how to die but not how to win. By the middle of the eighteenth century, Christian armies were consistently defeating Muslim ones, whether on the borders of the Ottoman empire or in the fast-diminishing Mughal empire in India.

The Muslim failure to adapt to military modernity is highlighted by the differing fortunes of Russia and the Ottoman empire. In 1600 Moscow seemed to envoys from western Europe almost as Asiatic a capital as Constantinople, but the Russians were to show a greater determination than the Ottomans in adopting European methods, particularly in military affairs. Czar Peter the Great destroyed the *steltsi*, the old reactionary military elite of Muscovy, in 1698; the Ottoman sultan did not crush the janissaries, his reactionary military elite, until 1826. The Russians brought in European military and naval advisers and adopted the latest European military technology. By the second half of the eighteenth century the Russian army and fleet were steadily shedding their foreign advisers and emerging as major forces on the European military scene. The Ottoman sultans brought in some European military and naval advisers and attempted technological modernization in areas such as artillery and warships, but the old conservative military groups usually managed to thwart most innovations, often in alliance with Muslim religious leaders. Instead of achieving a military modernization to match that of Russia, the Ottoman empire was to become the principal victim of growing Russian military power.

Thus by the first decades of the nineteenth century the Christian states of Europe could increasingly dominate Muslim states in land warfare as they had long done in sea warfare. The result was that the nineteenth century saw the peak of European imperialism around the world and Muslim populations were among its main victims. Islam gave those populations an organizing principle, often reinforced by Sufi brotherhoods, that allowed them to put up a stronger resistance than some other victims of European imperialism, but in the end even resisters like Abd el-Kader and Shamil had to give in to the military power of Christian Europe.

By the 1920s there were few truly independent Muslim states left in the world, and most Muslims lived under some form of colonial rule. Air power was now added to land and sea power to reinforce Christian military dominance. For a time the British even thought that air power alone might be sufficient to police some of the remaining Muslim resisters in their empire, but this view proved too optimistic and military garrisons were still necessary. European military domination of the Muslim world seemed unassailable, but after 1945 political changes made it irrelevant. Christian values became progressively less important in Western countries, while stressing secular values such as freedom and democracy undermined their will to dominate other peoples around the world. Militarily, the Anglo-French forces won at Suez in 1956, the French gained the upper hand against the Algerian rebels, and the Dutch overran the Indonesian nationalists. Politically, the three European powers were defeated by superpower hostility and critical international opinion, forcing them to withdraw from their Muslim colonies.

As decolonization came to an end in the 1970s, a new Western military power, or rather superpower, the United States of America, began to be increasingly active in the Muslim world and particularly the Middle East. The USA's three main concerns were to exclude Soviet influence during the Cold War; to ensure Western control of the region's oil supplies; and to defend the state of Israel, created in 1948. Despite earlier clashes with the Barbary pirates in the Mediterranean and the Moro rebels in the Philippines, the USA had no real record of past oppression in the Muslim world, unlike the Russians, British and French. It was now the leader of the Western world, however, and espoused secular materialist values that many religious Muslims found unacceptable. Their resentment of America was considerably sharpened by the Iranian revolution of 1979, which installed an Islamic fundamentalist regime openly hostile to the 'Great Satan'. Although the Americans supported Muslims in the Soviet–Afghan war of the 1980s and in the Bosnian conflict in the 1990s, they were increasingly viewed as the main enemy by Muslim fundamentalists. The growing presence of US air, land and sea forces in the Middle East from the late 1980s onwards only heightened fears among some Muslims of a new age of Western imperialism.

The rapid destruction of Saddam Hussein's Iraqi armed forces by the American-led coalition during the Gulf War of 1991 showed the impotence of even a supposedly strong Muslim military power in the face of superior American military technology. Despite the past pretensions of Egypt, Saudi Arabia and Pakistan, there is no Muslim state powerful enough to act as overall leader of the Muslim world on the Ottoman model. There is certainly no Muslim state today that can deploy the sort of military power that the Ottoman empire wielded in its prime. In terms of conventional warfare any future Christian–Muslim conflict will be no contest. The military domination of the USA on land, on sea and in the air is at the present time unassailable. It is for that reason that the emerging conflict has become increasingly concentrated on guerrilla warfare and terrorism, warfare in which the political dimension is as important as the military.

The swift US victories in Afghanistan in 2001 and in Iraq in 2003 confirmed American superiority in conventional warfare, yet these triumphs did not bring any lasting peace. In all the long centuries of Christian–Muslim conflict, never has the military imbalance between the two sides been greater, but the dominant West can apparently derive little comfort from that fact. In both Afghanistan and Iraq prolonged Islamist guerrilla resistance has worn down the USA and its allies. Temporary successes such as the US troop surge of 2007 in Iraq have not led to long-term peace and stability, while in both countries Western commitment to apparently endless struggles has faltered. Terrorist attacks on Western capitals such as Madrid, London and Paris continue to provide maximum publicity for Islamist militants, but the most important events take place in the Muslim heartland of the Middle East. The most significant recent development has been the rise to power of ISIS in both Syria and Iraq, creating the first jihadist state since the late nineteenth century. Although the USA and its allies remain wary of a return to large-scale Western military intervention in Muslim countries, the challenge posed by ISIS may not be defeated by air attacks and local forces alone. Even if the Christian–Muslim conflict of the past has taken on a new form, it seems unlikely to come to a swift end.

GLOSSARY OF
PLACE NAME CHANGES

PAST	PRESENT
Acre	Akko (Israel)
Adalia	Antalya (Turkey)
Adramyttium, Gulf of	Edremit, Gulf of (Turkey)
Adrianople	Edirne (Turkey)
Alcazarquivir	Ksar el Kebir (Morocco)
Aleppo	Halab (Syria)
Amida	Diyarbakir (Turkey)
Antioch	Antakya (Turkey)
Ascalon	Ashkelon, Ashqelon (Israel)
Asia Minor	Anatolia (Turkey)
Batavia	Jakarta (Indonesia)
Bone	Annaba (Algeria)
Bougie	Bejaia (Algeria)
Buda	Budapest (Hungary)
Calcutta	Kolkata (India)
Calicut	Kozhikode (India)
Candia	Iraklion (Greece)
Chanak	Canakkale (Turkey)
Constantinople	Istanbul (Turkey)
Dorylaeum	Eskisehir (Turkey)
Durazzo	Durres (Albania)
Edessa	Urfa (Turkey)
Gallipoli	Gelibolu (Turkey)
Goletta, La	Goulette, La (Tunisia)
Hattin	Hittin (Israel)
Iconium	Konya (Turkey)
Janina	Ioannina (Greece)
Jassy	Iasi (Romania)
Kairouan	Qayrawan (Tunisia)
Lepanto	Nafpaktos (Greece)
Manzikert	Malazgirt (Turkey)
Morea, the	Peloponnese, the (Greece)
Navarino	Pylos (Greece)

Negroponte	Euboea, Evvia (Greece)
Nicaea	Iznik (Turkey)
Nicomedia	Izmit (Turkey)
Nicopolis	Nikopol (Bulgaria)
Peterwardein, Petrovaradin	part of Novi Sad (Serbia)
Philippeville	Skikda (Algeria)
Plevna	Pleven (Bulgaria)
St Gotthard	Szentgotthard (Hungary)
Samosata	Samsat (Turkey)
San Stefano	Yesilkoy (Turkey)
Saragossa	Zaragoza (Spain)
Seringapatam	Srirangapatna (India)
Smyrna	Izmir (Turkey)
Temesvar	Timisoara (Romania)
Tenedos	Bozcaada (Turkey)
Thessalonica, Salonika	Thessaloniki (Greece)
Tiberias	Teverya (Israel)
Trebizond	Trabzon (Turkey)
Tripoli (Syria)	Tarabulus (Lebanon)
Tripoli (Libya)	Tarabulus (Libya)
Zenta	Senta (Serbia)

CHRONOLOGY

632	Death of the Prophet Muhammad
636	Arabs defeat Byzantines at River Yarmuk
638	Jerusalem captured by Arabs
642	Arabs force Byzantines out of Egypt
655	Arab fleet defeats Byzantines at the 'Battle of the Masts'
674–8	First Arab siege of Constantinople
698	Arabs capture Carthage
711	Arabs invade Visigothic Spain
717–18	Second Arab siege of Constantinople
720	Battle of Covadonga: beginning of Christian *Reconquista* in Iberia
732	Franks defeat Arabs in a battle between Poitiers and Tours
756	Umayyad state established in al-Andalus
778	Charlemagne's expedition to Saragossa and battle of Roncesvalles
801	Franks take Barcelona from Arabs
824	Arabs begin conquest of Crete from Byzantines
827	Arabs begin conquest of Sicily from Byzantines
846	Arabs raid Rome and sack St Peter's
880	Arabs expelled from southern Italy
904	Thessalonica sacked by Muslims
912–61	Abd al-Rahman III rules in al-Andalus; zenith of Muslim Iberia
961–9	Successful campaigns of Nicephorus Phocas: Byzantines recapture Crete (961), Cyprus (965) and Antioch (969)
975	John Tzimisces leads Byzantine army on successful campaign in Syria and Palestine
997	Almanzor sacks Santiago de Compostela
1009	Fatimid caliph orders destruction of Church of Holy Sepulchre in Jerusalem
1031	End of Umayyad caliphate at Córdoba; rise of *taifa* states in al-Andalus
1061	Normans begin conquest of Sicily from Muslims
1071	Seljuk Turks defeat Byzantine emperor at battle of Manzikert
1085	Alfonso VI of Castile takes Toledo from the Moors
1086	Almoravids defeat Alfonso at battle of Sagrajas
1091	Normans complete conquest of Sicily
1094	El Cid takes Valencia

1095	Pope Urban II calls for crusade to Holy Land
1096–9	First Crusade
1098	Crusaders take Antioch and Edessa
1099	Crusaders capture Jerusalem and establish crusader states of Outremer
1118	Alfonso I of Aragon takes Saragossa from Moors
1123	Venetian fleet destroys Fatimid Egyptian fleet off Ascalon; Venetians help crusaders to take Tyre (falls in 1124)
1144	Zengi takes Edessa from Christians
1147–8	Second Crusade
1147	Portuguese and crusaders take Lisbon from Moors
1148	Unsuccessful attack on Damascus ends Second Crusade
1176	Seljuk Turks defeat Byzantines at battle of Myriocephalon
1187	Saladin defeats Christian army at battle of Horns of Hattin and then captures Jerusalem
1189–92	Third Crusade
1191	Crusaders capture Acre
1192	Crusaders fail to take Jerusalem and make treaty with Saladin
1195	Almohads defeat Alfonso VIII of Castile at battle of Alarcos
1204	Fourth Crusade attacks Byzantine Christians rather than Muslims; Sack of Constantinople
1212	Almohads defeated by a combined Christian army at the battle of Las Navas de Tolosa; turning point of the *Reconquista*
1217–21	Fifth Crusade. Crusaders take Damietta in Egypt, then forced to withdraw
1223	Final expulsion of Muslims from Sicily
1228	Emperor Frederick II goes on crusade to the Holy Land
1229	Frederick's treaty with Muslims restores Jerusalem to Christian control
1236	Ferdinand III of Castile captures Córdoba
1238	James I of Aragon takes Valencia
1244	Muslims recapture Jerusalem from Christians; battle of La Forbie
1248	Ferdinand III takes Seville; soon Granada is the only Muslim state left in Iberia
1248–50	Crusade of Louis IX of France to Egypt
1268	Mamluk sultan Baybars takes Antioch
1270	Crusade of Louis IX to Tunis
1291	Mamluk sultan al-Ashraf Khalil captures Acre; the end of Outremer
1326	Ottoman Turks capture Bursa, which becomes their first capital
1344	Crusading league captures Smyrna
1354	Ottoman Turks capture Gallipoli, their first major foothold in Europe
1365	Peter I of Cyprus leads crusade to Alexandria
1369	Ottomans take Adrianople, which became their new capital
1389	Ottomans defeat Serbs at battle of Kosovo
1396	Ottomans defeat Franco-Hungarian crusader army at battle of Nicopolis

1402	Tamerlane defeats Ottomans at Ankara, then storms Smyrna
1426	Mamluks invade Cyprus and make its Christian king their vassal
1430	Ottomans capture Thessalonica
1444	Ottomans defeat Hungarian crusader army at Varna
1453	Ottomans capture Constantinople
1456	Hungarians repulse Ottoman attack on Belgrade
1461	Ottomans take Trebizond, the last remnant of the Byzantine empire
1481	Beginning of final war between Christians and Granada in Spain
1492	City of Granada surrendered to Ferdinand and Isabella; end of the *Reconquista*
1499	Ottoman fleet defeat the Venetians at the battle of Zonchio First Muslim revolt in the Alpujarras begins; ends 1501
1502	All Muslims in Castile ordered to convert to Christianity or leave
1521	Ottoman sultan Suleiman I takes Belgrade
1522	Suleiman attacks Rhodes and expels the Knights Hospitaller
1526	Suleiman defeats Hungarian king at battle of Mohács
1529	Unsuccessful siege of Vienna by Suleiman
1535	Emperor Charles v leads crusade to Tunis and takes the city from Barbarossa
1538	Barbarossa defeats Christian fleet under Andrea Doria at Preveza
1541	Charles v leads unsuccessful attempt to conquer Algiers
1551	Ottomans take Tripoli in Libya from the Hospitallers
1560	Ottomans defeat Spanish on land and sea at Djerba
1565	Hospitallers repulse Ottoman attack on Malta
1568–70	Second Muslim revolt in the Alpujarras; Christianized Moors (*moriscos*) revert to Islam, but are defeated
1570–71	Ottomans take Cyprus from the Venetians
1571	Fleet of the Christian Holy League defeats Ottoman fleet at the battle of Lepanto
1574	Ottomans recapture Tunis from the Spanish
1578	King Sebastian of Portugal leads crusade to Morocco, but is defeated and killed at battle of Alcazarquivir
1609	Final expulsion of Moriscos from Spain ordered
1645–69	War of Crete: Ottomans eventually take the island from Venetians
1664	Austrians defeat an invading Ottoman army at St Gotthard
1672–81	Ottoman campaigns against Poles and Russians in the Ukraine
1683	Ottoman siege of Vienna defeated by Austrian/Polish/German army
1684–7	Venetians take the Morea from Ottomans
1686	Austrians recapture the Hungarian capital Buda
1696	Russians capture Azov
1697	Austrian army under Prince Eugène defeats Ottomans at Zenta
1699	Treaty of Karlowitz; Ottomans make major territorial concessions to Christian powers
1711	Russian army under Peter the Great surrounded by Ottomans on River Pruth; Russians forced to come to terms
1714	Ottomans recapture the Morea from the Venetians

1716–18	Austro-Turkish war; Prince Eugène's victories force Ottomans to make concessions at Treaty of Passarowitz
1739	Treaty of Belgrade: Austrians and Russians make concessions to Ottomans after generally unsuccessful war with them
1757	British victory at battle of Plassey in Bengal begins their undermining of the Mughal empire in India
1768–74	Russo-Turkish war; major Russian successes such as the naval victory at Chesme (1770) and conquest of the Crimea (1771)
1774	Treaty of Kutchuk Kainardji; Ottomans make major concessions to the Russians and for the first time give up a Muslim population (Crimea) to Christian rule
1787–92	Russo-Turkish war; further Russian advances
1798	Napoleon invades the Ottoman province of Egypt
1799	British storm Seringapatam in India and kill Tipu Sultan of Mysore
1801–5	War between USA and Tripoli (Libya)
1803	British capture Delhi and take control of Mughal emperor
1804	Serbian uprising against Ottomans; first major rebellion by subject Christian peoples in the Balkans against Ottoman rule
1821	Start of the Greek war of independence
1827	British/French/Russian fleet defeats Ottoman/Egyptian fleet at battle of Navarino
1828–9	Russo-Turkish war
1830	French invasion of Algeria
1830–47	Franco-Algerian war
1832–59	Shamil leads Muslim resistance to Russians in the Caucasus
1832	Ottomans recognize independence of Greece; for the first time an independent nation has been carved out of the Ottoman empire
1839	British take control of Aden
1839–42	First Anglo-Afghan war
1853–6	Crimean war
1857	Indian Mutiny; British depose the last Mughal emperor (1858)
1860	French intervene in Lebanon to protect Maronites from Muslims
1875–6	Christian revolts in Ottoman Balkans; supported by Russia, Serbia and Montenegro
1877–8	Russo-Turkish war
1878	Congress of Berlin; Ottomans accept creation of a Bulgarian state
1878–80	Second Anglo-Afghan war
1881	French occupy Tunisia
1882	British occupy Egypt
1896–8	British conquest of Sudan
1899	The 'Mad Mullah' begins resistance to British in Somalia; crushed in 1920
1908	Young Turk revolution in Ottoman empire
1911–12	Italo-Turkish war; Italians take Libya and the Dodecanese Islands
1912	France declares a protectorate over Morocco
1912–13	The two Balkan wars; Ottomans largely driven out of Europe
1914–18	First World War; leads to defeat and division of Ottoman empire

CHRONOLOGY

1917	British capture Baghdad and Jerusalem; Balfour Declaration
1919–22	Turkish war of independence; drives Greeks, Armenians and allied powers out of Anatolia
1920	Anti-British revolt in Iraq
1921	Abd el Krim defeats Spanish at battle of Anual
1922	Ottoman sultanate abolished
1924	Ottoman caliphate abolished
1926	Abd el Krim surrenders in Morocco
1936–9	Arab revolt in Palestine against British over Jewish immigration
1939–45	Second World War
1941	British suppress revolt in Iraq
1945–9	Dutch oppose Indonesian nationalists, but eventually forced to grant independence
1947	British leave India, which is partitioned into Muslim state of Pakistan and largely Hindu state of India
1948	British leave Palestine; establishment of the state of Israel; first Arab–Israeli war
1953	USA and Britain aid overthrow of Mossadeq government in Iran
1954–62	Algerian war of liberation against the French
1956	Suez crisis; second Arab–Israeli war
1967	Third Arab–Israeli war (Six Day War); Israel occupies Old City of Jerusalem, the West Bank, Gaza and Sinai
1973	Fourth Arab–Israeli war (Yom Kippur War); Arab oil embargo on states friendly to Israel
1974	Turkey invades Cyprus and occupies the north of the island
1975–90	Christian–Muslim civil war in Lebanon
1979	Islamic revolution in Iran
1979–81	US hostages held in Iran; US rescue mission fails and crisis resolved by negotiation
1979–89	Soviet intervention in Afghanistan; US supports Muslim guerrillas
1980–88	War between Iran and Iraq
1982	Israeli invasion of Lebanon
1983	Islamic terrorist attacks on US and other Western troops in Beirut
1986	US air attacks on Libya
1990	Iraq invades Kuwait
1991	US-led coalition expels Iraqis from Kuwait (First Gulf War). End of USSR; Russians allow independent Muslim states to emerge in Central Asia, but less happy about those in the Caucasus
1991–5	Break-up of Yugoslavia; between 1992 and 1995 Muslim population of Bosnia fights Bosnian Serbs and, for a time, Bosnian Croats; US support for Muslims
1992–4	Russia helps Christian Armenia defeat Muslim state of Azerbaijan in dispute over Nagorno-Karabakh
1993	Failed US intervention in Somalia; first attack on World Trade Center, New York City, by Islamic terrorists
1994–6	Russia tries to suppress Chechen independence but is defeated
1994–6	Rise to power of the Taliban in Afghanistan

1998	Islamic terrorist attacks on US embassies in Kenya and Tanzania; US air attacks on Afghanistan and Sudan
1999	US-led coalition attacks Yugoslavia (Serbia) to protect Muslim Albanians in Kosovo; Russians invade and occupy Chechnya, but fail to end guerrilla resistance
2001	(11 September) Islamic terrorists use hijacked airliners to attack the Pentagon in Washington, DC, and to destroy the World Trade Center in New York City; USA attacks Afghanistan and overthrows the Taliban regime
2003	USA and Britain invade Iraq and overthrow Saddam Hussein
2004	Battles at Fallujah and Najaf in Iraq
	Terror attack in Madrid, Spain
2005	Terror attack in London, UK
2006	Sectarian civil war in Iraq
	Increased fighting in Afghanistan
2007	US troop surge in Iraq
2008	Terror attack in Mumbai, India
2009	Start of US troop surge in Afghanistan
	Russians declare victory in Chechnya
2010	US combat operations end in Iraq
2011	Revolts of the 'Arab Spring'
	Libyan civil war
	Start of Syrian civil war
2013	Most US and NATO combat operations end in Afghanistan
2014	ISIS captures Mosul and other Iraqi cities
	Start of US bombing of ISIS targets in Iraq and Syria
	ISIS fails to capture Kobani in Syria
2015	Russia joins bombing campaign against ISIS
	Terror attacks in Paris, France
	Iraqis drive ISIS out of Tikrit and Ramadi

SELECT BIBLIOGRAPHY

(Please note that certain titles are relevant to more than one section.)

GENERAL

Abulafia, D., *The Great Sea: A Human History of the Mediterranean* (London, 2001)
—, ed., *The Mediterranean in History* (London, 2003)
Akbar, M. J., *The Shade of Swords: Jihad and the Conflict between Islam and Christianity* (London, 2002)
Ali, T., *The Clash of Fundamentalisms: Crusades, Jihads and Modernity* (London and New York, 2002)
Almond, I., *Two Faiths, One Banner: When Muslims Marched with Christians across Europe's Battlefields* (London, 2008)
Ansary, T., *Destiny Disrupted: A History of the World Through Islamic Eyes* (New York, 2010)
Armstrong, K., *A History of Jerusalem: One City, Three Faiths* (London, 1996)
—, *Islam: A Short History* (London, 2000)
—, *The Battle for God: Fundamentalism in Judaism, Christianity and Islam* (London, 2000)
—, *Fields of Blood: Religion and the History of Violence* (London, 2015)
Aslan, R., *No God But God: The Origins, Evolution, and Future of Islam* (New York, 2006)
Axworthy, M., *A History of Iran: Empire of the Mind*, 3rd edn (New York, 2015)
Black, J., *War and the World, 1450–2000* (London, 2000)
—, *Naval Power: A History of Warfare and the Sea from 1500* (Basingstoke, 2009)
Bonner, M., *Jihad in Islamic History: Doctrine and Practice* (Princeton, NJ, 2006)
Boot, M., *Invisible Armies: An Epic History of Guerrilla Warfare from Ancient Times to the Present* (New York, 2013)
Burleigh, M., *Blood and Rage: A Cultural History of Terrorism* (London, 2008)
Cardini, F., *Europe and Islam* (English translation, Oxford, 2001)
Castillo, D., *The Maltese Cross: A Strategic History of Malta* (Westport, CT, 2006)
Chandler, D., *Atlas of Military Strategy: The Art, Theory and Practice of War, 1618–1878* (London, 1980)
Darwin, J., *After Tamerlane: The Global History of Empire since 1405* (New York, 2008)
Davies, N., *Europe: A History* (Oxford, 1996)

De Souza, P., *Seafaring and Civilization: Maritime Perspectives on World History* (London, 2001)

Duffy, C., *Siege Warfare: The Fortress in the Early Modern World, 1494–1660* (London, 1979)

—, *The Fortress in the Age of Frederick the Great and Vauban* (London, 1985)

Duncan, A., and M. Opatowski, *War in the Holy Land* (Stroud, 1998)

Encyclopaedia of Islam, 2nd edn, 11 vols (Leiden, 1960–2002)

Esposito, J. L., ed., *The Oxford History of Islam* (Oxford, 1999)

—, *Islam: The Straight Path*, 4th edn (Oxford, 2010)

Findley, C. V., *The Turks in World History* (New York, 2004)

Fletcher, R., *The Cross and the Crescent: Christianity and Islam from Muhammad to the Reformation* (London, 2003)

Freeman, D. B., *The Straits of Malacca: Gateway or Gauntlet?* (London, 2003)

Grousset, R., *The Empire of the Steppes: A History of Central Asia* (English translation, New Brunswick, NJ, 1970)

Hall, R., *Empires of the Monsoon: A History of the Indian Ocean and its Invaders* (London, 1996)

Halm, H., *The Shiites: A Short History*, 2nd edn (Princeton, NJ, 2007)

Hanson, V. D., *Why the West has Won: Carnage and Culture from Salamis to Vietnam* (London, 2001); as *Carnage and Culture: Landmark Battles in the Rise of Western Power* (New York, 2001)

Hazleton, L., *After the Prophet: The Epic Story of the Shia-Sunni Split in Islam* (New York, 2009)

—, *The First Muslim: The Story of Muhammad* (New York, 2014)

Hildinger, E., *Warriors of the Steppe: A Military History of Central Asia, 500 BC to AD 1700* (New York, 1997)

Hodgson, M.G.S., *The Venture of Islam*, 3 vols (Chicago, 1974)

Hordern, P., and N. Purcell, *The Corrupting Sea: A Study of Mediterranean History* (Oxford, 2000)

Hourani, A., *A History of the Arab Peoples* (London, 1991)

Jelavich, B., *History of the Balkans*, 2 vols (Cambridge, 1983)

Julien, C. A., *History of North Africa: Tunisia, Algeria, Morocco – From the Arab Conquests to 1830* (London and New York, 1970)

Karsh, E., *Islamic Imperialism: A History* (New Haven, CT, 2006)

Kennedy, P. M., *The Rise and Fall of the Great Powers: Economic Change and Military Conflict from 1500 to 2000* (London, 1988)

King, C., *The Black Sea: A History* (Oxford and New York, 2004)

Kissinger, H., *Diplomacy* (London, 1995)

Lapidus, I. M., *A History of Islamic Societies*, 2nd edn (Cambridge, 2002)

Lewis, B., *The Middle East: 2000 Years of History from the Rise of Christianity to the Present Day* (London, 1995)

Lewis, D. L., *God's Crucible: Islam and the Making of Europe, 570–1215* (New York, 2007)

McHugo, J., *A Concise History of the Arabs* (New York, 2013)

Mandaville, P., *Islam and Politics*, 2nd edn (London, 2014)

Mansel, P., *Constantinople: City of the World's Desire, 1453–1924* (Harmondsworth, 1995)

—, *Levant: Splendour and Catastrophe in the Mediterranean* (London, 2009)

Mansfield, P., *The Arabs*, 2nd edn (Harmondsworth, 1985)

—, *A History of the Middle East* (Harmondsworth, 1992)

McNeill, W. H., *The Pursuit of Power: Technology, Armed Forces and Society since AD 1000* (Oxford, 1983)

Naylor, P. C., *North Africa: A History from Antiquity to the Present* (Austin, TX, 2009)

Norwich, J. J., *The Middle Sea: A History of the Mediterranean* (London, 2006)

O'Shea, S., *Sea of Faith: Islam and Christianity in the Medieval Mediterranean World* (Vancouver, 2006)

Pagden, A., *Worlds at War: The 2,500 Year Struggle between East and West* (New York, 2008)

Paine, L., *The Sea and Civilization: A Maritime History of the World* (New York, 2013)

Parry, V. J., and M. E. Yapp, eds, *War, Technology and Society in the Middle East* (Oxford, 1975)

Partington, J. R., *A History of Greek Fire and Gunpowder* (Baltimore, MD, 1999)

Partner, P., *God of Battles: Holy Wars of Christianity and Islam* (London, 1997)

Pearson, M., *The Indian Ocean* (London, 2003)

Pemsel, H., *Atlas of Naval Warfare* (English translation, London, 1977)

Polk, W. R., *Violent Politics: A History of Insurgency, Terrorism, and Guerrilla War from the American Revolution to Iraq* (New York, 2007)

Pryor, J. H., *Geography, Technology and War: Studies in the Maritime History of the Mediterranean, 649–1571* (Cambridge, 1988)

Roberts, J. M., *Penguin History of Europe* (Harmondsworth, 1997)

Robinson, F., ed., *The Cambridge Illustrated History of Islam* (Cambridge, 1996)

Rodgers, W. L., *Naval Warfare under Oars, 4th to 16th Centuries: A Study of Strategy, Tactics and Ship Design* (Annapolis, MD, 1939; reprinted 1967)

Rogan, E., *The Arabs: A History* (New York, 2009)

Rotberg, R. I., and T. K. Rabb, eds, *The Origin and Prevention of Major Wars* (Cambridge, 1989)

Ruthven, M., *Islam in the World*, 2nd edn (London, 2000)

—, with A. Nanji, *Historical Atlas of Islam* (Cambridge, MA, 2004)

Sebag Montefiore, S., *Jerusalem: The Biography* (London, 2011)

Scammell, G. V., *The World Encompassed: The First European Maritime Empires, 800–1650* (London, 1981)

—, *The First Imperial Age: European Overseas Expansion, c. 1400–1715* (London, 1989)

Setton, K. M., *Western Hostility to Islam and Prophecies of Turkish Doom* (Philadelphia, PA, 1992)

Sicker, M., *The Islamic World in Ascendancy: From the Arab Conquests to the Siege of Vienna* (Westport, CT, 2000)

Soucek, S., *A History of Inner Asia* (Cambridge, 2000)

Tolan, J., H. Laurens and G. Veinstein, *Europe and the Islamic World: A History* (Princeton, NJ, 2012)

Wheatcroft, A., *Infidels: The Conflict between Christendom and Islam, 638–2002* (London, 2003)

THE ARAB CONQUESTS

Abun-Nasr, J. M., *A History of the Maghrib in the Islamic Period* (Cambridge, 1987)
Ahmad, A., *A History of Islamic Sicily* (Edinburgh, 1975)
Butler, A., *The Arab Conquest of Egypt* (Oxford, 1978)
Collins, R., *The Arab Conquest of Spain, 710–797*, revised edn (Oxford, 1995)
Crawford, P., *The War of the Three Gods: Romans, Persians and the Rise of Islam* (Barnsley, 2013)
Crone, P., *Slaves on Horses: The Evolution of the Islamic Polity* (Cambridge, 1980)
Donner, F. M., *The Early Islamic Conquests* (Princeton, NJ, 1981)
—, ed., *The Expansion of the Early Islamic State* (Burlington, VT, 2008)
Fahmy, A. M., *Muslim Sea-Power in the Eastern Mediterranean from the Seventh to the Tenth Century AD: Studies in Naval Organisation* (London, 1950)
Gil, M., *A History of Palestine, 634–1099* (English translation, Cambridge, 1997)
Holland, T., *In the Shadow of the Sword: The Battle for Global Empire and the End of the Ancient World* (London, 2012)
Hoyland, R. G., *In God's Path: The Arab Conquests and the Creation of an Islamic Empire* (New York, 2015)
Kennedy, H., *The Prophet and the Age of the Caliphates: The Islamic Near East from the Sixth to the Eleventh Century* (London, 1986)
—, *The Armies of the Caliphs: Military and Society in the Early Islamic State* (London, 2001)
—, *Mongols, Huns and Vikings* [also Arabs and Turks] (London, 2002)
—, *The Court of the Caliphs: The Rise and Fall of Islam's Greatest Dynasty* [the Abbasids] (London, 2004)
—, *The Great Arab Conquests* (London, 2007)
Lewis, B., *The Arabs in History*, 6th edn (Oxford, 1993)
Pipes, D., *Slave Soldiers and Islam: The Genesis of a Military System* (New Haven, CT, 1981)
Santosuosso, A., *Barbarians, Marauders and Infidels: The Ways of Medieval Warfare* (Boulder, CO, and Oxford, 2004)
Taha, A. D., *The Muslim Conquest and Settlement of North Africa and Spain* (London, 1989)

THE BYZANTINE EMPIRE

Angold, M., *The Byzantine Empire, 1025–1204: A Political History*, 2nd edn (London, 1997)
Bartusis, M. C., *The Late Byzantine Army: Arms and Society, 1204–1453* (Philadelphia, PA, 1992)
Bonner, M. D., *Aristocratic Violence and Holy War: Studies in the Jihad and the Arab–Byzantine Frontier* (New Haven, CT, 1996)
Decker, M. J., *The Byzantine Art of War* (Yardley, PA, 2013)
Freely, J., *Storm on Horseback: The Seljuk Warriors of Turkey* (London, 2008)
Haldon, J., *Warfare, State and Society in the Byzantine World, 565–1204* (London, 1999)
—, *Byzantium: A History* (Stroud, 2000)

—, *The Byzantine Wars: Battles and Campaigns of the Byzantine Era* (Stroud, 2001)

—, *Byzantium at War, AD 600–1453* (Oxford, 2002)

Hillenbrand, C., *Turkish Myth and Muslim Symbol: The Battle of Manzikert* (Edinburgh, 2007)

Kaegi, W., *Byzantium and the Early Islamic Conquests* (Cambridge, 1991)

Kazhdan, A. P., ed., *The Oxford Dictionary of Byzantium*, 3 vols (New York and Oxford, 1991)

Luttwak, E. N., *The Grand Strategy of the Byzantine Empire* (Cambridge, MA, 2009)

Mango, C., ed., *The Oxford History of Byzantium* (Oxford, 2002)

McGeer, E., *Sowing the Dragon's Teeth: Byzantine Warfare in the Tenth Century* (Washington, DC, 1995)

Nicol, D. M., *The End of the Byzantine Empire* (London, 1979)

—, *Byzantium and Venice: A Study in Diplomatic and Cultural Relations* (Cambridge, 1988)

—, *The Last Centuries of Byzantium, 1261–1453*, 2nd edn (Cambridge, 1993)

Nicolle, D., J. Haldon and S. Turnbull, *The Fall of Constantinople: The Ottoman Conquest of Byzantium* (Oxford, 2007)

Norwich, J. J., *Byzantium: The Early Centuries* (London, 1988)

—, *Byzantium: The Apogee* (London, 1991)

—, *Byzantium: The Decline and Fall* (London, 1995)

Peacock, A.C.S., *The Great Seljuk Empire* (Edinburgh, 2015)

Pringle, D., *The Defence of Byzantine Africa from Justinian to the Arab Conquest*, revised edn (Oxford, 2001)

Pryor, J. H., and E. M. Jeffreys, *The Age of the Dromōn: The Byzantine Navy, c. 500–1204* (Leiden, 2006)

Regan, G., *First Crusader: Byzantium's Holy Wars* (Stroud, 2001)

Runciman, S., *The Fall of Constantinople, 1453* (Cambridge, 1965)

Treadgold, W., *Byzantium and its Army, 284–1081* (Stanford, CA, 1995)

—, *A History of the Byzantine State and Society* (Stanford, CA, 1997)

Whittow, M., *The Making of Orthodox Byzantium, 600–1025* (London, 1996)

THE *RECONQUISTA*

Bisson, T. N., *The Medieval Crown of Aragon: A Short History* (Oxford, 1986)

Brett, M., and E. Fentress, *The Berbers* (Oxford, 1996)

Carr, R., ed., *Spain: A History* (Oxford, 2000)

Collins, R., *Early Medieval Spain: Unity in Diversity, 400–1000*, 2nd edn (London, 1995)

Downey, K., *Isabella: The Warrior Queen* (New York, 2014)

Fernandez-Armesto, F., *Ferdinand and Isabella* (London, 1975)

Fletcher, R., *The Quest for El Cid* (London, 1989)

—, *Moorish Spain* (London, 1992)

Forey, A., *The Templars in the Corona de Aragon* (London, 1973)

Fromherz, A. J., *The Almohads: The Rise of an Islamic Empire* (London, 2010)

Glick, T. F., *Islamic and Christian Spain in the Early Middle Ages* (Princeton, NJ, 1979)

Harvey, L. P., *Islamic Spain, 1250–1500* (Chicago, 1990)

Hillgarth, J. N., *The Spanish Kingdoms, 1250–1516*, 2 vols (Oxford, 1976–8)
Kennedy, H., *Muslim Spain and Portugal: A Political History of al-Andalus* (Harlow, 1996)
Livermore, H. V., *A New History of Portugal*, 2nd edn (Cambridge, 1976)
Lomax, D. W., *The Reconquest of Spain* (London, 1978)
Lowney, C., *A Vanished World: Muslims, Christians, and Jews in Medieval Spain* (Oxford, 2006)
Mackay, A., *Spain in the Middle Ages: From Frontier to Empire, 1000–1500* (London, 1977)
Messier, R. A., *The Almoravids and the Meanings of Jihad* (Santa Barbara, CA, 2010)
O'Callaghan, J. F., *A History of Medieval Spain* (Ithaca, NY, 1993)
—, *Reconquest and Crusade in Medieval Spain* (Philadelphia, PA, 2003)
Prescott, W. H., *The Art of War in Spain: The Conquest of Granada, 1481–1492*, ed. A. D. McJoynt (London, 1995)
Reilly, B. F., *The Kingdom of Leon-Castilla under Queen Urraca, 1109–1126* (Princeton, NJ, 1982)
—, *The Kingdom of Leon-Castilla under King Alfonso VI, 1065–1109* (Princeton, NJ, 1988)
—, *The Contest of Christian and Muslim Spain, 1031–1157* (Oxford, 1992)
—, *The Medieval Spains* (Cambridge, 1993)
—, *The Kingdom of Leon-Castilla under King Alfonso VII, 1126–1157* (Philadelphia, PA, 1998)
Wasserstein, D., *The Rise and Fall of the Party-Kings: Politics and Society in Islamic Spain, 1002–1086* (Princeton, NJ, 1985)
—, *The Caliphate in the West: An Islamic Political Institution in the Iberian Peninsula* (Oxford and New York, 1993)
Woodward, G., *Spain in the Reigns of Isabella and Ferdinand, 1474–1516* (London, 1997)

THE CRUSADES, SICILY AND VENICE

Abulafia, D., *Frederick II: A Medieval Emperor* (Oxford, 1988)
Angold, M., *The Fourth Crusade* (London, 2003)
Asbridge, T. S., *The First Crusade: A New History* (Oxford, 2004)
—, *The Crusades: The War for the Holy Land* (London, 2010)
Barber, M., *The New Knighthood: A History of the Order of the Temple* (Cambridge, 1994)
Cahen, C., *The Formation of Turkey: The Seljukid Sultanate of Rum, Eleventh to Fourteenth Century* (Harlow and New York, 2001)
Cobb, P. M., *The Race for Paradise: An Islamic History of the Crusades* (Oxford, 2014)
Crowley, R., *City of Fortune: How Venice Won and Lost a Maritime Empire* (London, 2011)
Douglas, D. C., *The Norman Achievement, 1050–1100* (London, 1969)
—, *The Norman Fate, 1100–1154* (London, 1976)
Edbury, P. W., *The Kingdom of Cyprus and the Crusades, 1191–1374* (Cambridge, 1991)
Finley, M. I., and Smith, D. M., *A History of Sicily*, 3 vols (London, 1968)

Firestone, R., *Jihad: The Origin of Holy War in Islam* (New York and Oxford, 1999)
Forey, A., *The Military Orders from the Twelfth to the Early Fourteenth Centuries* (London, 1992)
France, J., *Victory in the East: A Military History of the First Crusade* (Cambridge, 1994)
—, *Western Warfare in the Age of the Crusades, 1000–1300* (London, 1999)
—, *The Crusades and the Expansion of Catholic Christendom, 1000–1714* (London, 2006)
Frankopan, P., *The First Crusade: The Call from the East* (London, 2012)
Gillingham, J., *Richard the Lionheart* (London, 1989)
Glubb, J. B., *Soldiers of Fortune: The Story of the Mamlukes* (London, 1973)
Harris, J., *Byzantium and the Crusades* (London, 2002)
Hill, G., *A History of Cyprus*, 4 vols (Cambridge, 1940–52)
Hillenbrand, C., *The Crusades: Islamic Persepectives* (Edinburgh, 1999)
Hindley, G., *Saladin* (London, 1976)
—, *The Crusades: History of Armed Pilgrimages and Holy Jihad* (London, 2003)
Holt, P. M., *The Age of the Crusades: The Near East from the Eleventh Century to 1517* (London, 1986)
Hooper, N., and M. Bennett, *Cambridge Illustrated Atlas of Warfare: The Middle Ages, 768–1487* (Cambridge, 1996)
Houben, H., *Roger II of Sicily: A Ruler between East and West* (Cambridge, 2002)
Housley, N. J., *The Later Crusades, 1274–1580: From Lyons to Alcazar* (Oxford, 1992)
—, *Fighting for the Cross: Crusading to the Holy Land* (New Haven, CT, 2008)
Irwin, R., *The Middle East in the Middle Ages: The Early Mamluk Sultanate, 1250–1382* (London, 1986)
Johnson, J. T., *The Holy War Idea in Western and Islamic Traditions* (University Park, PA, 1997)
Jordan, W. C., *Louis IX and the Challenge of the Crusade: A Study in Rulership* (Princeton, NJ, 1979)
Keen, M., ed., *Medieval Warfare: A History* (Oxford, 1999)
Kennedy, H., *Crusader Castles* (Cambridge, 1994)
Lane, F. C., *Venice: A Maritime Republic* (Baltimore, MD, 1973)
Lewis, A. R., *Naval Power and Trade in the Mediterranean, AD 500–1100* (Princeton, NJ, 1951)
—, and T. J. Runyan, *European Naval and Maritime History, 300–1500* (Bloomington, IN, 1985)
Lewis, B., *The Assassins: A Radical Sect in Islam* (London, 1967)
Lilie, R. J., *Byzantium and the Crusader States, 1096–1204* (English translation, Oxford, 1993)
Lyons, M. C., and D.E.P. Jackson, *Saladin: The Politics of the Holy War* (Cambridge, 1982)
Maalouf, A., *The Crusades Through Arab Eyes* (English translation, London, 1984)
Madden, T. F., *Venice: A New History* (New York, 2012)
Marshall, C., *Warfare in the Latin East, 1192–1291* (Cambridge, 1992)
Matthew, D., *The Norman Kingdom of Sicily* (Cambridge, 1992)
Mayer, H. E., *The Crusades*, 2nd edn (English translation, Oxford, 1988)
McNeill, W. H., *Venice: The Hinge of Europe, 1081–1797* (Chicago, 1974)
Morgan, D., *The Mongols* (Oxford, 1986)

Nicholson, H. J., *The Knights Hospitaller* (Woodbridge, 2001)

Nicolle, D., *Medieval Warfare Source Book*, 2 vols (London, 1995–6)

—, *Fighting for the Faith: The Many Fronts of Medieval Crusade and Jihad, 1000–1500 AD* (Barnsley, 2007)

Norwich, J. J., *The Normans in the South, 1016–1130* (London, 1967)

—, *The Kingdom in the Sun, 1130–1194* (London, 1970)

—, *A History of Venice* (Harmondsworth, 1983)

—, *Sicily: An Island at the Crossroads of History* (New York, 2015)

Phillips, J., *Defenders of the Holy Land: Relations between the Latin East and the West, 1119–1187* (Oxford, 1996)

—, *The Fourth Crusade and the Sack of Constantinople* (London, 2004)

—, *Holy Warriors: A Modern History of the Crusades* (London, 2009)

Powell, J. M., *Anatomy of a Crusade, 1213–21* (Philadelphia, PA, 1986)

Prawer, J., *The Latin Kingdom of Jerusalem: European Colonialism in the Middle Ages* (London, 1972)

Regan, G., *Lionhearts: Saladin and Richard I* (London, 1998)

Reston, J., *Warriors of God: Richard the Lionheart and Saladin in the Third Crusade* (London, 2001)

Richard, J., *Saint Louis: Crusader King of France* (English translation, Cambridge, 1992)

—, *The Crusades, c. 1071–c. 1291* (English translation, Cambridge, 1999)

Riley-Smith, J., *The Knights of St John in Jerusalem and Cyprus, c. 1050–1310* (London, 1967)

—, *The First Crusade and the Idea of Crusading* (London, 1986)

—, *The Crusades: A Short History* (London, 1987)

—, *The Atlas of the Crusades* (London, 1991)

—, *The First Crusaders, 1095–1131* (Cambridge, 1997)

—, ed., *The Oxford History of the Crusades* (Oxford, 1999)

—, *The Crusades: A History*, 3rd edn (London, 2014)

Rose, S., *Medieval Naval Warfare, 1000–1500* (London, 2002)

Rubenstein, J., *Armies of Heaven: The First Crusade and the Quest for Apocalypse* (New York, 2011)

Runciman, S., *A History of the* Crusades, 3 vols (Cambridge, 1951–4)

Setton, K. M., ed., *The Papacy and the Levant, 1204–1571*, 4 vols (Philadelphia, PA, 1976–84)

—, ed., *A History of the Crusades*, 2nd edn, 5 vols (Madison, WI, 1969–89)

Seward, D., *The Monks of War: The Military Religious Orders* (London, 1972)

Smail, R. C., *Crusading Warfare, 1097–1193*, 2nd edn (Cambridge, 1995)

Thorau, P., *The Lion of Egypt: Sultan Baybars I and the Near East in the Thirteenth Century* (English translation, London and New York, 1992)

Tyerman, C., *England and the Crusades, 1095–1588* (Chicago and London, 1988)

—, *Fighting for Christendom: Holy War and the Crusades* (Oxford, 2004)

Tyerman, C., *God's War: A New History of the Crusades* (London, 2006)

Walsh, M. J., *Warriors of the Lord: The Military Orders of Christendom* (Arlesford, 2003)

Waterson, J., *The Knights of Islam: The Wars of the Mamluks* (London, 2007)

—, *The Ismaili Assassins: A History of Medieval Murder* (Barnsley, 2008)

THE OTTOMAN EMPIRE (TO 1500)

Ayalon, D., *Gunpowder and Firearms in the Mamluk Kingdom*, 2nd edn (London, 1978)

Babinger, F., *Mehmed the Conqueror and his Time* (English translation, Princeton, NJ, 1978)

Bak, J. M., and B. K. Kiraly, eds, *From Hunyadi to Rakoczi: War and Society in Late Medieval and Early Modern Hungary* (Brooklyn, NY, 1982)

Cook, M. A., ed., *A History of the Ottoman Empire to 1730: Chapters . . . by V. J. Parry and Others* (Cambridge, 1976)

Crowley, R., *Constantinople: The Last Great Siege* (London, 2006)

David, G., and P. Fodor, eds, *Ransom Slavery Along the Ottoman Borders: Early Fifteenth – Early Eighteenth Centuries* (Leiden, 2007)

Engel, P., *The Realm of St Stephen: A History of Medieval Hungary, 895–1526* (English translation, London, 2001)

Finkel, C., *Osman's Dream: The Story of the Ottoman Empire, 1300–1923* (London, 2005)

Fisher, A. W., *The Crimean Tatars* (Stanford, CA, 1978)

Freely, J., *Mehmet II* (London, 2009)

Goffman, D., *The Ottoman Empire and Early Modern Europe* (Cambridge, 2002)

Goodwin, G., *The Janissaries* (London, 1994)

Goodwin, J., *Lords of the Horizons: A History of the Ottoman Empire* (London, 1998)

Held, J., *Hunyadi: Legend and Reality* (Boulder, CO, 1985)

Imber, C., *The Ottoman Empire, 1300–1650: The Structure of Power* (Basingstoke and New York, 2002)

Inalcik, H., *The Ottoman Empire: The Classical Age, 1300–1600* (English translation, London, 1973)

—, *The Ottoman Empire: Conquest, Organisation and Economy* (London, 1978)

Kafadar, C., *Between Two Worlds. The Construction of the Ottoman State* (Berkeley, CA, 1995)

Lowry, H. W., *The Nature of the Early Ottoman State* (Albany, NY, 2003)

Malcolm, N., *Kosovo: A Short History* (London, 1998)

Mazower, M., *The Balkans: From the End of Byzantium to the Present Day* (London, 2000)

McCarthy, J., *The Ottoman Turks: An Introductory History to 1923* (Harlow, 1997)

Nicolle, D., *Nicopolis, 1396* (Oxford, 1999)

Shaw, S., and E. K. Shaw, *History of the Ottoman Empire and Modern Turkey*, 2 vols (Cambridge, 1976–7)

Stavrianos, L. S., *The Balkans since 1453* (New York, 2000)

Sugar, P. F., *Southeastern Europe under Ottoman Rule, 1354–1804* (Seattle, WA, 1977)

—, and P. Hanak, eds, *A History of Hungary* (London, 1990)

Uyar, M., and E. J. Erickson, *A Military History of the Ottomans: From Osman to Ataturk* (Santa Barbara, CA, 2009)

Wheatcroft, A., *The Ottomans* (London, 1993)

THE SIXTEENTH CENTURY

Aksan, A. D., and G. Goffman, eds, *The Early Modern Ottomans: Remapping the Empire* (Cambridge, 2007)

Allen, B. W., *The Great Siege of Malta: The Epic Battle between the Ottoman Empire and the Knights of St John* (Lebanon, NH, 2015)

Allen, W.E.D., *Problems of Turkish Power in the Sixteenth Century* (London, 1963)

Anderson, R. C., *Naval Wars in the Levant, 1559–1853* (Liverpool, 1952)

Arnold, T., *The Renaissance at War* (London, 2001)

Bicheno, H., *Crescent and Cross: The Battle of Lepanto, 1571* (London, 2003)

Black, J., *Cambridge Illustrated Atlas of Warfare: Renaissance to Revolution, 1492–1792* (Cambridge, 1996)

—, ed., *European Warfare, 1453–1815* (London, 1999)

Bobrick, B., *Fearful Majesty: The Life and Reign of Ivan the Terrible* (New York, 1987)

Bovill, E. W., *The Battle of Alcazar: An Account of the Defeat of Don Sebastian of Portugal at El Ksar el Kebir* (London, 1952)

Boxer, C. R., *The Portuguese Seaborne Empire, 1415–1825* (London, 1969)

Bradford, E., *The Great Siege* [Malta 1565] (London, 1961)

—, *The Sultan's Admiral: The Life of Barbarossa* (London, 1969)

Braudel, F., *The Mediterranean and the Mediterranean World in the Age of Philip II*, 2 vols (English translation, London, 1972)

Bridge, A., *Suleiman the Magnificent* (London, 1983)

Brockman, W. E., *The Two Sieges of Rhodes, 1480–1522* (London, 1969)

Brummett, P., *Ottoman Seapower and Levantine Diplomacy in the Age of Discovery* (Albany, NY, 1994)

Capponi, N., *Victory of the West: The Story of the Battle of Lepanto* (English translation, London, 2006)

Carr, M., *Blood and Faith: The Purging of Muslim Spain* (New York, 2009)

Casale, G., *The Ottoman Age of Exploration* (New York, 2010)

Chaudhuri, K. N., *Trade and Civilisation in the Indian Ocean: An Economic History from the Rise of Islam to 1750* (Cambridge, 1985)

Cipolla, C. M., *Guns and Sails in the Early Phase of European Expansion, 1400–1700* (London, 1965)

Clot, A., *Suleiman the Magnificent: The Man, his Life, his Epoch* (English translation, London, 1992)

Cook, W. F., *The Hundred Years War for Morocco: Gunpowder and the Military Revolution in the Early Modern Muslim World* (Boulder, CO, and Oxford, 1994)

Crowley, R., *Empires of the Sea: The Final Battle for the Mediterranean, 1521–1580* (London, 2008)

—, *Conquerors: How Portugal Seized the Indian Ocean and Forged the First Global Empire* (London, 2015)

Dale, S. F., *Islamic Society on the South Asian Frontier: The Mappilas of Malabar, 1498–1922* (Oxford, 1980)

—, *The Muslim Empires of the Ottomans, Safavids, and Mughals* (Cambridge, 2010)

David, G., and P. Fodor, eds, *Hungarian–Ottoman Military and Diplomatic Relations in the Age of Suleyman the Magnificent* (Budapest, 1994)

Davis, R. C., *Christian Slaves, Muslim Masters: White Slavery in the Mediterranean, the Barbary Coast and Italy, 1500–1800* (Basingstoke and New York, 2003)
—, *Holy War and Human Bondage: Tales of Christian-Muslim Slavery in the Early Modern Mediterranean* (Santa Barbara, CA, 2009)
Earle, P., *Corsairs of Malta and Barbary* (London, 1970)
—, *The Pirate Wars* (London, 2003)
Elliott, J., *Imperial Spain, 1469–1716* (London, 1963)
Faroqhi, S., *The Ottoman Empire and the World around It* (London, 2004)
Farrukh, K., *Iran at War, 1500–1988* (Oxford, 2011)
Fisher, G., *Barbary Legend: War, Trade and Piracy in North Africa, 1415–1830* (Oxford, 1957)
Glete, J., *Warfare at Sea, 1500–1650: Maritime Conflicts and the Transformation of Europe* (London, 1999)
Greene, M., *Catholic Pirates and Greek Merchants: A Maritime History of the Early Modern Mediterranean* (Princeton, NJ, 2010)
Guilmartin, J. F., *Galleons and Galleys* (London, 2002)
—, *Gunpowder and Galleys: Changing Technology and Mediterranean Warfare at Sea in the Sixteenth Century*, revised edn (London, 2003)
Hanlon, G., *The Twilight of a Military Tradition: Italian Aristocrats and European Conflicts, 1560–1800* (London, 1997)
Harvey, L. P., *Muslims in Spain, 1500 to 1614* (Chicago and London, 2005)
Hattendorf, J. B., and R. W. Unger, eds, *War at Sea in the Middle Ages and Renaissance* (Woodbridge and Rochester, NY, 2002)
Heers, J., *The Barbary Corsairs: Warfare in the Mediterranean, 1480–1580* (English translation, London, 2003)
Hess, A. C., *The Forgotten Frontier: A History of the Sixteenth Century Ibero-African Frontier* (Chicago, 1978)
Jamieson, A. G., *Lords of the Sea: A History of the Barbary Corsairs* (London, 2012)
Kamen, H., *Spain, 1469–1714: A Society in Conflict*, 2nd edn (London, 1991)
—, *Philip of Spain* (New Haven, CT, and London, 1997)
—, *Spain's Road to Empire: The Making of a World Power, 1492–1763* (London, 2002)
Kann, R. A., *A History of the Habsburg Empire, 1526–1918* (Berkeley, CA, 1974)
Kirk, T. A., *Genoa and the Sea: Policy and Power in an Early Modern Maritime Republic, 1559–1684* (Baltimore, MD, 2006)
Kortepeter, C. M., *Ottoman Imperialism during the Reformation: Europe and the Caucasus* (New York, 1972)
Kunt, I. M., and C. Woodhead, eds, *Suleyman the Magnificent and his Age: The Ottoman Empire in the Early Modern World* (London and New York, 1995)
Malcolm, N., *Agents of Empire: Knights, Corsairs, Jesuits, and Spies in the 16th Century Mediterranean World* (London, 2015)
Maltby, W., *The Reign of Charles v* (Basingstoke and New York, 2002)
Matar, N., *Turks, Moors and Englishmen in the Age of Discovery* (New York, 1999)
—, *Europe through Arab Eyes, 1578–1727* (New York, 2008)
McNeill, W. H., *Europe's Steppe Frontier, 1500–1800* (Chicago, 1964)
Murphey, R., *Ottoman Warfare, 1500–1700* (London, 1999)
Oman, C., *A History of the Art of War in the Sixteenth Century* (London, 1937; reprinted 1999)

Ozbaran, S., *The Ottoman Response to European Expansion: Studies on Ottoman–Portuguese Relations in the Indian Ocean and Ottoman Administration in the Arab Lands during the Sixteenth Century* (Istanbul, 1994)

Padfield, P., *Tide of Empires: Decisive Naval Campaigns in the Rise of the West*, vol. I: *1481–1654* (London, 1979)

Pankhurst, R., *The Ethiopians: A History* (Oxford, 1998)

Parker, G., *The Military Revolution: Military Innovation and the Rise of the West, 1500–1800*, 2nd edn (Cambridge, 1996)

—, *The Grand Strategy of Philip II* (New Haven, CT, and London, 1998)

—, *Imprudent King: A New Life of Philip II* (New Haven, CT, 2014)

Pearson, M. N., *Merchants and Rulers in Gujarat: The Response to the Portuguese in the Sixteenth Century* (Berkeley, CA, 1976)

Perjes, G., *The Fall of the Medieval Kingdom of Hungary: Mohacs 1526–Buda 1541* (English translation, Boulder, CO, 1989)

Petrie, C., *Don John of Austria* (London, 1967)

Reston, J., *Defenders of the Faith: Charles V, Suleyman the Magnificent, and the Battle for Europe, 1520–1536* (New York, 2009)

Richards, J. F., *The Mughal Empire* (Cambridge, 1993)

Rogerson, B., *The Last Crusaders: The Hundred-year Battle for the Centre of the World* (London, 2009)

Russell-Wood, A.J.R., *The Portuguese Empire, 1415–1808: A World on the Move* (Baltimore, MD, 1998)

Savory, R. N., *Iran under the Safavids* (Cambridge, 1980)

Sire, H.J.A., *The Knights of Malta* (New Haven, CT, and London, 1994)

Streusand, D. E., *Islamic Gunpowder Empires: Ottomans, Safavids, and Mughals* (Boulder, CO, 2011)

Subrahmanyam, S., *The Portuguese Empire in Asia, 1500–1700* (London, 1992)

—, *The Career and Legend of Vasco da Gama* (Cambridge, 1997)

Tinniswood, A., *Pirates of Barbary* (London, 2010)

Vaughan, D., *Europe and the Turk: A Pattern of Alliances, 1350–1700* (Liverpool, 1954)

Weiss, G. L., *Captives and Corsairs: France and Slavery in the Early Modern Mediterranean* (Stanford, CA, 2011)

Williams, P., *Empire and the Holy War in the Mediterranean* (London, 2014)

Wolf, J. B., *The Barbary Coast: Algiers under the Turks, 1500–1830* (New York, 1979)

RUSSIA, AUSTRIA AND OTTOMAN DECLINE (TO 1815)

Aksan, V., *An Ottoman Statesman in War and Peace: Ahmed Resmi Efendi, 1700–1783* (Leiden, 1995)

—, *Ottoman Wars, 1700–1850: An Empire Besieged* (Harlow, 2007)

Allison, R. J., *The Crescent Obscured: The United States and the Muslim World, 1776–1815* (New York, 1995)

Baer, M. D., *Honored by the Glory of Islam: Conversion and Conquest in Ottoman Europe* (New York, 2008)

Barker, T. M., *Double Eagle and Crescent: Vienna's Second Turkish Siege and its Historical Setting* (Albany, NY, 1967)

Black, J., *Warfare in the Eighteenth Century* (London, 1999)

Brewer, D., *Greece, the Hidden Centuries: Turkish Rule from the Fall of Constantino*
to Greek Independence (London, 2010)

Childs, J., *Warfare in the Seventeenth Century* (London, 2001)

Davies, B. L., *The Russo-Turkish War, 1768–1774: Catherine II and the Ottoman Empire*
(London, 2015)

—, ed., *Warfare in Eastern Europe, 1500–1800* (Leiden, 2012)

Davies, N., *God's Playground: A History of Poland*, 2 vols (Oxford, 1981)

Dearden, S., *A Nest of Corsairs: The Fighting Karamanlis of Tripoli* (London, 1976)

Duffy, C., *Russia's Military Way to the West: Origins and Nature of Russian Military
Power, 1700–1800* (London, 1981)

Evans, R.J.W., *The Making of the Habsburg Monarchy, 1550–1700: An Interpretation*
(Oxford, 1979)

Fedorowicz, J. K., ed., *A Republic of Nobles: Studies in Polish History to 1864*
(Cambridge, 1982)

Fichtner, P. S., *Terror and Toleration: The Habsburg Empire Confronts Islam, 1526–1850*
(London, 2007)

Field, J. A., *America and the Mediterranean World, 1776–1882* (Princeton, NJ, 1969)

Finkel, C., *The Administration of Warfare: The Ottoman Military Campaign in
Hungary, 1593–1606* (Vienna, 1988)

Fisher, A. W., *The Russian Annexation of the Crimea, 1772–1783* (Cambridge, 1970)

Fuller, W. C., *Strategy and Power in Russia, 1600–1914* (New York, 1992)

Hochedlinger, M., *Austria's Wars of Emergence: War, State and Society in the
Habsburg Monarchy, 1683–1797* (Harlow, 2003)

Hughes, L., *Russia in the Age of Peter the Great* (New Haven, CT, 1998)

Ingrao, C. W., *The Habsburg Monarchy, 1618–1815*, revised edn (Cambridge, 2000)

Ingrao, C., N. Samardzic and J. Pesalj, eds, *The Treaty of Passarowitz, 1718*
(West Lafayette, IN, 2011)

Keep, J.L.H., *Soldiers of the Tsar: Army and Society in Russia, 1462–1874* (Oxford,
1985)

Kilmeade, B., and D. Yaeger, *Thomas Jefferson and the Tripoli Pirates: The Forgotten
War that Changed American History* (New York, 2015)

Khodarkovsky, M., *Russia's Steppe Frontier: The Making of a Colonial Empire,
1500–1800* (Bloomington, IN, 2002)

LeDonne, J. P., *The Russian Empire and the World, 1700–1917: The Geopolitics
of Expansion and Containment* (New York, 1997)

Leiner, F. C., *The End of Barbary Terror: America's 1815 War against the Pirates
of North Africa* (New York, 2006)

Lloyd, C., *English Corsairs on the Barbary Coast* (London, 1981)

Longworth, P., *The Art of War: The Life and Achievements of Field Marshal Suvorov,
1729–1800* (London, 1965)

—, *The Cossacks* (London, 1969)

Love, R. W., *History of the US Navy*, 2 vols (Harrisburg, PA, 1992)

Madariaga, I. de, *Russia in the Age of Catherine the Great* (New Haven,
CT, 1981)

Mitchell, D. W., *A History of Russian and Soviet Sea Power* (London, 1974)

O'Rourke, S., *The Cossacks* (Manchester, 2007)

Phillips, E. J., *The Founding of Russia's Navy* (Westport, CT, 1995) cock, T., *Breaking the Chains: The Royal Navy's War on White Slavery* (Annapolis, MD, 2006)

Quataert, D., *The Ottoman Empire, 1700–1922* (Cambridge, 2000)

Ralston, D. B., *Importing the European Army: The Introduction of European Military Techniques and Institutions into the Extra-European World, 1600–1914* (Chicago, 1996)

Roider, K. A., *Austria's Eastern Question, 1700–1790* (Princeton, NJ, 1982)

Rothenberg, G. E., *The Austrian Military Border in Croatia, 1522–1747* (Urbana, IL, 1960)

—, *The Military Border in Croatia, 1740–1881: A Study of an Imperial Institution* (Chicago, 1966)

Sebag Montefiore, S., *Prince of Princes: The Life of Potemkin* (London, 2000)

Setton, K. M., *Venice, Austria, and the Turks in the Seventeenth Century* (Philadelphia, PA, 1991)

Shaw, S., *Between Old and New: The Ottoman Empire under Sultan Selim III, 1789–1807* (Cambridge, MA, 1971)

Stiles, A., *Russia, Poland and the Ottoman Empire, 1725–1800* (London, 1991)

Stevens, C., *Russia's Wars of Emergence, 1460–1730* (Harlow, 2007)

Stone, D. R., *A Military History of Russia: From Ivan the Terrible to the War in Chechnya* (Westport, CT, 2006)

Stoye, J. W., *The Siege of Vienna*, revised edn (Edinburgh, 2000)

Subtelny, O., *Ukraine: A History*, 2nd edn (Toronto, 1994)

Sumner, B., *Peter the Great and the Ottoman Empire* (Oxford, 1950)

Toll, I., *Six Frigates: The Epic Story of the Founding of the US Navy* (New York, 2006)

Wheatcroft, A., *The Enemy at the Gate: Habsburgs, Ottomans and the Battle for Europe* (London, 2008)

Woodward, D., *The Russians at Sea* (London, 1965)

MUSLIM LANDS AND EUROPEAN IMPERIALISM

Al-Sayyid Marsot, A. L., *Egypt in the Reign of Muhammad Ali* (Cambridge, 1984)

Aldrich, R., *Greater France: A History of French Overseas Expansion* (Basingstoke, 1996)

Allen, W.E.D., and P. Muratoff, *Caucasian Battlefields: A History of the Wars on the Turco-Caucasian Border, 1828–1921* (Cambridge, 1953)

Anderson, M. S., *The Eastern Question, 1774–1923: A Study in International Relations* (London, 1966)

Ansary, T., *Games Without Rules: The Often Interrupted History of Afghanistan* (New York, 2012)

Barry, Q., *War in the East: A Military History of the Russo-Turkish War 1877–78* (Solihull, 2012)

Baumgart, W., *The Crimean War, 1853–1856* (London, 1999)

Bayly, C. A., *Imperial Meridian: The British Empire and the World, 1780–1830* (London, 1989)

Black, J., *The British Seaborne Empire* (New Haven, CT, and London, 2004)

Blanch, L., *The Sabres of Paradise* (London, 1960)

Blaxland, G., *Objective: Egypt* (London, 1966)

Blunt, W., *Desert Hawk: Abd el Kader and the French Conquest of Algeria* (London, 1947)

Brewer, D., *The Flame of Freedom: The Greek War of Independence, 1821–1833* (London, 2001)

Clayton, A., *France, Soldiers and Africa* (London, 1988)

Clogg, R., *A Concise History of Greece*, 2nd edn (Cambridge, 2002)

Cole, J., *Napoleon's Egypt: Invading the Middle East* (London, 2007)

Colley, L., *Captives: Britain, Empire and the World, 1600–1850* (London, 2002)

Dalrymple, W., *The Last Mughal: The Fall of a Dynasty, Delhi, 1857* (London, 2006)

—, *Return of a King: The Battle for Afghanistan, 1839–42* (New York, 2013)

Daly, J.C.K., *Russian Seapower and the Eastern Question, 1827–41* (Annapolis, MD, 1991)

Daly, M. W., ed., *The Cambridge History of Egypt*, vol. II: *Modern Egypt from 1517 to the End of the Twentieth Century* (Cambridge, 1998)

Daniel, E. L., *The History of Iran* (Westport, CT, 2000)

Danziger, R., *Abd al-Qadir and the Algerians: Resistance to the French and Internal Consolidation* (New York, 1977)

David, S., *The Indian Mutiny 1857* (London, 2002)

Fahmy, K., *All the Pasha's Men: Mehmed Ali, his Army, and the Making of Modern Egypt* (Cambridge, 1997)

—, *Mehmed Ali* (New York, 2008)

Figes, O., *Crimea: The Last Crusade* (London, 2010)

Forrest, D., *Tiger of Mysore: The Life and Death of Tipu Sultan* (London, 1970)

Forsyth, J., *The Caucasus: A History* (Cambridge, 2013)

Gammer, M., *Muslim Resistance to the Tsar: Shamil and the Conquest of Chechnia and Daghestan* (London, 1994)

—, *The Lone Wolf and the Bear: Three Centuries of Chechen Defiance of Russian Rule* (London, 2006)

Glenny, M., *The Balkans, 1804–1999: Nationalism, War and the Great Powers* (London, 2000)

Griffin, N., *Caucasus: Mountain Men and Holy Wars* (London, 2001)

Headrick, D. R., *The Tools of Empire: Technology and European Imperialism in the Nineteenth Century* (Oxford, 1981)

Heathcote, T. A., *The Afghan Wars, 1839–1919*, 2nd edn (Staplehurst, Kent, 2003)

Holt, P. M., *Egypt and the Fertile Crescent, 1516–1922: A Political History* (London, 1966)

—, *The Mahdist State in the Sudan, 1881–1898: A Study of its Origins, Development and Overthrow*, 2nd edn (Oxford, 1970)

—, and M. W. Daly, *The History of the Sudan from the Coming of Islam to the Present Day*, 4th edn (London and New York, 1988)

Ingram, E., *In Defence of British India: Great Britain in the Middle East, 1775–1842* (London, 1984)

James, L., *Raj: The Making and Unmaking of British India* (London, 1997)

Kanya-Forstner, A. S., *The Conquest of the Western Sudan: A Study of French Military Imperialism* (Cambridge, 1969)

Kappeler, A., *The Russian Empire: A Multiethnic History* (English translation, Harlow, 2001) arsh, E., and I. Karsh, *Empires of the Sand: The Struggle for Mastery of the Middle East, 1789–1923* (Cambridge, MA, and London, 1999)

Keay, J., *The Honourable Company: A History of the English East India Company* (London, 1991)

—, *India: A History* (London, 2000)

Kiernan, V. G., *European Empires from Conquest to Collapse, 1815–1960* (London, 1982)

King, C., *The Ghost of Freedom: A History of the Caucasus* (New York, 2008)

Kiser, J. W., *Commander of the Faithful: The Life and Times of Emir Abd el-Kader* (Cambridge, 2008)

Lambert, A., *The Crimean War: British Grand Strategy, 1853–56* (Manchester, 1990)

Langensiepen, B., and A. Guleryuz, *The Ottoman Steam Navy, 1828–1923* (London, 1995)

Lewis, I. M., *A Modern History of the Somali: Nation and State in the Horn of Africa*, 4th edn (Oxford, 2002)

Lieven, D., *Empire: The Russian Empire and its Rivals* (London, 2000)

Loyn, D., *Butcher and Bolt: Two Hundred Years of Foreign Engagement in Afghanistan* (London, 2008)

Macfie, A. L., *The Eastern Question, 1774–1923* (London, 1989)

Malcolm, N., *Bosnia: A Short History* (London, 1994)

McCarthy, J., *Death and Exile: Ethnic Cleansing of the Ottoman Muslims, 1821–1922* (Princeton, NJ, 1995)

—, *The Ottoman Peoples and the End of Empire* (London, 2001)

McElwee, W., *The Art of War: Waterloo to Mons* (London, 1974)

Menning, B., *Bayonets before Bullets: The Russian Imperial Army, 1861–1914* (Bloomington, IN, 1992)

Miller, S. G., *A History of Modern Morocco* (Cambridge, 2013)

Motadel, D., ed., *Islam and the European Empires* (Oxford, 2014)

Neillands, R., *The Dervish Wars: Gordon and Kitchener in the Sudan, 1880–1898* (London, 1996)

O'Ballance, E., *Afghan Wars, 1839 to the Present Day*, revised edn (London, 2002)

Palmer, A., *The Decline and Fall of the Ottoman Empire* (London, 1992)

Pavlowitch, S. K., *A History of the Balkans, 1804–1945* (Harlow, 1999)

Peers, D. M., ed., *Warfare and Empire: Contact and Conflict between European and Non-European Military and Maritime Forces and Cultures* (Aldershot, 1997)

Pennell, C. R., *Morocco since 1830: A History* (London, 2000)

Porch, D., *The Conquest of the Sahara* (London, 1984)

—, *The Conquest of Morocco* (London, 1986)

—, *The French Foreign Legion* (London, 1991)

—, *Wars of Empire* (London, 2000)

Ricklefs, M. C., *A History of Modern Indonesia since c. 1200*, 3rd edn (Stanford, CA, 2001)

Rodogno, D., *Against Massacre: Humanitarian Interventions in the Ottoman Empire, 1815–1914* (Princeton, NJ, 2011)

Rogers, P. G., *A History of Anglo-Moroccan Relations to 1900* (London, 1977)

Seton-Watson, H., *The Russian Empire, 1801–1917* (Oxford, 1967)

Sked, A., *The Decline and Fall of the Habsburg Empire, 1815–1918* (London, 1989)

Strathern, P., *Napoleon in Egypt* (London, 2007)

Vatikiotis, P. J., *The History of Modern Egypt: From Muhammad Ali to Mubarak*, 4th edn (London, 1991)

Woodhouse, C. M., *The Battle of Navarino* (London, 1965)

Wright, J., *Libya* (London, 1969)

Yapp, M. E., *The Making of the Modern Middle East, 1798–1923* (London, 1987)

Zurcher, E. J., ed., *Arming the State: Military Conscription in the Middle East and Central Asia, 1775–1925* (London, 1999)

THE TWENTIETH CENTURY AND BEYOND

Abdullah, T., *A Short History of Iraq*, 2nd edn (Harlow, 2011)

Alvarez, J. E., *The Betrothed of Death: The Spanish Foreign Legion during the Rif Rebellion, 1920–1927* (Westport, CT, and London, 2001)

Ambrose, S. E., and D. G. Brinkley, *Rise to Globalism: American Foreign Policy since 1938*, 8th edn (New York and London, 1997)

Andrew, C., *For the President's Eyes Only: Secret Intelligence and the American Presidency from Washington to Bush* (London, 1995)

Andrew, C. M., and A. S. Kanya-Forstner, *France Overseas: The Great War and the Climax of French Imperial Expansion* (London, 1981)

Ansari, A., *Modern Iran since 1921: The Pahlavis and After* (Harlow, 2003)

Arjomand, S. A., *The Turban for the Crown: The Islamic Revolution in Iran* (New York and Oxford, 1988)

Atkinson, R., *Crusade: The Untold Story of the Persian Gulf War* (Boston, MA, 1993)

Auerswald, D. P., and S. M. Saideman, *NATO in Afghanistan: Fighting Together, Fighting Alone* (Princeton, NJ, 2014)

Axworthy, M., *Revolutionary Iran: A History of the Islamic Republic* (New York, 2013)

Bailey, J., R. Iron and H. Strachan, eds, *British Generals in Blair's Wars* (Farnham, 2013)

Balakian, P., *The Burning Tigris: A History of the Armenian Genocide* (New York, 2003)

Balfour, S., *Deadly Embrace: Morocco and the Road to the Spanish Civil War* (Oxford, 2002)

Barker, A. J., *The Neglected War: Mesopotamia 1914–1918* (London, 1967)

Barr, J., *A Line in the Sand: The Anglo-French Struggle for the Middle East, 1914–1948* (New York, 2011)

Bergen, P. L., *Holy War Inc.: Inside the Secret World of Osama Bin Laden* (London, 2001)

—, *The Longest War: The Enduring Conflict between America and Al-Qaeda* (New York, 2011)

—, *Manhunt: The Ten-year Search for Bin Laden – From 9/11 to Abbottabad* (New York, 2012)

—, and D. Rothenberg, eds, *Drone Wars: Transforming Conflict, Law, and Policy* (Cambridge, 2014)

Bethell, N., *The Palestine Triangle: The Struggle between the British, the Jews and the Arabs, 1935–48* (London, 1979)

..l, J. A., *The Eagle and the Lion: The Tragedy of American–Iranian Relations* (New Haven, CT, and London, 1988)

Biondich, M., *The Balkans: Revolution, War, and Political Violence since 1878* (New York, 2011)

Bolger, D., *Why We Lost: A General's Inside Account of the Iraq and Afghanistan Wars* (New York, 2014)

Boot, M., *The Savage Wars of Peace: Small Wars and the Rise of American Power* (New York, 2002)

Bowden, M., *Guests of the Ayatollah: The First Battle in America's War with Militant Islam* (New York, 2006)

—, *The Finish: The Killing of Osama Bin Laden* (New York, 2012)

Bowden, T., *The Breakdown of Public Security: The Case of Ireland, 1916–1921, and Palestine, 1936–1939* (London and Beverly Hills, CA, 1977)

Braithwaite, R., *Afgantsy: The Russians in Afghanistan, 1979–89* (New York, 2011)

Bregman, A., *Israel's Wars: A History since 1947*, 2nd edn (London and New York, 2002)

—, *A History of Israel* (Basingstoke, 2002)

Bruce, A.P.C., *The Last Crusade: The Palestine Campaign in the First World War* (London, 2002)

Budiansky, S., *Air Power: The Men, Machines and Ideas that Revolutionized War from Kitty Hawk to Gulf War II* (New York, 2004)

Bullock, D. L., *Allenby's War: The Palestine-Arabian Campaign, 1916–1918* (London, 1988)

Burg, S. L., and P. S. Shoup, *The War in Bosnia-Herzegovina: Ethnic Conflict and International Intervention* (London, 1999)

Burke, J., *Al-Qaeda: Casting a Shadow of Terror* (London, 2003)

—, *The 9/11 Wars* (London, 2011)

—, *The New Threat from Islamic Militancy* (London, 2015)

Burleigh, M., *Small Wars, Faraway Places: Global Insurrection and the Making of the Modern World, 1945–1965* (London, 2013)

Catherwood, C., *Churchill's Folly: How Winston Churchill created Modern Iraq* (London, 2004)

Cesari, J., ed., *Muslims in the West after 9/11* (London, 2008)

Clayton, A., *The British Empire as a Superpower, 1919–39* (Basingstoke, 1986)

—, *The Wars of French Decolonization* (London, 1994)

Cleveland, W. L., *A History of the Modern Middle East*, 3rd edn (Boulder, CO, 2004)

Cloughley, B., *A History of the Pakistan Army: Wars and Insurrections*, 4th edn (Oxford, 2014)

Cockburn, A., *Kill Chain: The Rise of the High-tech Assassins* (New York, 2015)

Cockburn, P., *The Occupation: War and Resistance in Iraq* (London, 2007)

—, *Muqtada al-Sadr and the Fall of Iraq* (London, 2008)

—, *The Rise of Islamic State: ISIS and the New Sunni Revolution* (London, 2015)

Cohen, M. J., and M. Kolinsky, eds, *Britain and the Middle East in the 1930s: Security Problems, 1935–39* (Basingstoke, 1992)

Cole, P., and B. McQuinn, eds, *The Libyan Revolution and its Aftermath* (Oxford, 2015)

Coll, S., *Ghost Wars: The Secret History of the CIA, Afghanistan and Bin Laden* (New York, 2004)

Collins, J. J., *Understanding War in Afghanistan* (Washington, DC, 2011)

Cooley, J., *Unholy Wars: Afghanistan, America and International Terrorism* (London, 1999)

Corbin, J., *The Base: In Search of al-Qaeda* (London, 2002)

Cordesman, A. H., *The Iraq War: Strategy, Tactics and Military Lessons* (Westport, CT, 2003)

Crist, D., *The Twilight War: The Secret History of America's Thirty-year Conflict with Iran* (New York, 2012)

Cunningham, J., and W. Maley, eds, *Australia and Canada in Afghanistan: Perspectives on a Mission* (Toronto, 2015)

Dupree, L., *Afghanistan* (Oxford, 1997)

Dyer, G., *Don't Panic: ISIS, Terror, and Today's Middle East* (Toronto, 2015)

Erickson, E. J., *Ordered to Die: A History of the Ottoman Army in the First World War* (Westport, CT, 2001)

—, *Defeat in Detail: The Ottoman Army in the Balkans, 1912–1913* (Westport, CT, 2003)

—, *Gallipoli and The Middle East, 1914–1918* (London, 2012)

Fairweather, J., *The Good War: Why We Couldn't Win the War or the Peace in Afghanistan* (New York, 2014)

Falls, C., *A Hundred Years of War*, 2nd edn (London, 1961)

Ferguson, N., *Colossus: The Rise and Fall of the American Empire* (London, 2004)

Filkins, D., *The Forever War* (New York, 2008)

Fisk, R., *Pity the Nation: Lebanon at War*, 2nd edn (Oxford, 1992)

—, *The Great War for Civilisation: The Conquest of the Middle East* (London, 2006)

Fleming, S. E., *Primo de Rivera and Abd-el-Krim: The Struggle in Spanish Morocco, 1923–1927* (New York and London, 1991)

Ford, R., *Eden to Armageddon: The First World War in the Middle East* (London, 2009)

Freedman, L., *The Cold War: A Military History* (London, 2001)

—, *A Choice of Enemies: America Confronts the Middle East* (London, 2008)

—, and E. Karsh, *The Gulf Conflict, 1990–1991: Diplomacy and War in the New World Order* (London, 1994)

Friedman, N., *Desert Victory: The War for Kuwait* (Annapolis, MD, 1991)

Fromkin, D., *A Peace to End all Peace: Creating the Modern Middle East, 1914–1922* (Harmondsworth, 1989)

Furneaux, R., *Abdel Krim: Emir of the Rif* (London, 1967)

Galbraith, P. W., *The End of Iraq* (New York, 2006)

Galeotti, M., *Russia's Wars in Chechnya, 1994–2009* (Oxford, 2014)

Gall, C., *The Wrong Enemy: America in Afghanistan, 2001–2014* (New York, 2014)

—, and T. de Waal, *Chechnya: A Small Victorious War* (London, 1997)

Gall, S., *War Against the Taliban: Why it All Went Wrong in Afghanistan* (London, 2012)

Gilbert, M., *Israel: A History* (London, 1998)

Glenny, M., *The Fall of Yugoslavia: The Third Balkan War*, 3rd edn (London, 1996)

Gordon, M., and B. Trainor, *Cobra II: The Inside Story of the Invasion and Occupation of Iraq* (New York, 2006)

Griffin, M., *Reaping the Whirlwind: Afghanistan, Al-Qaida, and the Holy War* (London, 2003)

~unther, M. M., *The Kurds: A Modern History* (London, 2015)

Hall, R. C., *The Balkan Wars, 1912–1913: Prelude to the First World War* (London, 2000)

—, *War in the Balkans: An Encyclopedic History from the Fall of the Ottoman Empire to the Breakup of Yugoslavia* (Santa Barbara, CA, 2014)

Hansen, S. J., *Al Shabaab in Somalia* (Oxford, 2013)

Hiro, D., *Islamic Fundamentalism* (London, 1988)

—, *The Longest War: The Iran–Iraq Conflict* (London, 1989)

—, *Desert Shield to Desert Storm* (London, 1992)

—, *War Without End: The Rise of Islamist Terrorism and Global Response* (London and New York, 2002)

Hokayem, E., *Syria's Uprising and the Fracturing of the Levant* (London, 2013)

Hooton, E. R., *Prelude to the First World War: The Balkan Wars, 1912–1913* (Stroud, 2014)

Horne, A., *A Savage War of Peace: Algeria, 1954–1962* (London, 1977)

Hughes, M., *Allenby and British Strategy in the Middle East, 1917–1919* (London, 1999)

Huntington, S. P., *The Clash of Civilizations and the Remaking of World Order* (New York, 1996)

Ignatieff, M., *Virtual War: Kosovo and Beyond* (London, 2000)

Isby, D., *Afghanistan, Graveyard of Empires: A New History of the Borderland* (New York, 2010)

Johnson, C., *The Sorrows of Empire* (New York, 2004)

Johnson, R., *The Afghan Way of War: How and Why They Fight* (New York, 2012)

Jones, S. G., *In the Graveyard of Empires: America's War in Afghanistan* (New York, 2009)

Kagan, K., *The Surge: A Military History* (New York, 2009)

Karnow, S., *In Our Image: America's Empire in the Philippines* (New York, 1989)

Karsh, E., *The Iran–Iraq War, 1980–1988* (Oxford, 2002)

Keay, J., *Sowing the Wind: The Seeds of Conflict in the Middle East* (London, 2003)

Kedourie, E., *England and the Middle East: The Destruction of the Ottoman Empire, 1914–1921*, new edn (London, 1987)

Keegan, J., *The Iraq War* (London, 2004)

Kervokian, R., *The Armenian Genocide: A Complete History* (London, 2011)

Khosrokhavar, F., *Suicide Bombers: Allah's New Martyrs* (London, 2005)

Kimmerling, B., and J. S. Migdal, *Palestinians: The Making of a People* (New York, 1993)

Kinzer, S., *Overthrow: America's Century of Regime Change from Hawaii to Iraq* (New York, 2006)

Kyle, K., *Suez: Britain's End of Empire in the Middle East* (London, 1991; reprinted 2003)

Lang, E., and J. Stein, *The Unexpected War: Canada in Kandahar* (Toronto, 2008)

Laqueur, W., *Guerrilla: A Historical and Critical Study* (London, 1977)

—, *Terrorism* (London, 1977)

—, *The New Terrorism: Fanaticism and the Arms of Mass Destruction* (Oxford and New York, 1999)

—, *No End to War: Terrorism in the Twenty-first Century* (New York and London, 2003)

Lawrence, Q., *Invisible Nation: How the Kurds' Quest for Statehood is Shaping Iraq and the Middle East* (New York, 2008)

Le Sueur, J. D., *Algeria since 1989: Between Terror and Democracy* (London, 2010)

Ledwidge, F., *Losing Small Wars: British Military Failure in Iraq and Afghanistan* (London, 2011)

Lesch, D. W., and M. L. Haas, eds, *The Arab Spring: Change and Resistance in the Middle East* (New York, 2012)

Lewis, B., *What Went Wrong? Western Impact and Middle Eastern Response* (London, 2002)

—, *The Crisis of Islam: Holy War and Unholy Terror* (London, 2003)

Lippold, K., *Front Burner: Al Qaeda's Attack on the USS 'Cole'* (New York, 2012)

Longrigg, S. H., *Iraq, 1900–1950* (London, 1953)

Macfie, A. L., *The End of the Ottoman Empire, 1908–1923* (Harlow, 1998)

Macmillan, M., *Peacemakers: The Paris Conference of 1919* (London, 2001)

Maley, W., *The Afghanistan Wars [1979–2001]* (Basingstoke and New York, 2002)

Mango, A., *Ataturk* (London, 1999)

Marlowe, J., *Rebellion in Palestine* (London, 1946)

McHugo, J., *Syria: A History of the Last Hundred Years* (New York, 2015)

McLoughlin, L. J., *Ibn Saud: Founder of a Kingdom* (Basingstoke, 1993)

McMeekin, S., *The Berlin-Baghdad Express: The Ottoman Empire and Germany's Bid for World Power, 1898–1918* (Cambridge, MA, 2010)

—, *The Ottoman Endgame: War, Revolution, and the Making of the Modern Middle East, 1908–1923* (London, 2015)

Millett, A. R., P. Maslowski and W. B. Feis, *For the Common Defense: A Military History of the United States from 1607–2012*, 3rd edn (New York, 2012).

Milton, G., *Paradise Lost. Smyrna 1922: The Destruction of Islam's City of Tolerance* (London, 2008)

Milton-Edwards, B., *The Israeli-Palestinian Conflict* (London, 2008)

—, *Islamic Fundamentalism since 1945*, 2nd edn (London, 2013)

Mitchell, R., *The Society of the Muslim Brothers* (Oxford, 1969)

Monroe, E., *Britain's Moment in the Middle East, 1914–1971*, revised edn (London, 1981)

Moran, D., *Wars of National Liberation* (London, 2000)

Morell, M., and B. Harlow, *The Great War of Our Time: The CIA's Fight Against Terrorism – From Al Qaida to ISIS* (New York, 2015)

Motadel, D., *Islam and Nazi Germany's War* (New York, 2014)

Moyar, M., *A Question of Command: Counterinsurgency from the Civil War to Iraq* (New Haven, CT, 2009)

Murray, W., and R. H. Scales, *The Iraq War: A Military History* (Cambridge, MA, and London, 2003)

Murray, W., and K. M. Woods, *The Iran–Iraq War: A Military and Strategic History* (Cambridge, 2014)

Nasr, V., *The Shia Revolution: How Conflicts within Islam will Shape the Future* (New York, 2006)

Naylor, S., *Relentless Strike: The Secret History of Joint Special Operations Command* (New York, 2015)

Neillands, R., *A Fighting Retreat: The British Empire, 1947–1997* (London, 1996)

Omissi, D. E., *Air Power and Colonial Control: The Royal Air Force, 1919–1939* (Manchester, 1990)

Oren, M., *Six Days of War: June 1967 and the Making of the Modern Middle East* (Oxford, 2002)

—, *Power, Faith, and Fantasy: America and the Middle East, 1776 to the Present* (New York, 2007)

Packer, G., *The Assassin's Gate: America in Iraq* (New York, 2006)

Paget, J., *Last Post: Aden, 1964–67* (London, 1969)

Palmer, M. A., *Guardians of the Gulf: A History of America's Expanding Role in the Persian Gulf, 1833–1992* (New York, 1992)

Pavkovic, A., *The Fragmentation of Yugoslavia: Nationalism and War in the Balkans*, 2nd edn (Basingstoke, 2000)

Pennell, C. R., *A Country with a Government and a Flag: The Rif War in Morocco, 1921–1926* (Wisbech, 1986)

Pokalova, E., *Chechnya's Terrorist Network: The Evolution of Terrorism in Russia's North Caucasus* (Santa Barbara, CA, 2015)

Polk, W. R., *The United States and the Arab World*, 3rd edn (Cambridge, MA, 1975)

—, *The Arab World Today*, 5th edn (Cambridge, MA, 1991)

—, *Understanding Iraq: The Whole Sweep of Iraqi History from Genghis Khan's Mongols . . . to the American Occupation* (New York, 2005)

Porath, Y., *The Emergence of the Palestinian Arab National Movement*, vol. II: *1929–1939: From Riots to Rebellion* (London, 1977)

Rasanayagam, A., *Afghanistan: A Modern History* (London and New York, 2003)

Rashid, A., *Taliban: Islam, Oil and the New Great Game in Central Asia* (London, 2000)

—, *Jihad: The Rise of Militant Islam in Central Asia* (New Haven, CT, and London, 2002)

—, *Descent into Chaos: How the War against Islamic Extremism is being Lost in Pakistan, Afghanistan, and Central Asia* (London, 2008)

—, *Pakistan on the Brink: The Future of Pakistan, Afghanistan, and the West* (London, 2012)

Reid, W., *Empire of Sand: How Britain Made the Middle East* (Edinburgh, 2013)

Reynolds, M. A., *Shattering Empires: The Clash and Collapse of the Ottoman and Russian Empires, 1908–1918* (Cambridge, 2011)

Ricks, T., *Fiasco: The American Military Adventure in Iraq* (New York, 2006)

Ricks, T., *The Gamble: General David Petraeus and the American Military Adventure in Iraq, 2006–2008* (New York, 2009)

Rogan, E., *The Fall of the Ottomans: The Great War in the Middle East, 1914–1920* (London, 2015)

Roy, O., *Islam and Resistance in Afghanistan*, 2nd edn (Cambridge, 1990)

Ruthven, M., *A Fury for God: The Islamist Attack on America*, revised edn (London, 2004)

Rutledge, I., *Enemy on the Euphrates: The British Occupation of Iraq and the Great Arab Revolt, 1914–1921* (London, 2014)

Scahill, J., *Dirty Wars: The World is a Battlefield* (New York, 2013)

Schulze, K. E., *The Arab-Israeli Conflict*, 2nd edn (London, 2008)

Segev, T., *One Palestine, Complete: Jews and Arabs under the British Mandate* (English translation, London and New York, 2000)

Shepherd, N., *Ploughing the Sand: British Rule in Palestine* (London, 1999)

Shlaim, A., *The Iron Wall: Israel and the Arab World* (London, 2000)

Simons, G., *Iraq: From Sumer to Post-Saddam*, 3rd edn (Basingstoke and New York, 2004)

Sluglett, P., *Britain in Iraq, 1914–32* (London, 1976)

Smith, M., *Boko Haram: Inside Nigeria's Unholy War* (London, 2015)

Smith, M. L., *Ionian Vision: Greece in Asia Minor, 1919–1922* (London, 1998)

Smith, S., *Allah's Mountains: The Battle for Chechnya*, revised edn (London, 2001)

Spiegel, S. L., *The Other Arab-Israeli Conflict: Making America's Middle East Policy, from Truman to Reagan* (Chicago, 1985)

Talbot, I., *Pakistan: A Modern History* (London, 1998)

Tomsen, P., *The Wars of Afghanistan* (New York, 2011)

Townshend, C., *Britain's Civil Wars: Counterinsurgency in the Twentieth Century* [includes Palestine, Iraq, etc.] (London, 1986)

—, *When God Made Hell: The British Invasion of Mesopotamia and the Creation of Iraq, 1914–1921* (London, 2010)

Tripp, C., *A History of Iraq*, 2nd edn (Cambridge, 2002)

Tyler, P., *A World of Trouble: The White House and the Middle East – From the Cold War to the War on Terror* (New York, 2009)

Ulrichsen, K. C., *The First World War in the Middle East* (Oxford, 2014)

Urban, M., *War in Afghanistan* (London, 1990)

Walker, J., *Aden Insurgency: The Savage War in South Arabia, 1962–67* (London, 2004)

Ward, S. R., *Immortal: A Military History of Iran and its Armed Forces* (Washington, DC, 2009)

Warrick, J., *Black Flags: The Rise of ISIS* (New York, 2015)

Wawro, G., *Quicksand: America's Pursuit of Power in the Middle East* (New York, 2010)

Weiner, T., *Legacy of Ashes: The History of the CIA* (New York, 2007)

West, B., *The Strongest Tribe: War, Politics, and the Endgame in Iraq* (New York, 2008)

—, *The Wrong War: Grit, Strategy, and the Way Out of Afghanistan* (New York, 2011)

Weymouth, T., and S. Henig, eds, *The Kosovo Crisis: The Last American War in Europe?* (Harlow, 2001)

Woods, C., *Sudden Justice: America's Secret Drone Wars* (New York, 2015)

Woodward, B., *Obama's Wars* (New York, 2010)

Woolman, D., *Rebels in the Rif: Abd el Krim and the Rif Rebellion* (Stanford, CA, and Oxford, 1969)

Wright, L., *The Looming Tower: Al-Qaeda and the Road to 9/11* (New York, 2006)

Yapp, M. E., *The Near East since the First World War* (London, 1991)

Yergin, D., *The Prize: The Epic Quest for Oil, Money and Power* (London, 1991)

Zurcher, E. J., *Turkey: A Modern History*, 2nd edn (London, 1998)

Acknowledgements

A short book covering nearly fourteen centuries of history is necessarily dependent on secondary works. These I have found in a variety of libraries, both large and small, and I wish to express my thanks to them: in the United Kingdom, the British Library in London and the Herefordshire Library Service, particularly the libraries in Hereford and Leominster; in Canada, the library of the University of British Columbia and the Vancouver Central Public Library (both in British Columbia) and Hinton Municipal Library in Alberta; and in the United States, the Library of Congress in Washington, DC.

I must thank Professor Jeremy Black for his support; Michael Leaman and his team at Reaktion Books for their assistance; and András Bereznay for producing the maps.

INDEX